J W WATERHOUSE

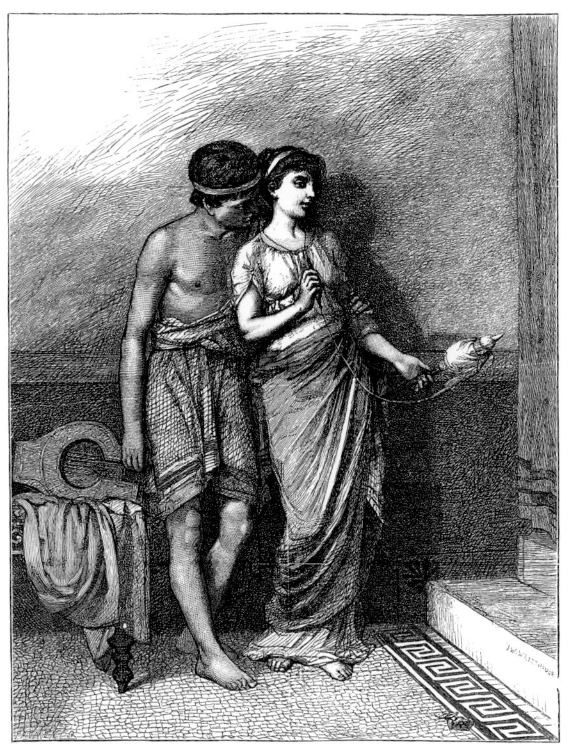

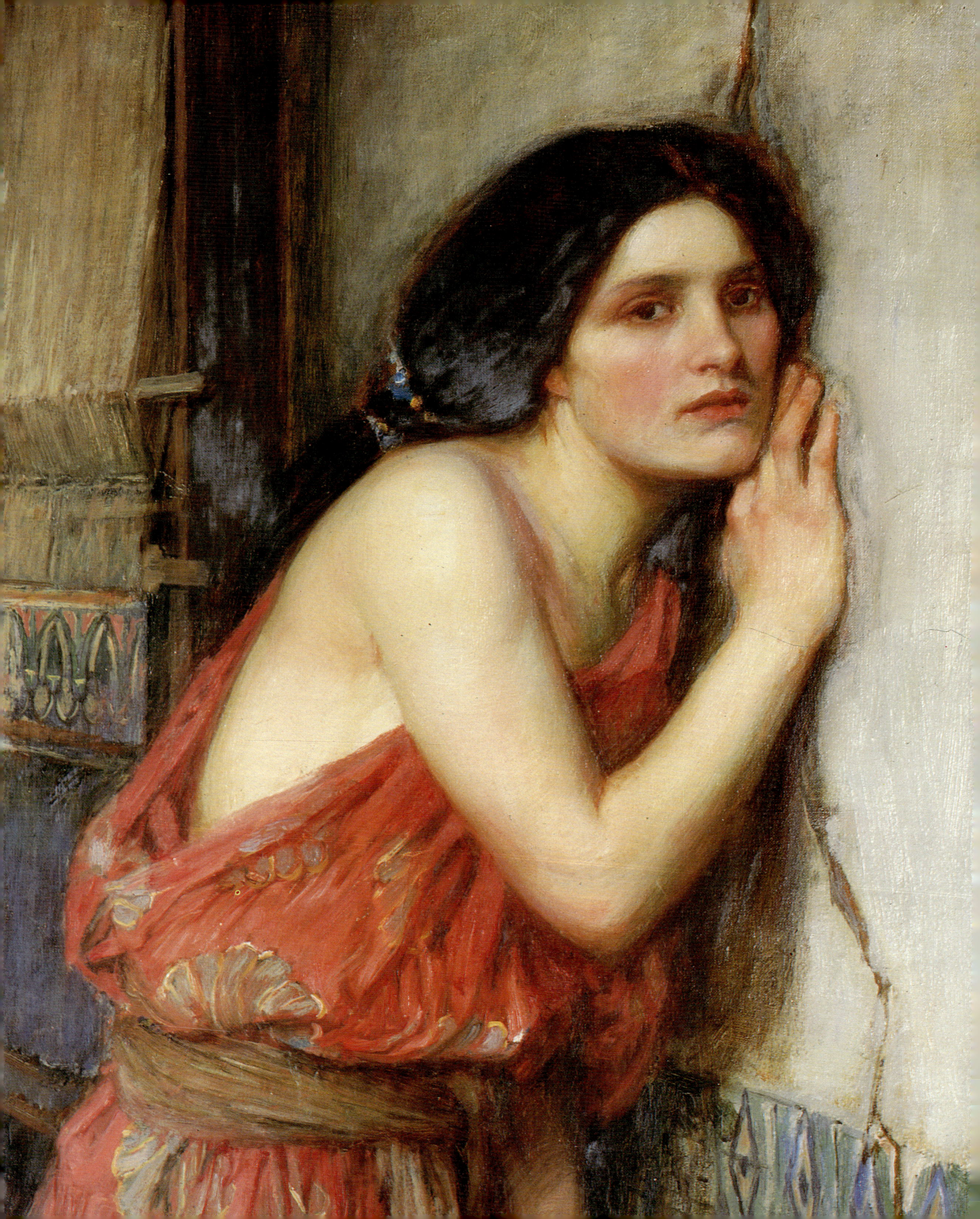

J W WATERHOUSE

Anthony Hobson

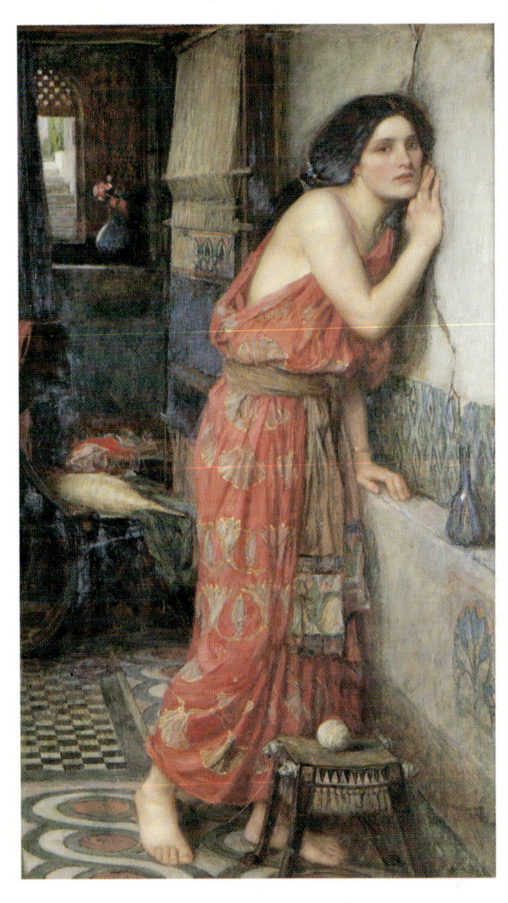

Φ

ACKNOWLEDGEMENTS

18, 32 South Australian Government Grant; 7, 46 Towneley Hall Art Gallery and Museums, Burnley Borough Council; 35 Falmouth Art Gallery (Falmouth Town Council); 48 Hammersmith and Fulham Archives; 20 photo courtesy Paul Mellon Centre; 8 by courtesy of the Board of Trustees of the Victoria and Albert Museum; 30 reproduced by permission of the National Gallery of Victoria; 3 reproduced by permission of Tyne and Wear Museums Service; 85 Art Gallery of Ontario, Toronto. Gift of Mrs Phillip B Jackson, 1971; 62 reproduced by kind permission of the Harris Museum and Art Gallery, Preston; 22 by permission of Sheffield City Art Galleries.

Phaidon Press Limited
140 Kensington Church Street
London W8 4BN

Printed in paperback 1992
Reprinted in paperback 1993

A CIP catalogue record for this book is available from the British Library.

ISBN 0 7148 2864 5

Printed in Hong Kong

Cover. *The Lady of Shalott*, 1888 (detail). 60¼ x 78¾ in (153 x 200 cm). London, Tate Gallery.

Half Title. *Whispered Words*, 1875. 40 x 30 in (102 x 76 cm). From an engraving after the original, *Illustrated London News*, 28 August, 1875.

Title page and frontispiece. *Thisbe*, 1909 (and detail). Oil on canvas, 38 x 23½ in (97 x 60 cm). Courtesy, Sotheby's.

NOTE: All works are in oils and on canvas unless otherwise stated.

Contents

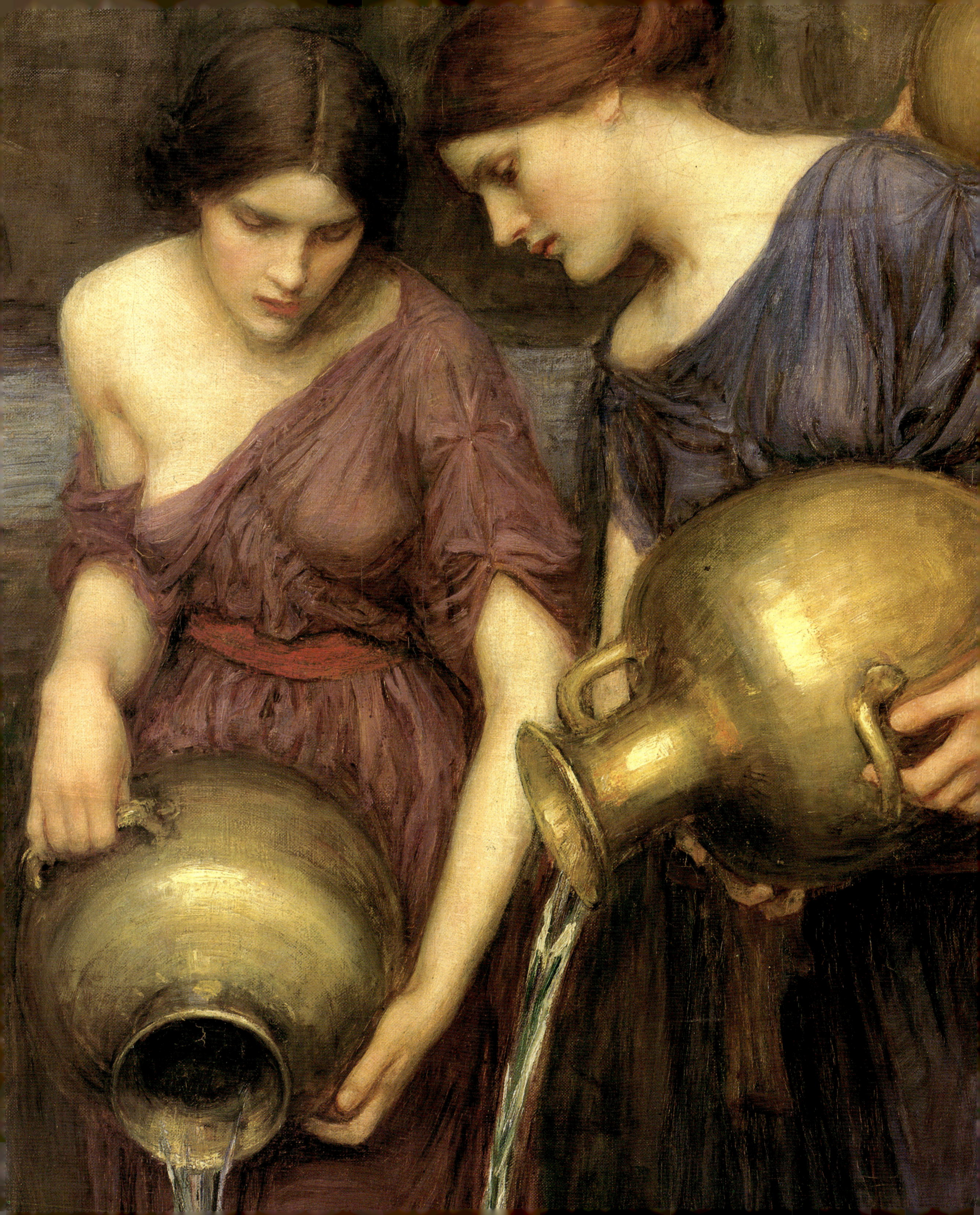

Preface

IN THE TEN years since my doctoral thesis was transformed into *The Art and Life of J.W. Waterhouse*, RA, published by Studio Vista, the artist has remained continually in my thoughts, affecting my own work as a painter and my view of European art in general as I regularly lectured and corresponded about him. Outside the study and studio much has happened, too. Waterhouse's paintings have progressively increased in value – more so than most of his contemporaries' – and yet among the numerous owners of his pictures I have met more who appreciated them for their intrinsic beauty and meaning than for their investment potential.

1 Detail from *The Danaïdes* (Pl. 79)

Under the circumstances, then, it seemed appropriate to re-examine Waterhouse's work in the terms which account for his success: the paintings themselves. Indeed, the retiring nature of the artist made this an essential element in the original research; he left no such store of letters or diaries as have often proved to be a gold-mine for the biographer. The general interest in his paintings has manifestly increased, and fresh thoughts have been aroused about the nature of his art. Additionally, a number of pictures included in the original *catalogue raisonné* but then undiscovered have come to light, and as many as possible of these have been reproduced here. The catalogue and illustrations of *The Art and Life of J.W. Waterhouse*, RA, however, still form the most complete reference to the artist's work.

The acknowledgements voiced in the original book were both comprehensive and deeply felt. I reiterate them all *en bloc*, with fresh salutations to the staff of Christie's and Sotheby's, to Phaidon Press for giving me the opportunity to address the subject again, to the owners whose pictures are reproduced here for the first time, and to my wife, whose patient support has been invaluable in my pursuit of a great artist.

Anthony Hobson

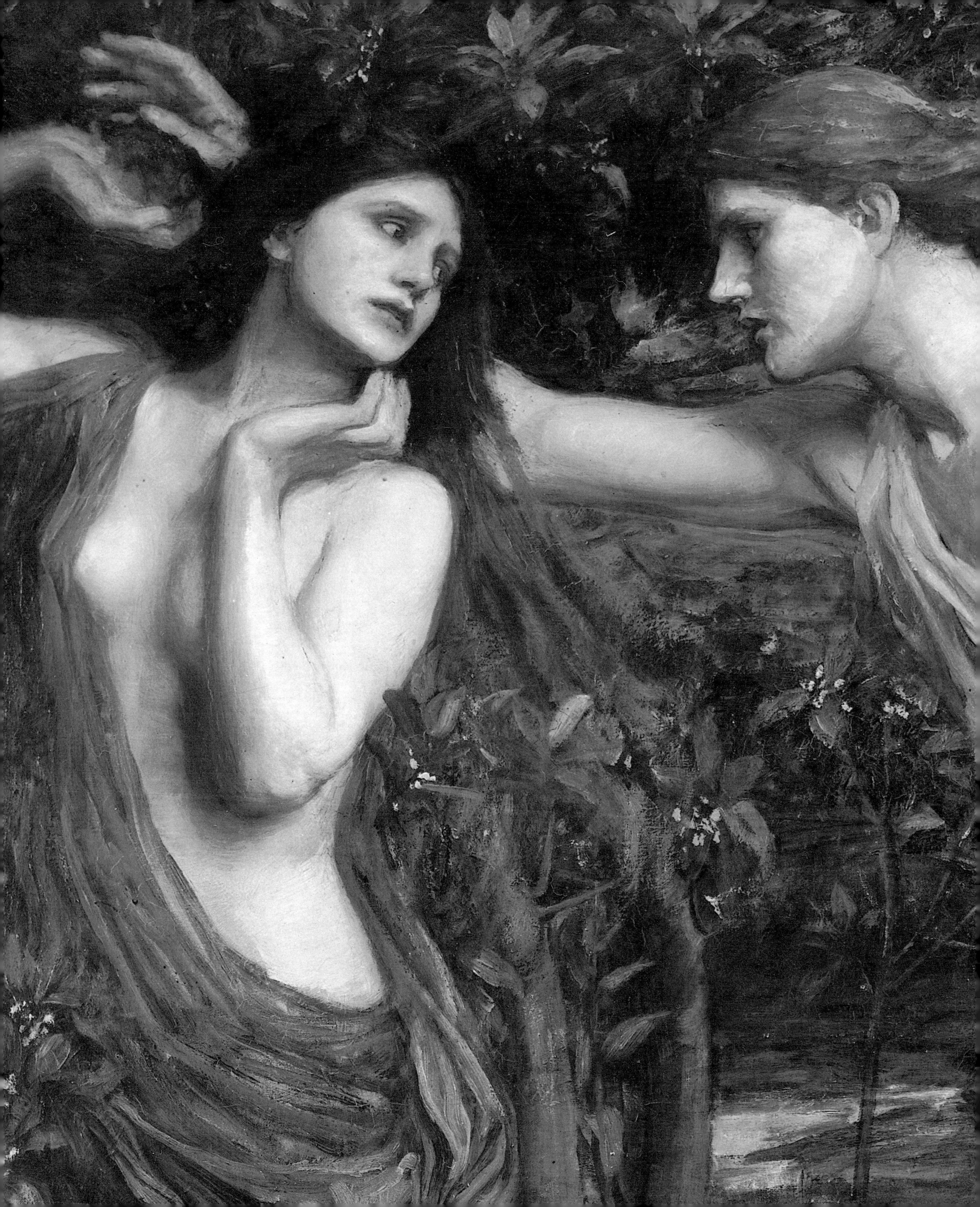

Introduction

FOR MOST PEOPLE the art of John William Waterhouse exerts an immediate and powerful appeal, attested in the nineteenth century by his popularity and continuing success and in the twentieth by the use of his pictures as a vehicle for advertising and by their ever-rising saleroom value.

2 Detail from *Apollo and Daphne* (Pl.66)

This appeal is not too difficult to define. Superficially, there is the perennially attractive image of the young innocent girl: in Waterhouse's art this has a quality which is timeless and yet has accorded with the fashionable taste both in his period and ours. But the roots go deeper, and they are shared by many of us. Waterhouse has been wrongly called Pre-Raphaelite, but he was a Romantic Classicist: he had the Northerner's love of legend and mystery, but his Italian birth lent a warm personality to his rendering of the classical myths, peopled as they were by superhuman beings.

Burne-Jones, a follower of the Pre-Raphaelites, managed to fix the image of Pre-Raphaelitism in a mould of his own making – that of the long-haired girl in the long dress. But his girls are anonymous and anaemic: Waterhouse's are individual, sensitive and warm-blooded: they are in fact the living models of his studio, with their own youth and their inimitable combination of modesty and sexuality imbued with the painter's creative imagination.

The other-worldly aspect of Waterhouse's own nature was given a sense of order by the classical heritage we all share and a personality by the personal quality of the Greek legends, a strong Southern softness akin to Botticelli's in which beauty is shared equally by good and evil and the only human differences are those of youth and age. There are no monsters in Waterhouse's story-telling as in Dürer's, or even Burne-Jones's, or occasionally that of Leighton – himself the foremost English Neoclassicist. And to his natural gifts as a pure painter, nurtured in his father's studio, Waterhouse brought the two other essentials of the great artist in the narrative field, an unerring sense of composition and the instinct for the moment in the story at which everything stands still for our contemplation.

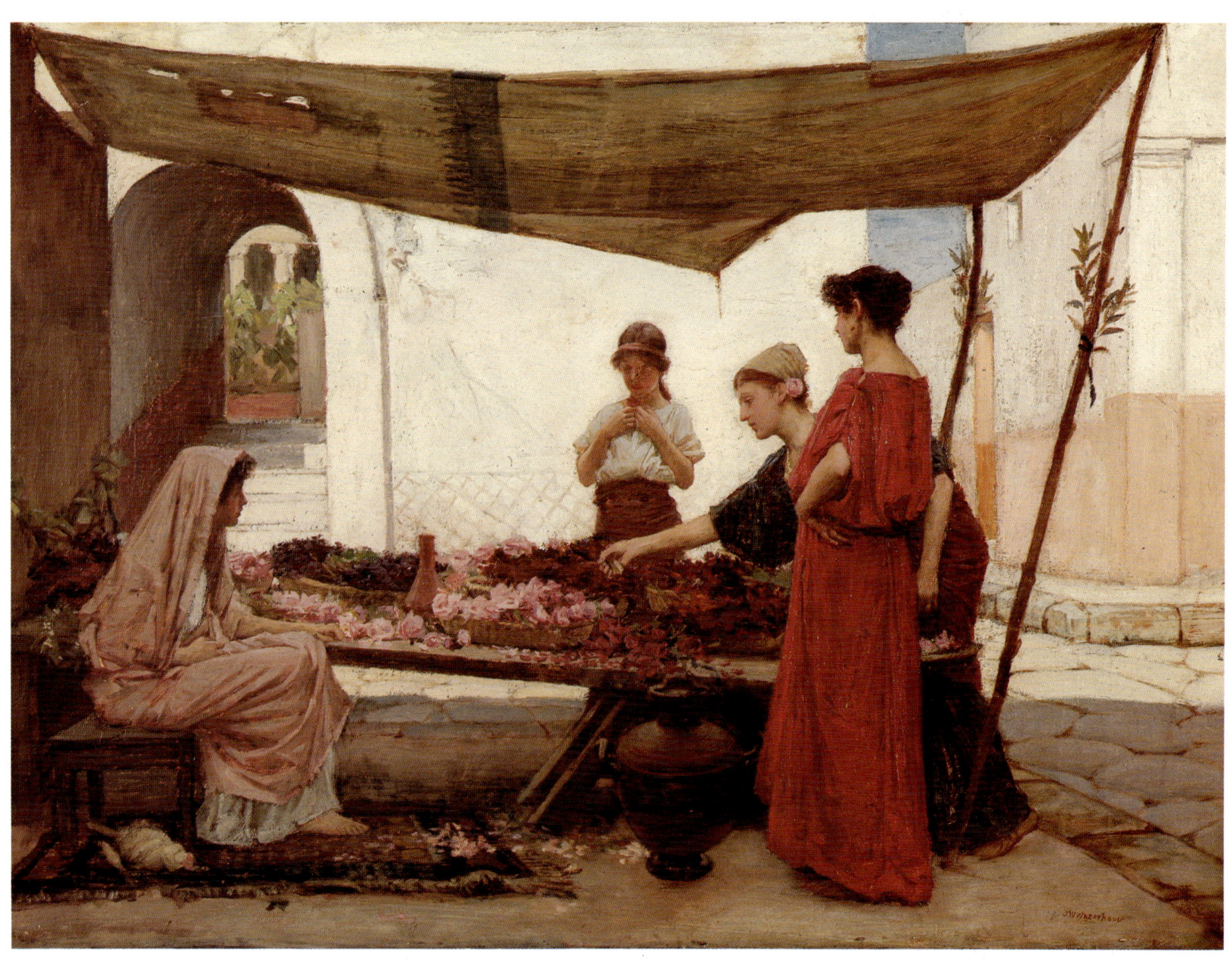

3 *A Flower Stall* (or *A Grecian Flower Market*), 1880. 22 × 31 in (56 × 79 cm). Newcastle-upon-Tyne, Laing Art Gallery

I

The Early Years

IT IS NOT mere fancy to ascribe the character and strength of Waterhouse's art to the fact that he was born in Rome, emerging thereby into a stream which had flowed for over two thousand years and brought with it the myths and legends of the Greeks; and it was to Italy that he continually returned for refreshment. A contemporary critic tells of his 'weeks of free wandering and dwelling in Italian cities and country', experiencing anew the atmosphere of his boyhood, while other young artists sought the heady society of Montparnasse or the intellectual milieus of Munich and Düsseldorf. He had absorbed the sounds and the understanding of the Italian language during the first six years of his life, and he was always known to his family as 'Nino' – short for Giovannino.

These visits continued through the early part of Waterhouse's mature career, producing numerous paintings of which *A Flower Market, Old Rome* (Pl.4), is a superb example, showing the action and characterization of the figures which came so naturally to him. Flowers, indeed, were a theme of paintings throughout his life, and the sunshine of the Mediterranean is evoked especially in such early pictures.

His father, William Waterhouse, was a Yorkshireman, an artist who practised with moderate but still adequate success in prosperous Victorian society. He too had been drawn to Rome early in his career, and regularly travelled there to stay a few months, copying Old Masters and painting pictures for the tourists, before returning to sell the remaining work in London exhibitions. Already a widower at twenty-nine, he then married Isabella Mackenzie, daughter of the Secretary of the old-established Union Club in Trafalgar Square. Within a few months they were in Rome, where John William was born on 6 April 1849, followed in 1851 by Edwin, in 1853 by Jessica and in 1855 by their brother Charles.

Nino inherited his talents from both parents. Isabella and her younger sister Jane both exhibited portraits at the Royal Academy, and his own facility in this branch of art was speedily evident, though applied mainly to his models. At school in Yorkshire, a facility for drawing did not immediately prompt a career as an artist, but he read ancient history constantly and pleasurably, storing up subjects which appear in later paintings. It was a working apprenticeship in his father's studio which eventually led to his entry to the Royal Academy Schools. Meanwhile, he was trying his hand. His first paintings were on old canvases re-used, and even in

A Flower Stall of 1880 (Pl.3) this economical habit persists: the heavy impasto on the sunlit wall conceals the buildings still visible through the thinly painted canopy.

Admission to the Royal Academy Schools was by specimens of drawing. The necessary basic ability was nurtured most frequently in the number of private art schools which offered their students to the R.A., but Waterhouse relied upon his father as tutor and on his own constant spare-time activity. During the previous fifty years three chalk drawings – from an antique figure, an anatomical figure and a skeleton – had been required, but by 1870 an intending student of painting had to submit only one specimen, 'a finished Drawing in Chalk, about two feet high, of an Undraped, Antique Statue'.

4 *A Flower Market, Old Rome*, 1886. 61 × 34½ in (155 × 88 cm) Private collection

In Waterhouse's case, an extraordinary sequence of events took place; not even, it would appear, due to the distinctions of age introduced some years later between candidates for different disciplines. His drawing of the Discobolus in the South Kensington Museum (now the Victoria and Albert Museum) faithfully recorded the false lights and shadows due to accumulated dust and dirt, and was understandably rejected. He then decided to apply as a sculptor, submitting a model in clay – possibly on the advice of William Waterhouse's friend, the sculptor Edward James Physick. After considerable labour this was completed and accepted and he was admitted as a Probationer in the Sculpture School on 28 July 1870.

His obligatory sponsor was, however, a painter: F.R. Pickersgill, an R.A. since 1857; and no doubt it was he who was able to return the young man to the field of painting. Waterhouse was already twenty-two, though that was average among the students who had spent some time in the private art schools. Pickersgill's own painting moved in the footsteps of Etty and of Titian, through history, literature and the Middle East, and although the influences on Waterhouse up to this time had been mainly classical, four Eastern subjects were among his earliest exhibits. Studies for the first two, *Bedouin Woman* and *The Slave*, are reflected in his sketchbooks (now preserved in the Victoria and Albert Museum), and the paintings were shown together with the classically derived *Undine* (Pl.9) in the 1872 Winter Exhibition of the Society of British Artists (not yet the R.B.A.) in Suffolk Street. The *Art Journal* complimented the Society for opening its doors so widely to 'the rising and yet nameless genius of the time' but, recalling that the S.B.A.'s Winter Exhibitions had been commenced as displays of sketches to relieve the pressure on the ordinary summer exhibitions, questioned the work in this particular exhibition as diminishing the normal high standards of the Society. However, Waterhouse was noted among the few whose pictures 'attract by their various qualities'.

Next year the S.B.A.'s Summer Exhibition included *The Unwelcome Companion: A Street Scene in Cairo* (Pl.7). Nino used his friends and relatives, including his sister Jessie, as models, and whatever costumes could be borrowed or contrived. The same girl in the same dress figured in his *Dancing Girl*, of which a line illustration appeared in the catalogue of the Aird collection in 1884.

The scenario of *The Unwelcome Companion* is obscure; perhaps it shows the girl

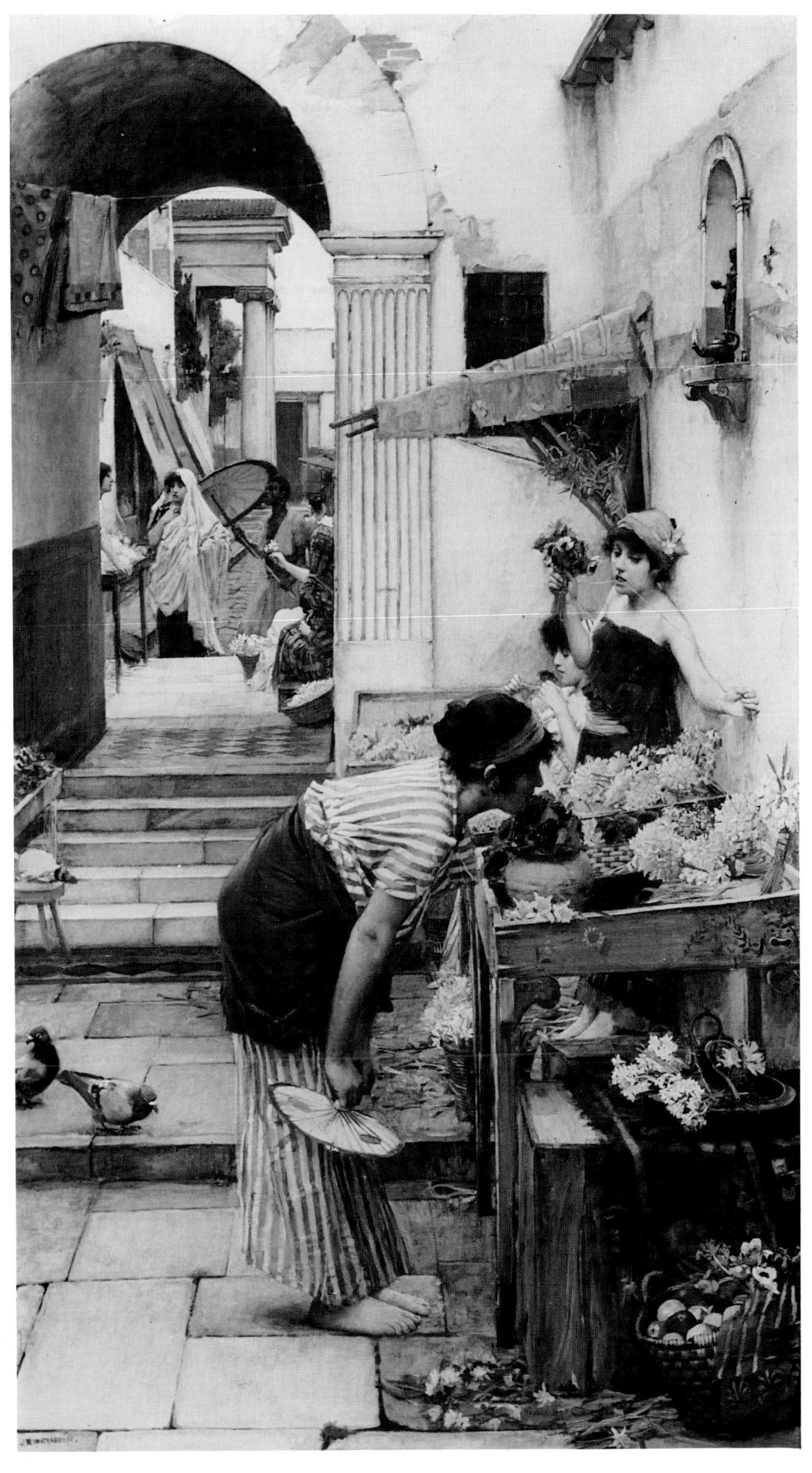

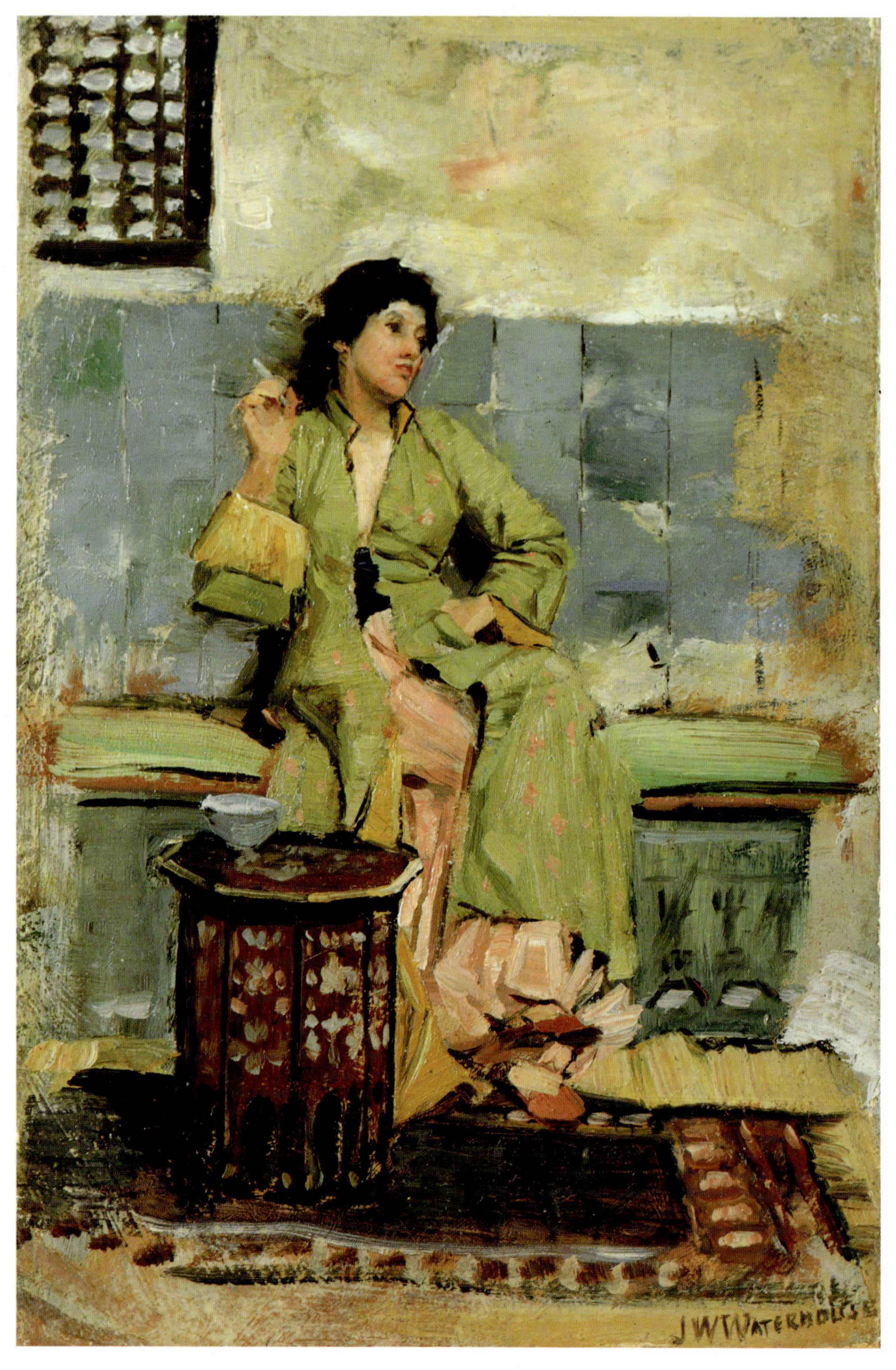

5 *An Eastern Reminiscence* (sketch), 1874. 9¾ × 6½ in (24.5 × 16.5 cm). Courtesy Peter Nahum

6 *La Fileuse*, 1874. Panel, 12½ × 10 in (31.7 × 25.6 cm). Collection Claudio Bruni Sakraischik

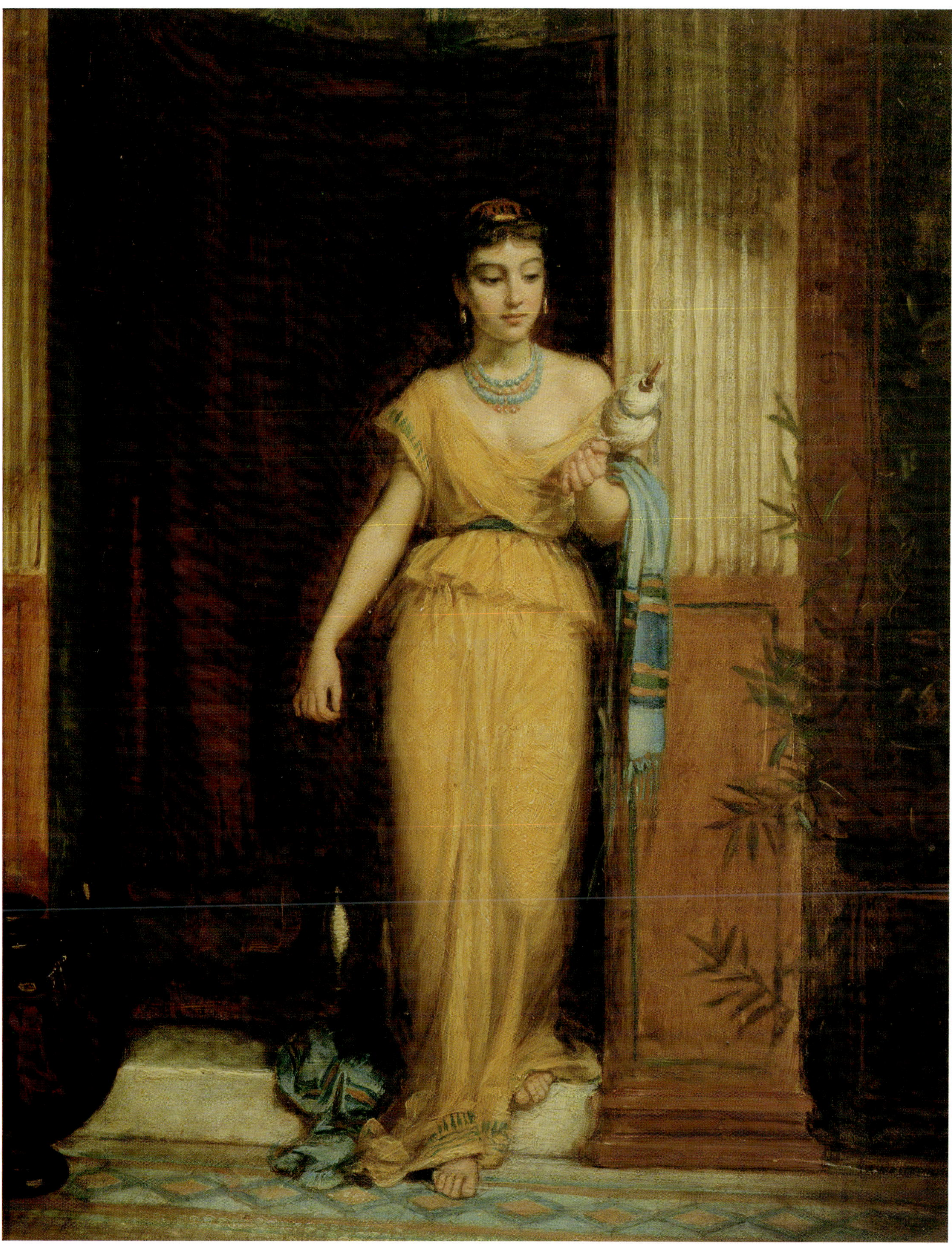

7 *The Unwelcome Companion: A Street Scene in Cairo*, 1873. 23¼ × 19½ in (59 × 49.5 cm). Burnley, Towneley Hall Art Gallery

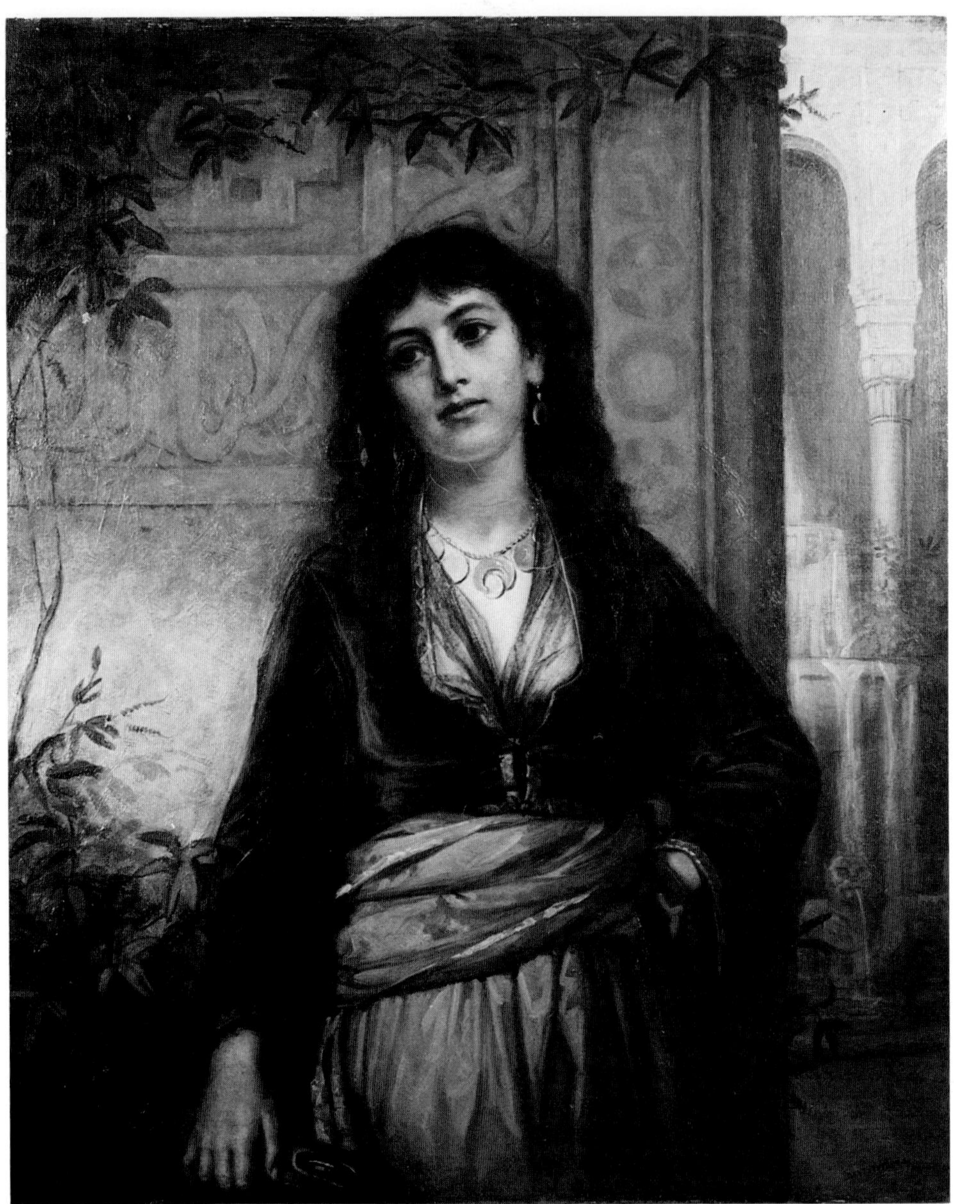

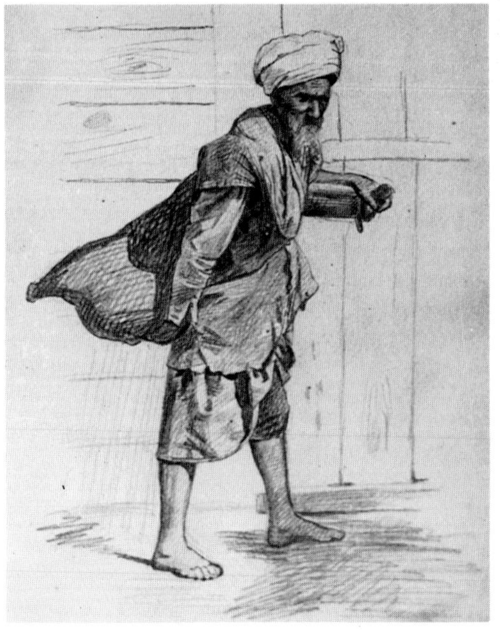

8 *Water Seller*, *c.* 1872. Pencil. London, Victoria & Albert Museum, Sketchbook E1103–1963

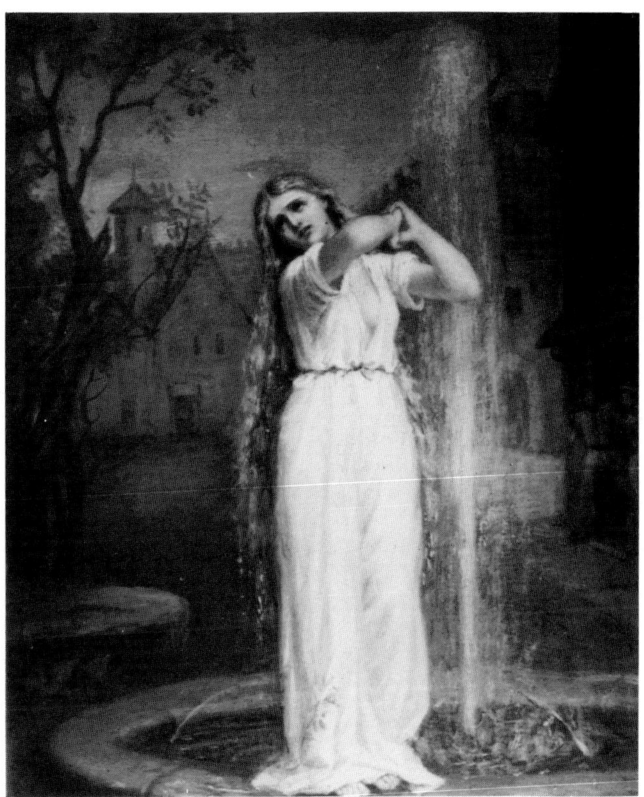

9 *Undine*, *c.*1872. Panel, 10 × 8 in (25 × 20 cm). Location unknown

catching her breath in a quiet corner after escaping from some follower. Donated by its owner to a public collection, this picture remained for many years under the incorrect (though perhaps understandable) title of *Spanish Tambourine Girl* until identified by the writer. The Victorian compulsion to tell a story was inescapable, but although Waterhouse was clearly developing the ability to compose a satisfying picture, he had not yet acquired that combination of an appropriate setting with the pose and gesture of the figure which within a few years was to make him an outstanding illustrator of the legends.

Some of these early pictures had no story to tell: they owe their undoubted charm to his sensitive painting of the female figure, as in *La Fileuse* (Pl.6), with its Graeco-Roman setting and the graceful yet positive rendering of hands and arms of which many lesser painters, including his father, fought shy. Another example shown in the 1874 Annual Exhibition of the Society of British Artists was the delightful small sketch in oils (Pl.5) for the painting *An Eastern Reminiscence*. This time Waterhouse received no compliments from the *Art Journal*, which was too busy castigating the S.B.A. for this 'indifferent collection ... numbering upwards of a thousand pictures ... for the most part so dull and uninspired as not to arouse criticism of any kind'. However, his paintings continued to appeal by their individual subject matter and their sound technique, and they regularly disappeared into private collections from which many have still not emerged, earning the young artist a respectable living. His favourite model at this time may well have been his sister: her name appears in the sentimental verse which accompanied *Whispered Words* (half-title page) in the 1875 Royal Academy, from where it was

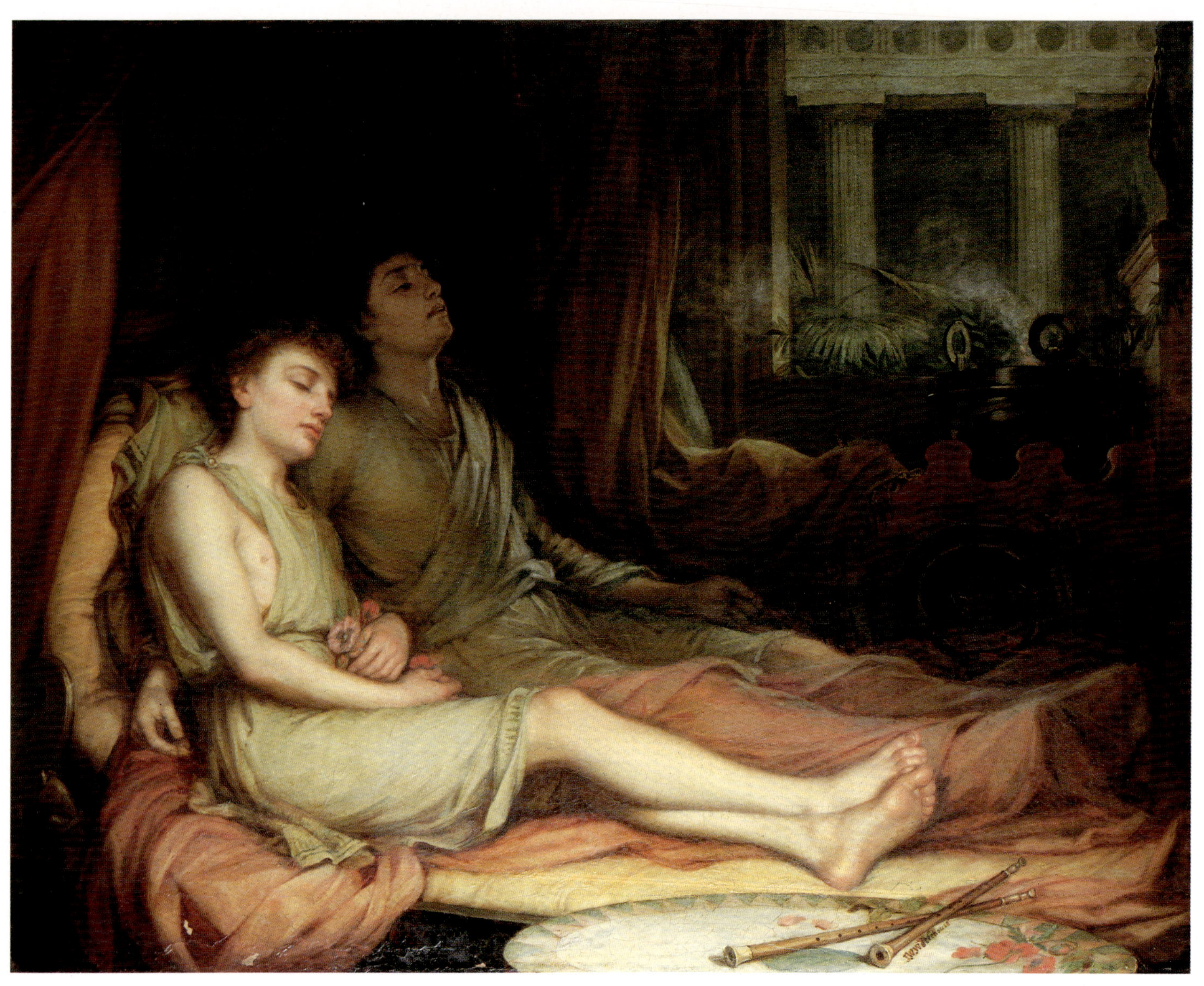

10 *Sleep and his Half-Brother Death*, 1874. 28 × 36 in (70 × 91 cm). Courtesy Sotheby's

11 *Two Little Italian Girls by a Village*, *c.*1875. 24 × 16 in (61 × 49 cm). Private collection

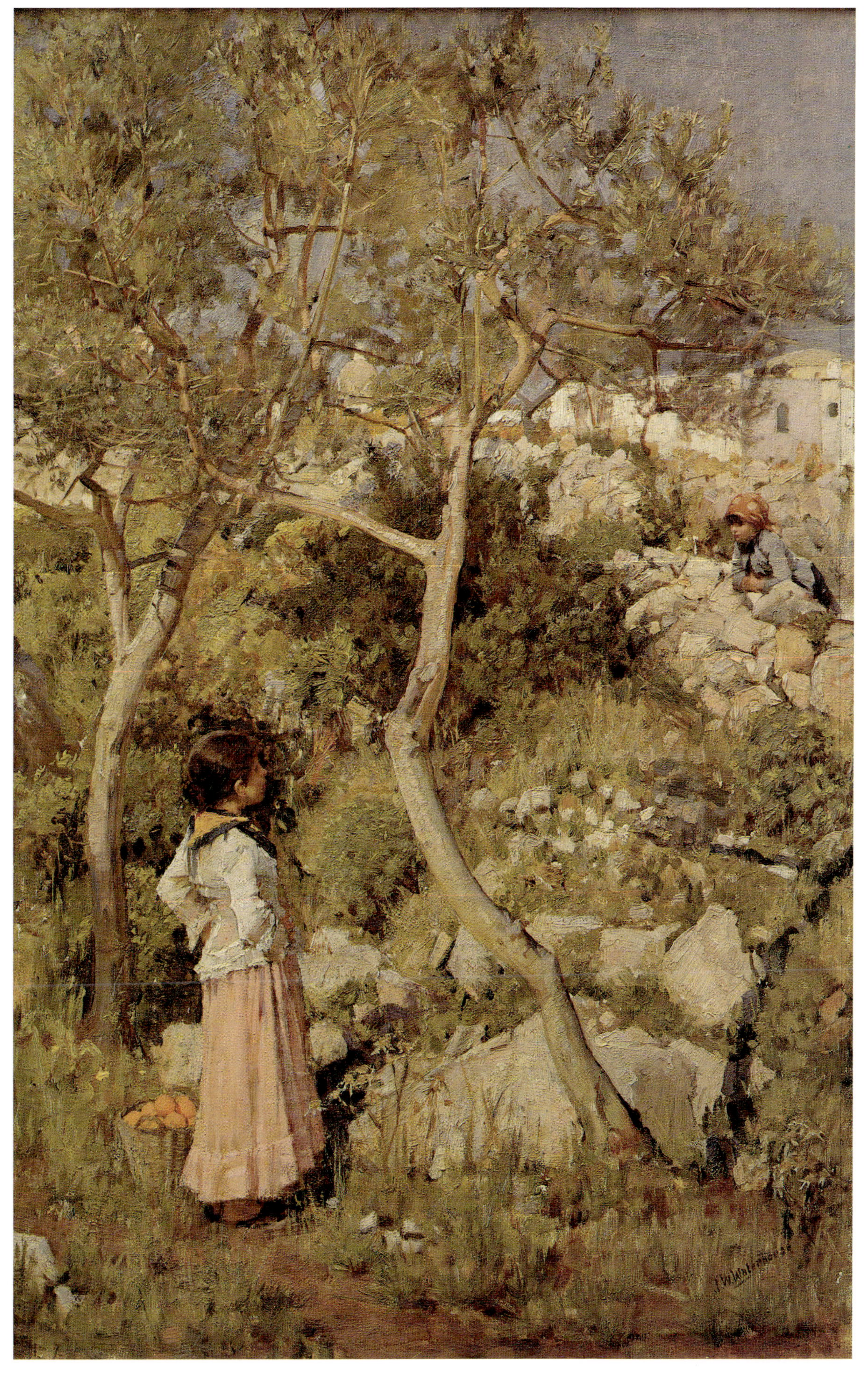
J.W. Waterhouse

bought by Mr (later the first baronet, Sir John) Aird, the engineer and contractor responsible for the removal of the Crystal Palace buildings from Hyde Park and their erection at Sydenham in 1854, and later for the construction of the great Aswan Dam across the Nile. The catalogue of Aird's noted collection of British art, including four Waterhouse paintings, was published in 1884 with line illustrations one of which suggests the same model and costume for Waterhouse's other 1875 exhibit, *Miranda*. Waterhouse never stylized the features of his models as did Burne-Jones, and this pretty girl is surely recognizable again in *A Flower Stall*.

It should be recalled that all this took place while Waterhouse was still a student. Competition for entry to the Academy Schools was fierce and fewer than half of his 128 fellow applicants for Probationership in 1870 finally became Students. But once there, the advantages were clear: seven years' tenure as a student, tutored in the Life School by Royal Academicians serving as monthly Visitors (Millais and Poynter were among the Visitors in 1871), and with considerable freedom about attendance; although it was necessary to qualify formally in order to pass to the Upper Schools. Whether painter or sculptor, the student would have had to produce certificates of attendance at an entire course in perspective and an entire course of lectures 'in order to be admitted to draw from the Nude Living Model'. There were also regulations relating to the various prizes and scholarships. Waterhouse's second place for the Silver Medal was his only achievement. His methods of study tended to be solitary and personal; drawing, painting and composing from memory after study in the museums inculcated and enhanced his ability to visualize. His natural facility in technique enabled him later to realize his visual concepts with an unerring directness, although in these early years he would test out his compositions in public: for instance, at the Dudley Gallery's annual Black and White Exhibition.

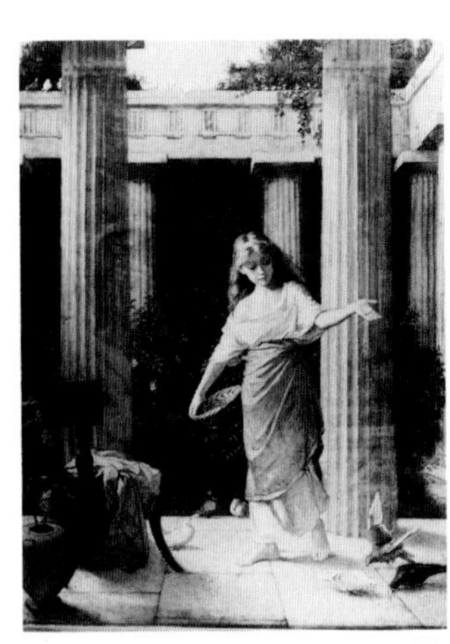

12 *In the Peristyle*, 1874. 26½ × 20½ in (67 × 52 cm). Rochdale Art Gallery

The Dudley Gallery's Winter Exhibition of 1874 included Waterhouse's *In The Peristyle* (Pl. 12). It showed the next major influence on him – that of Lawrence Alma-Tadema, who had settled in London with a European reputation in 1870 and was elected A.R.A. in 1876 and R.A. in 1879, was knighted in 1899 and admitted to the Order of Merit in 1905. Alma-Tadema's dazzling virtuosity concealed the prevailing triviality of his subject matter, which mainly presented in antique costume and settings the incidents of the Victorian drawing-room. But his careful research and his rendering of marble surfaces and architectural interiors with their figures in classical dress were an inspiration to many students, and he had a number of disciples among contemporary artists. This painting of Waterhouse's artfully follows the scheme of classical architecture, but already concentrates on the personality and action of the young model. It too suffered for many years in a municipal gallery under a commonplace title – *Feeding the Pigeons*.

Waterhouse's first Royal Academy exhibit, however, also in 1874, diverged from the classical theme and showed considerable depth of feeling. *Sleep and his Half-Brother Death* (Pl. 10) relates quite certainly to family tragedy. His talented mother, Isabella, had succumbed to the universal scourge of tuberculosis after the return from Italy and died when Nino was only eight years of age. The more recent loss of both his younger brothers from the same disease is reflected in this moving image of the two youthful figures merging into the shadows. A contemporary writer referred to 'the strange likeness and unlikeness of the recumbent figures ... the beauty of youth belongs to one as much as to the other'. In a later review of Waterhouse's career, the *Illustrated London News* made particular mention of this picture and ascribed it to the influence of G.F. Watts; but, great as was the stature of Watts (more especially in the following decade), this is a personal document rather than an allegorical exercise.

A lighter vein was, however, more characteristic of this time. Nino's return to Italy for periods of travel and study between 1876 and 1883 produced a number of charming pictures, showing his interest in colour and the play of light, with models posed out of doors and the conventions of the studio left behind. Typical of these is the picture of *Two Little Italian Girls by a Village* (Pl.11). His enjoyment of the subject is as evident as his skill in rendering it, and it is clear that he could have pursued this aspect of painting with as much success as his former fellow students at the Royal Academy, Stanhope Forbes and H.H. La Thangue. But they were the products of Paris and Brittany, not of Italy, and Waterhouse's thoughts were ever with the beings of history and mythology rather than with fisherfolk and farmers.

So he returned to Rome, to stories and events of the past, and to a world of mysteries which all his life he contrived to flesh out in forms somehow as tangible and certainly more warm-blooded than the sculpture of the Greeks, from whose legends the Romans largely derived their own religion and mythology. There were a number of paintings in which he set the scenes of the classical world: on-the-spot paintings of Roman streets and ruins, of the Colosseum and of Pompeii. Some of them utilized the accessories which Alma-Tadema had so carefully researched: *The Tibia* (the ancient double flute), the trappings of *A Pompeian Shop*, the columns, the couch and the peacock feather fan of *Dolce Far Niente*. Critics who had become accustomed to absorbing without much effort Alma-Tadema's views of everyday life among the ancients were happy to describe *After the Dance* (Pl.14) as a Roman interior with two Greek dancing girls – or alternatively a boy and a girl! Alma-Tadema's painting of the same title appeared in the same Royal Academy exhibition of 1876; a coincidence which, as one critic said, 'much exercised the simple-minded'; though the *Art Journal* distinguished Tadema's nude Bacchante as being 'faulty in drawing'.

There were more serious subjects, still in the Alma-Tadema mode, such as *A Sick Child brought into the Temple of Aesculapius* (Pl.15), exhibited at the Royal Academy in 1877. This is really an astonishing performance, which a small reproduction is inadequate to convey. Henry Blackburn in his *Academy Notes* described it as 'a large and carefully studied composition', and one's first impression on seeing the picture is of its magnitude, and of the boldness of the artist in attempting it. The figures appear life-size and those in the foreground are nearly

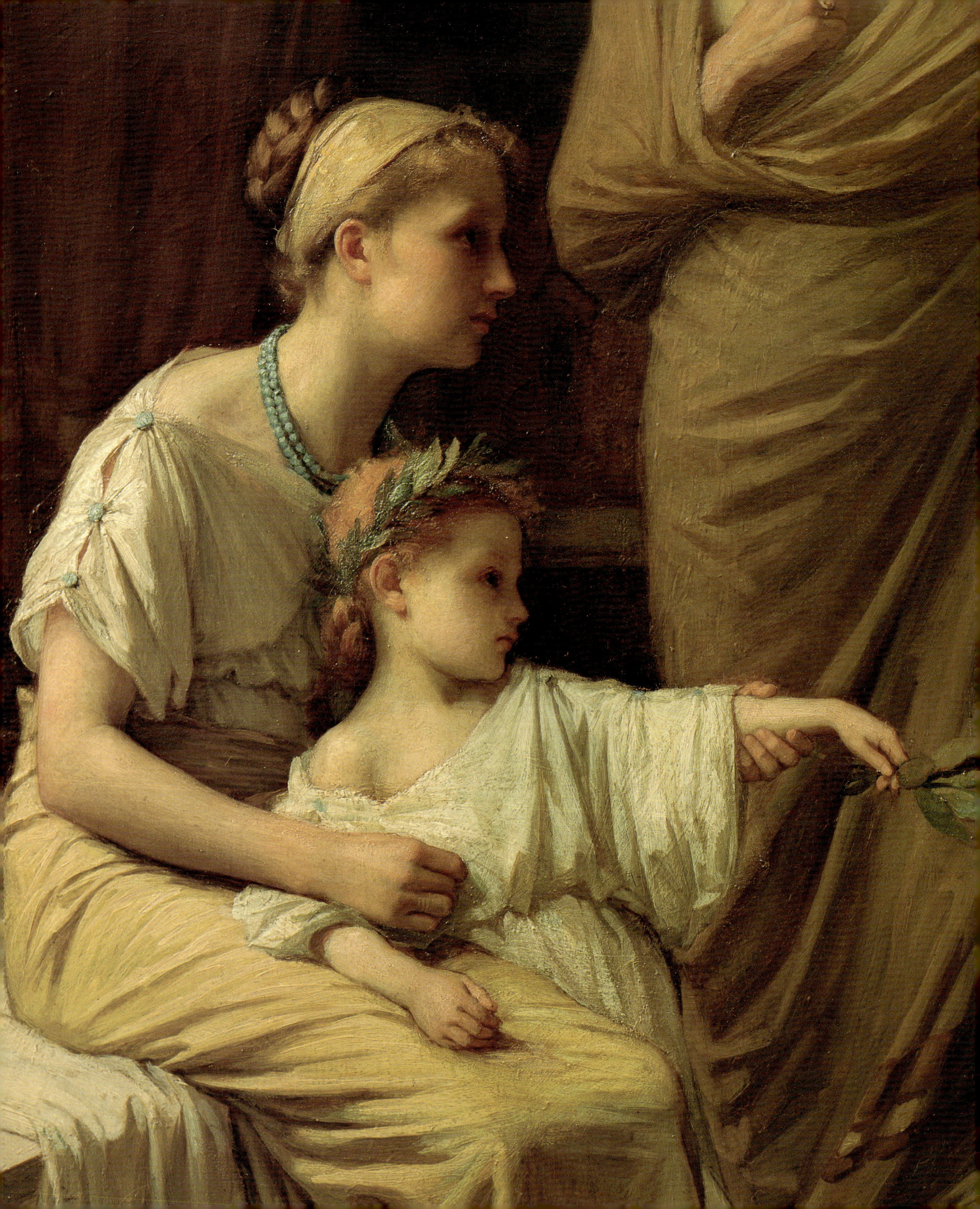

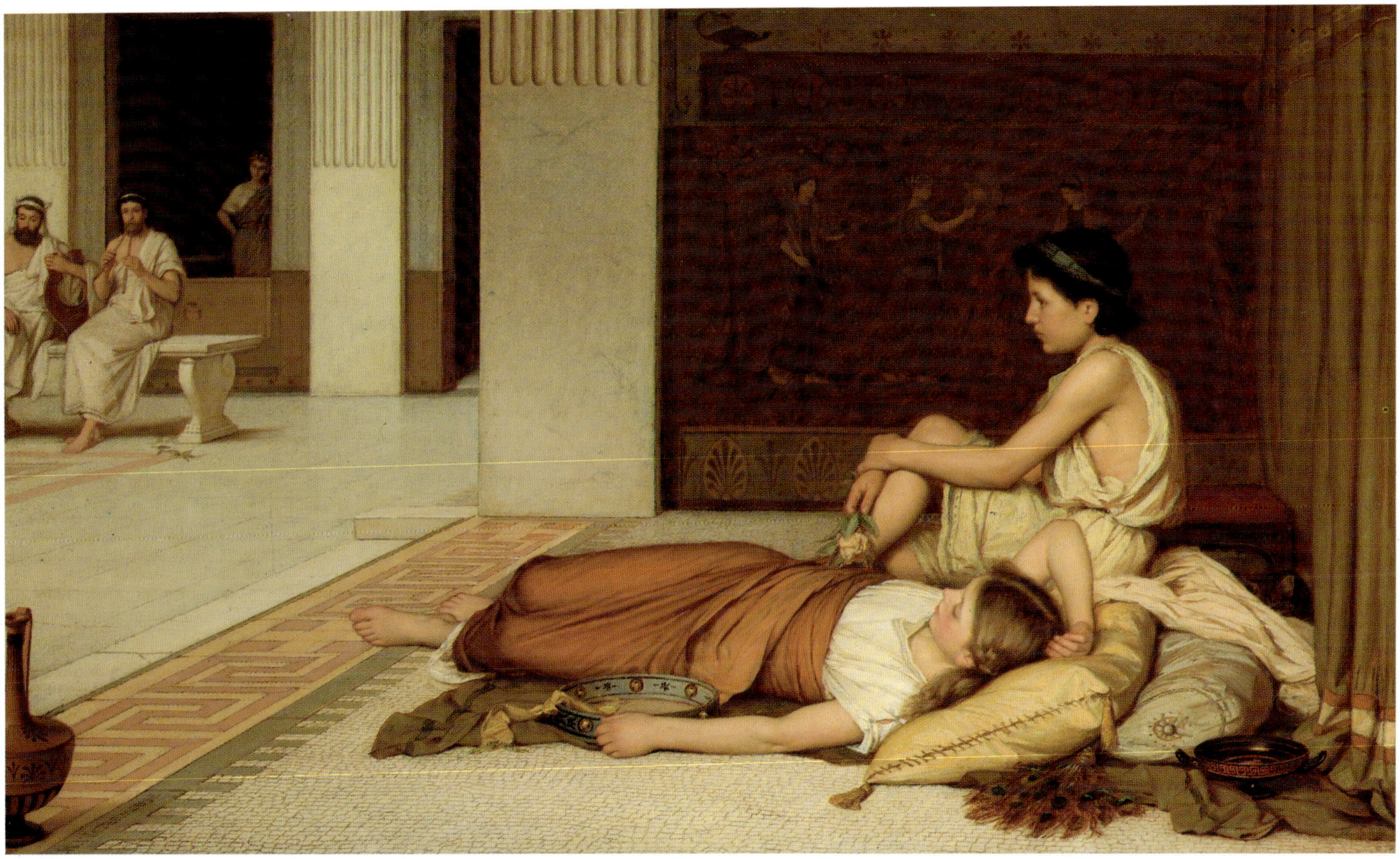

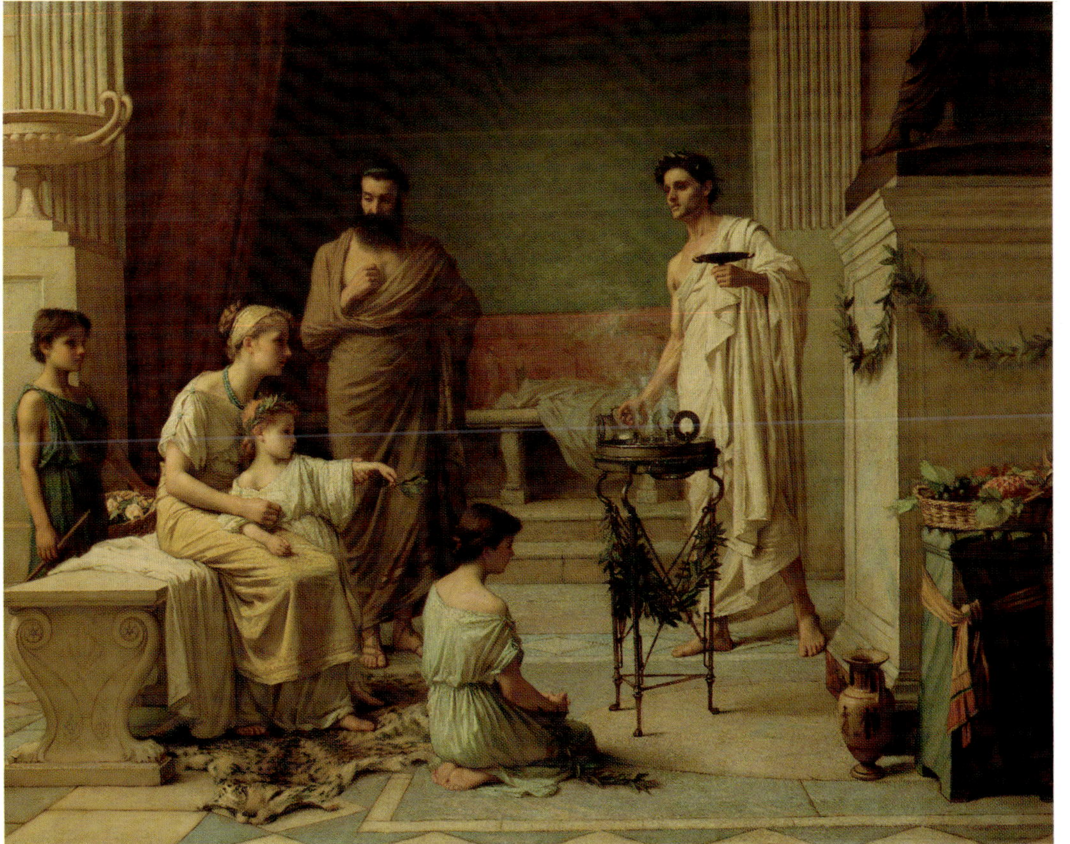

14 ABOVE *After the Dance*, 1876. 30 × 50 in (76.2 × 127 cm). Private collection

13 OPPOSITE Detail from *A Sick Child brought into the Temple of Aesculapius* (Pl. 15)

15 LEFT *A Sick Child brought into the Temple of Aesculapius*, 1877. 67 × 82 in (170 × 208 cm). Private collection

so, the canvas being a little under six feet by seven. A heavy frame (replacing an even heavier one) adds to its visual weight, and in contrast to the many smaller pictures by Alma-Tadema it creates the same impact that the nineteenth-century visitor to the Academy must have felt on approaching Leighton's *Captive Andromache*. Even today, one is simply embraced by the picture, and the experience a century ago – with the cinema still inconceivable – of entering into the picture space and into a scene in ancient Greece, perfectly reconstructed in full colour and architectural perspective, filled with apparently tangible objects and human beings expressing their emotions in look and gesture, must have been truly momentous. Even today photography offers nothing more except cinematic movement, and no still photograph, capturing a single moment, can attain the thoughtful perfection of the painter's creation over many months.

We should have to search the artist's sketchbooks to discover the beginnings of such a painting. At this time Waterhouse had not achieved – perhaps not considered – the fluent progress through larger and larger oil studies which we can observe later on. But that is of no consequence. His methods were perfectly adequate to execute the painting once conceived, and he had the innate ability to grasp the concept, visualize the action, construct the space in perspective, and secure the whole in a firm compositional framework. The geometry of the picture is immediately evident, based on the verticals and horizontals of the architecture, the two male figures standing at the same height, with the boy at the left and the plinth of the statue at the right. But there is also a carefully conceived inner structure, a sweeping curve directed downwards by the father's hand and arm, through the body of the mother, assisted by the drapery angled on the seat, to that of the older child, whose feet and leg slant upwards with the feet of the tripod leading like points on a graph to the foot of the priest, where the inward curve begins again. How cunningly all this leads our eyes into the composition, at the focal point of which the sick child's hand, pale against the dark drapery, weakly presents the leafy offering.

Waterhouse's colour has still to attain its final brilliance and delicacy; the shadows are dark rather than luminous (and by this one can date the oil sketch for *The Lady Clare* which recently came to light) but the flesh tones are finely rendered. The older children are almost certainly the two who appeared the previous year in *After the Dance*. A final pointer to the controlled brilliance of the artist's technique is to be found on the left of the picture, where between the meticulously painted flesh-tones and drapery of son and mother the basket of flowers is rendered with fiercely vital brush-strokes of impasto.

The artistic hierarchy of the period still placed the history painter at the top of the tree, and it was natural that classical history as well as classical myth should occupy Waterhouse's attention. *The Remorse of the Emperor Nero after the Murder of his Mother* (Pl.16), exhibited in the Royal Academy of 1878, was a formidable subject for interpretation through a single figure, yet the Victorian artist was not afraid to tackle hurdles of this difficulty, where he laid himself open to either approval or censure in the forthright criticism of the day. In this case Waterhouse received both. Blackburn's *Academy Notes* called it a 'powerful picture' and, said the *Art Journal*, 'the agony of the man is made painfully manifest'. The *Illustrated London News*, however, though conceding that this 'grovelling figure' of apparently forty years of age was 'gaunt, haggard and remorseful enough in appearance', pointed out that Nero was in fact very fat and under thirty at the time. Its comment on the artist's 'considerable ambition' in the attempt, though, does credit to the Victorians when gesture and expression have today all but disappeared from twentieth-century 'fine art'.

No doubt the inspiration for these works came largely from Alma-Tadema, but the differences not merely in size but in depth of subject are already apparent, and Waterhouse finally decided to leave the train of that acknowledged master at a peak of his own achievement. The 1882 *Diogenes* (Pl.17) is a large, sunny canvas, precise in its rendering of the architecture and the texture of the marble, flexible in the linked figures of the light-hearted girls, so unaffectedly posed. Yet all are firmly welded into an unerring composition towards which the artist had progressed in earlier exhibited pictures such as *A Summer's Day in Greece* and the loosely structured *Diogenes* of the Aird collection. In this final picture, our eyes move downwards without straying between the horizontal bounds of the temple roof and the stone pavement, from the closed circle of the parasol to that of the philosopher's tub.

It was then to the old Empire that Waterhouse turned in 1883 for his first major exercise in history: *The Favourites of the Emperor Honorius* (Pl.18). The Victorian painter was always seeking an unusual or startling subject to make his next Academy exhibit stand out from the rest; preferably one which he could conceal from the world until it was too late for any rival to copy or plagiarize it. Nevertheless, Waterhouse's subjects were never sensational or shocking; they were products of his own reading of history, legend or poetry, and the paintings themselves prove his deep involvement with them. Flavius Honorius is not one of the more familiar or admirable figures of ancient Rome. He ascended the throne as 'Emperor of the West' in the year 395, establishing his court first at Milan and then, in fear of the barbarians, at Ravenna. Lazy by nature, he depended on able generals like Constantius and his own guardian and father-in-law, the Vandal Stilicho, to save Italy from the invading forces, exerting himself only in the support of the orthodox Church and the persecution of heathens and heretics.

Once again the composition of the picture is scrupulously organized, not merely to direct the eye, but in so doing to explain the situation. Two smaller oils show the artist's way of achieving his objectives, and also indicate how very much of a painter and visualizer he was, rather than a linear draughtsman and designer. He always went straight from his first concept to colour and the brush, making progress on the canvas in contrast to Leighton's almost interminable series of chalk studies and squared-up compositions. Here the first oil sketch (Pl.19) is very small, less than eight inches high, but the theme is established: Honorius is feeding his pet

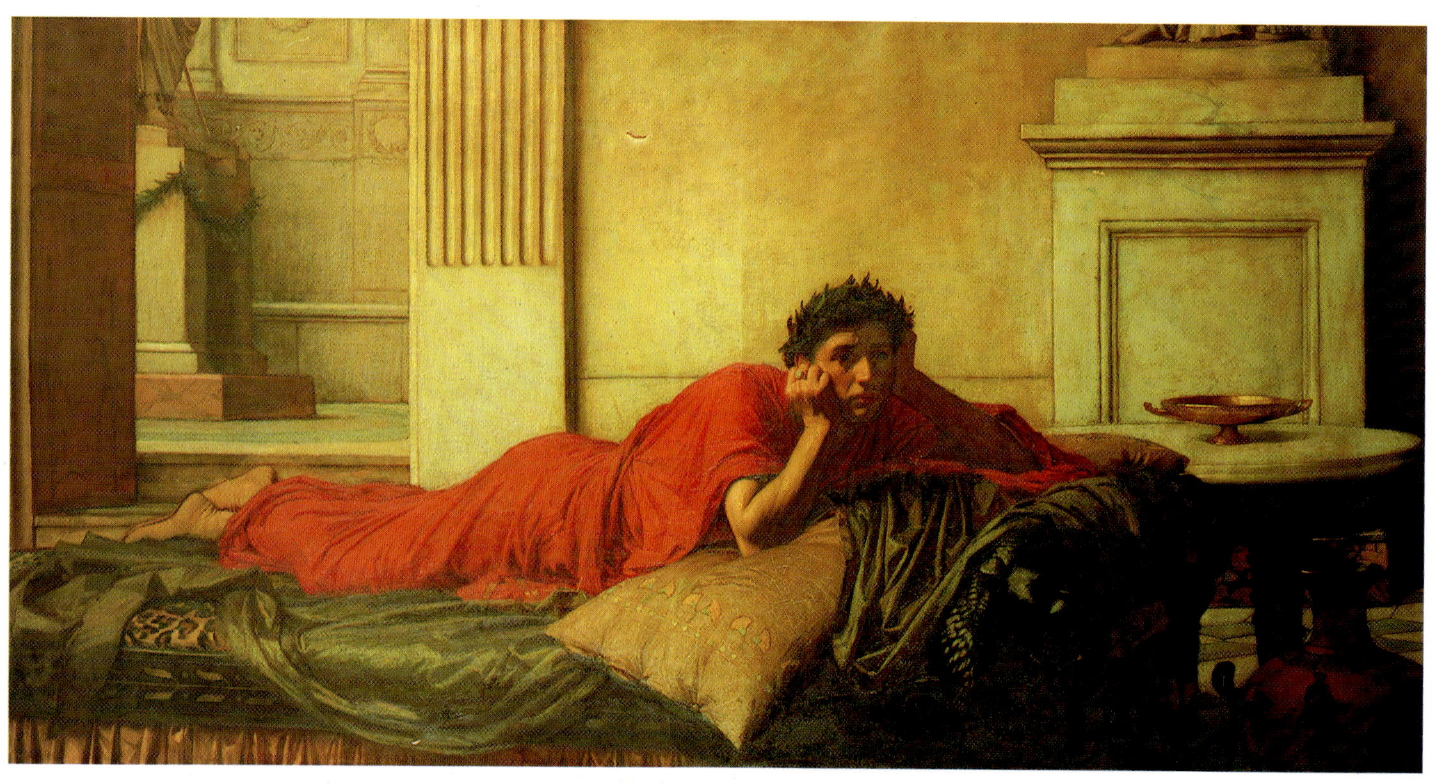

16 *The Remorse of Nero after the Murder of his Mother*, 1878. 37 × 66 in (94 × 168 cm). Courtesy Sotheby's

17 *Diogenes*, 1882. 82 × 53 in (208 × 135 cm). Sydney, Art Gallery of New South Wales

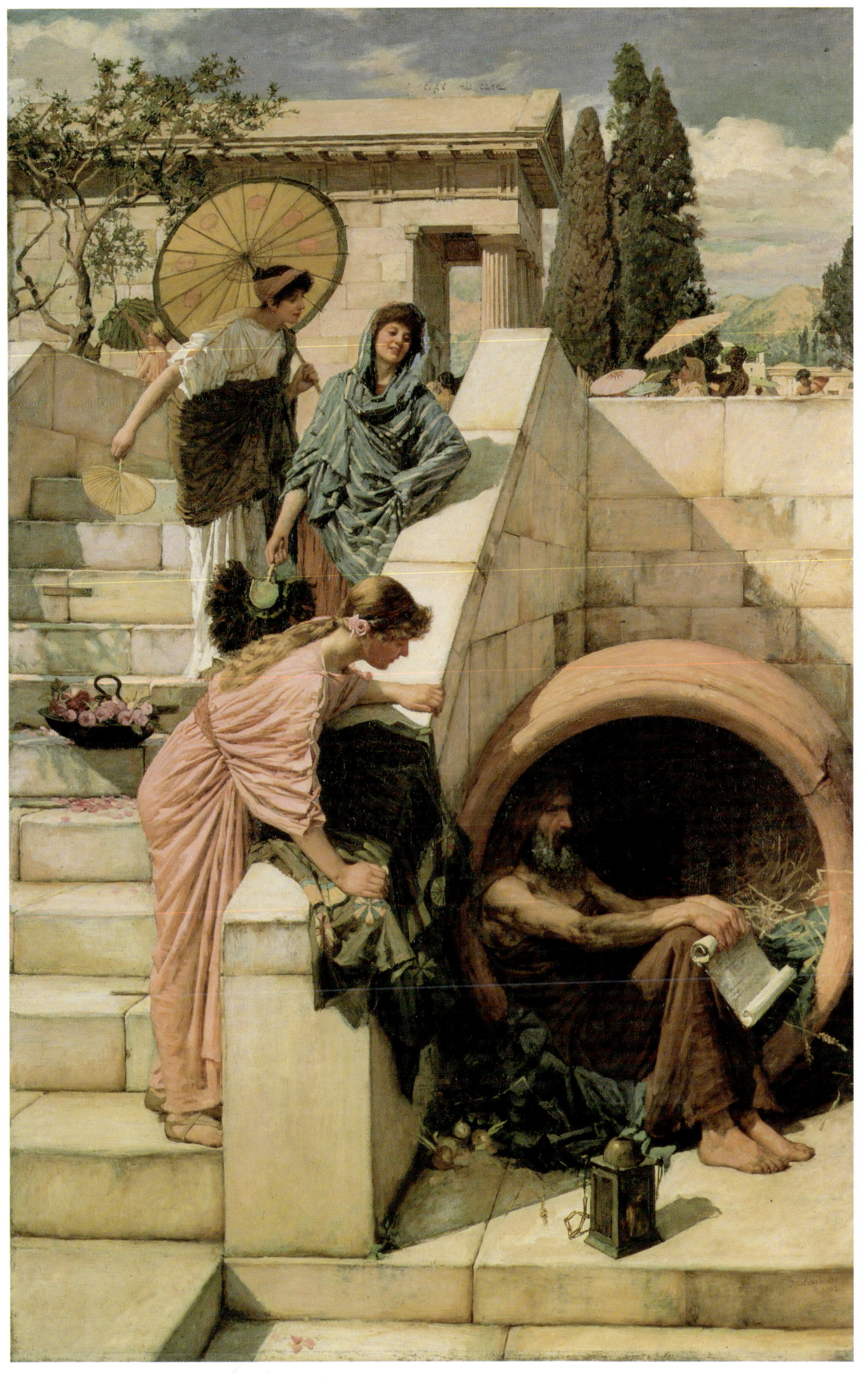

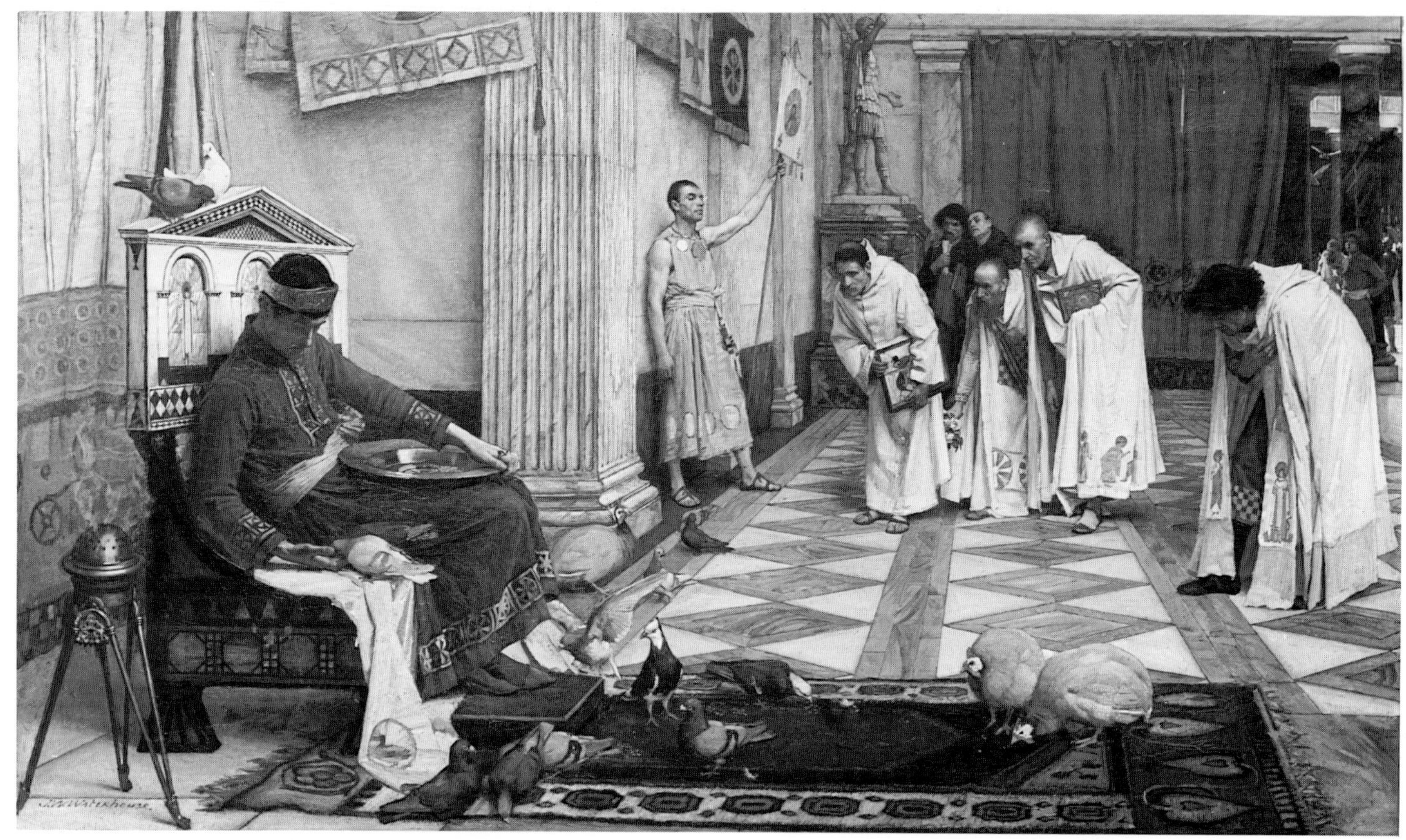

18 *The Favourites of the Emperor Honorius*, 1883. 46¼ × 79½ in (117 × 202 cm). Adelaide, Art Gallery of South Australia

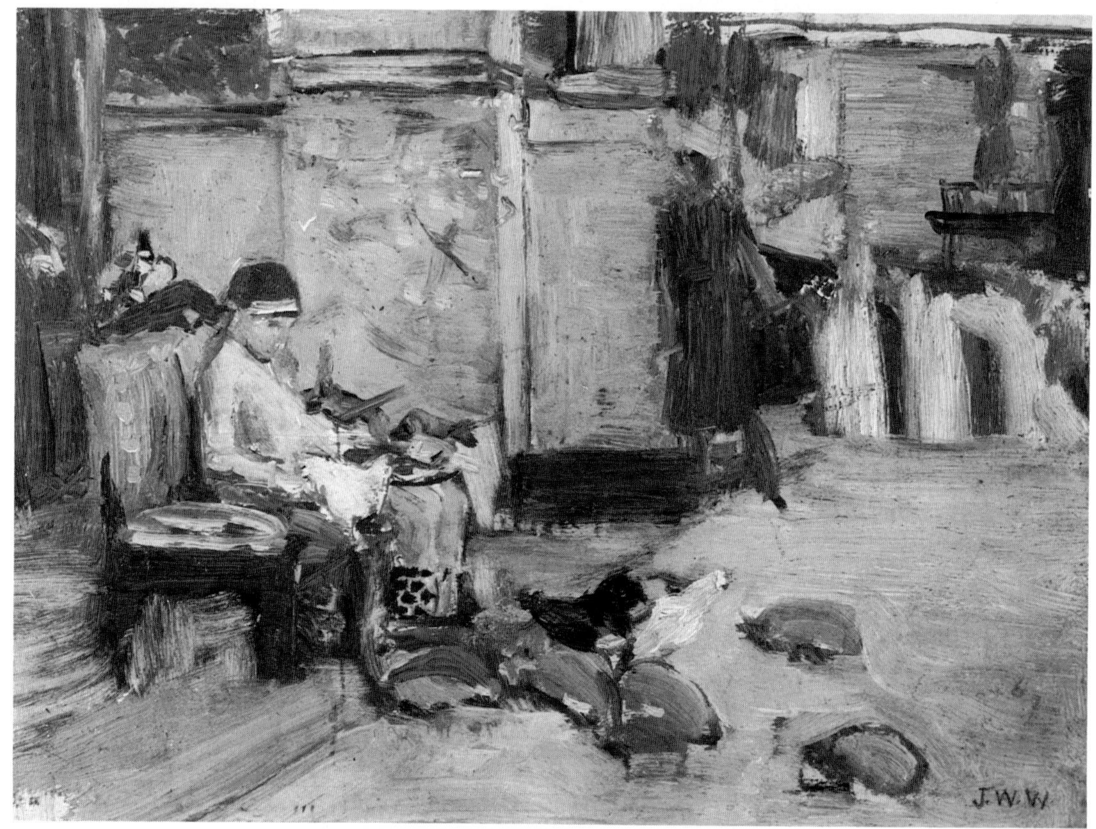

19 *The Favourites of the Emperor Honorius* (oil sketch), *c.* 1883. Board 7¾ × 11 in (20 × 28 cm). John Physick, Esq

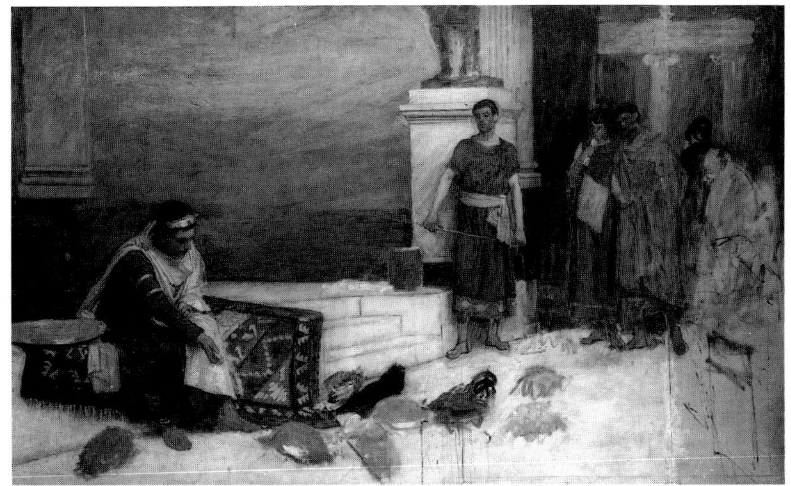

20 *The Favourites of the Emperor Honorius* (study), *c.* 1883. 37 × 65 in (94 × 165 cm). Private collection

birds while councillors await his attention, and the central figure of an attendant separates him from them.

In the intermediate study (Pl. 20) the councillors are brought forward in an expanded audience chamber. The emperor's attention is concentrated on his tame pigeons and the large guinea-fowl, to which the painter devoted little work at this stage (when this canvas came up in a twentieth-century saleroom it was described as *Roman Emperor and Tortoises*: another instance of the extraordinary disappearance of picture titles). Waterhouse as always is primarily absorbed in the painting of the figures, but the story is not yet properly told. The central figure of the attendant is an unwanted focus of attention, standing four-square against the pedestal of the statue and more imposing than the seated monarch. And all are too much in repose to suggest a situation fraught with tension.

The final picture resolves all the problems. Honorius and his pets – the 'favourites' – occupy a space of their own, defined and restricted by the darkness of the carpet and of his garments; the others are palely clad. The central attendant is moved, stiffened in posture, turned away and reduced to the scale of the councillors, who wait tensely, caught half bent in their obeisance, with eyes anxiously fixed on the emperor. He is supremely relaxed, apparently unconscious of their presence. The mental gulf between them lies in their attitudes and expressions, and the artist has completed their physical separation by the great column in the centre and – the final subtle combination of all these forces – the removal of the golden tray to the emperor's left hand, forming the ultimate barrier to communication. No story could be better told in one still picture; and, as we shall see again and again in Waterhouse's painting, it is the moment of stillness – selected, sought and finally captured on the canvas – which is one of the chief marks of his genius.

As Waterhouse's reputation increased, the destinations of these large paintings, each the principal work of one year, began to include the major public galleries. In the latter years of the nineteenth century the great museums of Australia were building up their art collections, and this picture went immediately from the Royal Academy Summer Exhibition to the Art Gallery of South Australia, Adelaide.

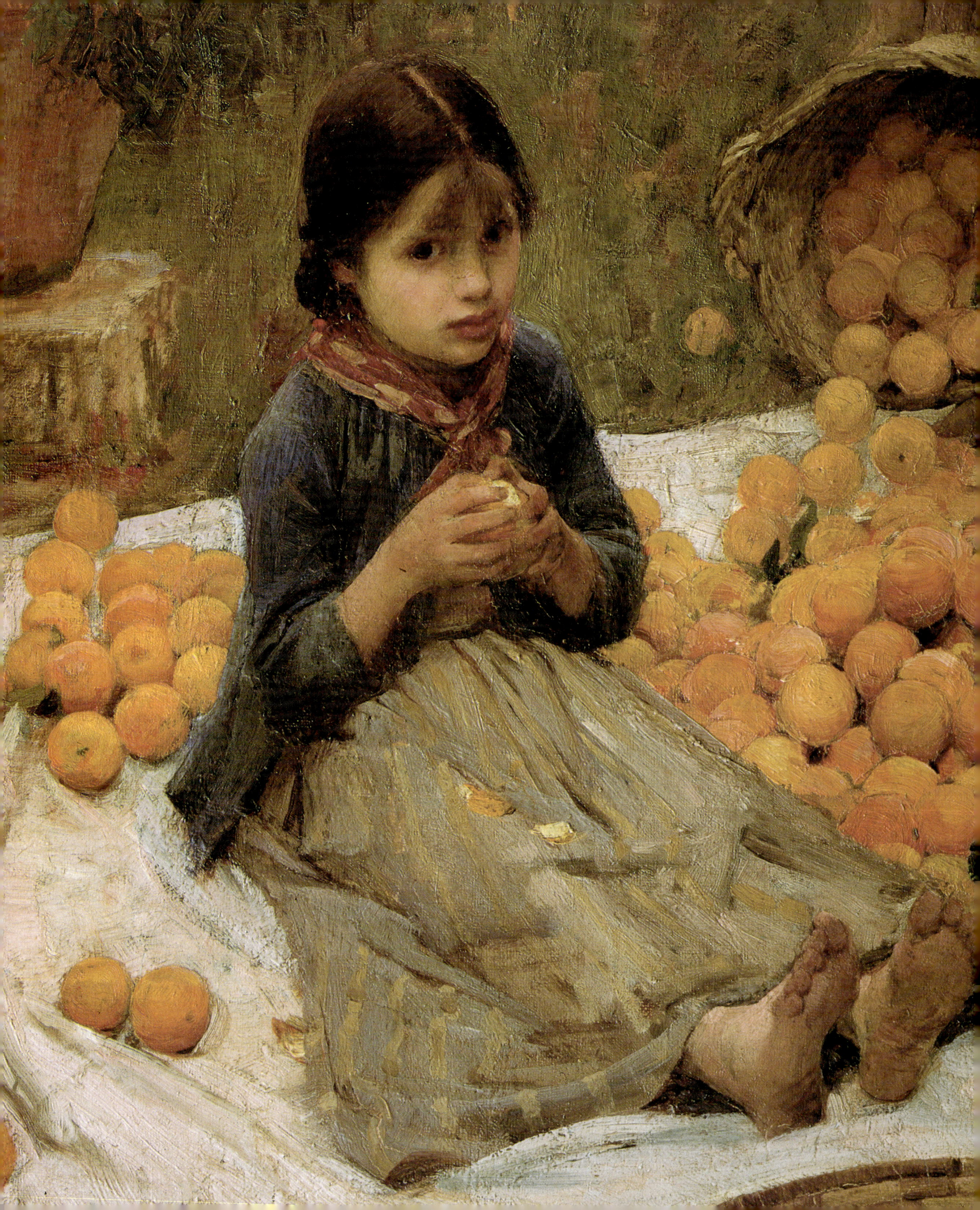

2

Primrose Hill

ON 8 SEPTEMBER 1883, John William Waterhouse married Esther Kenworthy at the parish church of St Mary, Ealing. He was then thirty-four and she twenty-five. His portrait of her about this time (Pl. 22) shows dark eyes and rounded features but no great beauty. The painting, however, sums up his extraordinary capabilities with the brush. The young woman's head is modelled with marvellous strength and subtlety, flesh and bone expressed with the chiaroscuro of a follower of Velasquez. By contrast, the modish shape of the beribboned straw hat is laid in with powerful strokes of impasto, in which colour and texture are unhesitatingly defined.

21 Detail from *The Orange Gatherers* (Pl. 28)

The couple moved into No. 3, Primrose Hill Studios, a group of twelve dwellings round a courtyard off Fitzroy Road, just north of Regent's Park. They had been custom-built in 1880 as artists' residences, each with a spacious north-lit studio. All the occupiers had keys to the gate at the top of the entry, and if they went out without them they had to ring the bell at the side gate in Kingstown Street to be re-admitted by the caretaker.

The combination of security, privacy and a community of artists encouraged long-lasting friendships like that between Nino and Esther Waterhouse and Maurice Greiffenhagen and his wife. The Waterhouses relinquished No. 3 in 1888 to the Greiffenhagens and moved to No. 6, which was very slightly larger and where they remained for another twelve years. Another great friend and an excellent painter, William Logsdail, who occupied No. 4 from 1889 to 1892, recalled in his memoirs the visits of postmen bearing the acceptance notices for the Royal Academy exhibitions, the walk across Regent's Park to the Academy on Varnishing Day and in the evening the celebratory dinner with champagne at Blanchard's in Beak Street. It was in the dedicated yet convivial atmosphere of Primrose Hill Studios that Waterhouse was to paint his finest pictures.

The major work of the following year, 1884, was *Consulting the Oracle* (Pl. 23), which together with the *Honorius* helped to consolidate his reputation. This large painting is another object lesson in composition, where Waterhouse used again with even greater deliberation the simple, logical and highly effective device which the writer has ventured to call 'the keyhole composition'. This refers not to some telescopic view of the scene but to the keyhole shape of the figure grouping, in

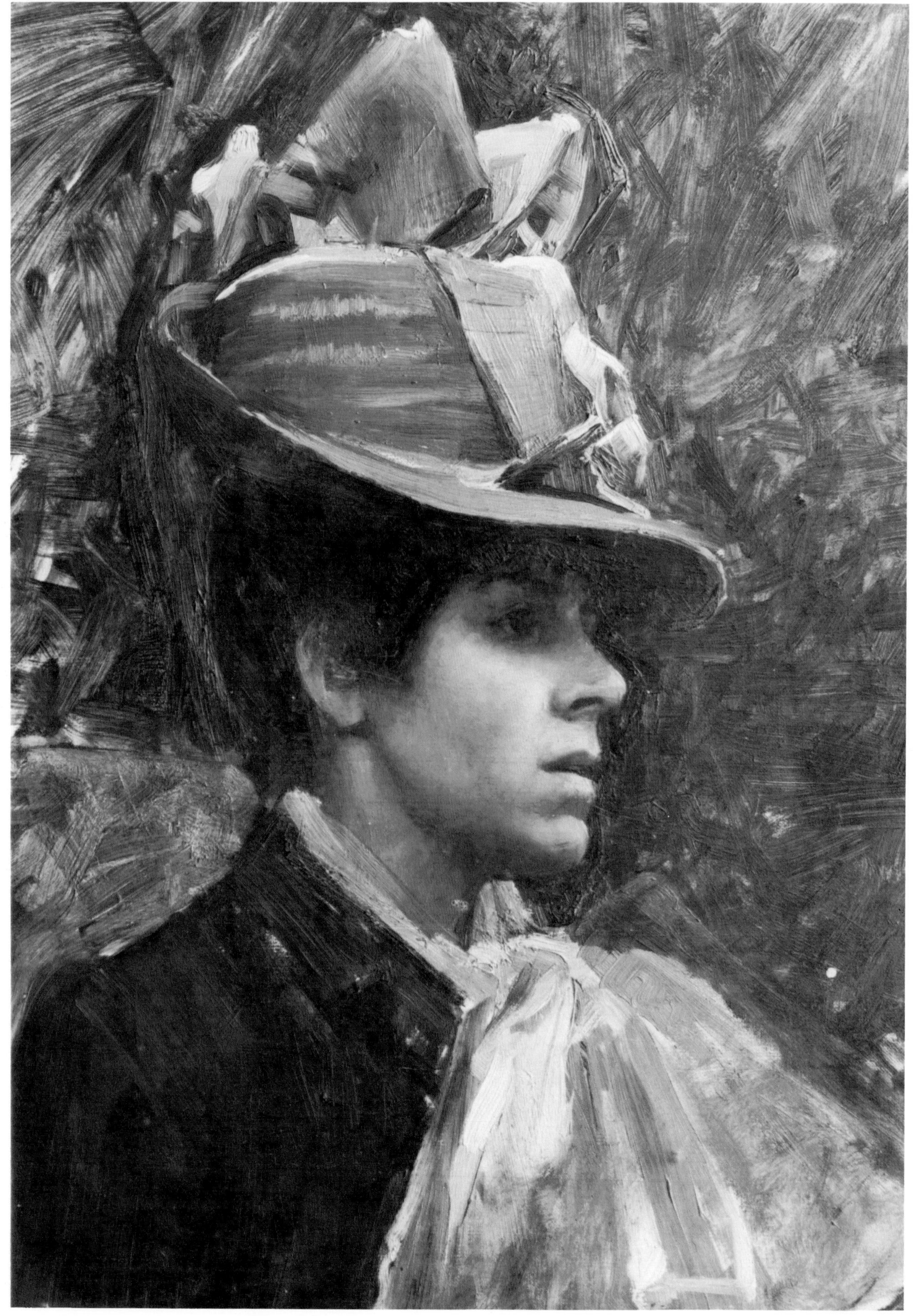

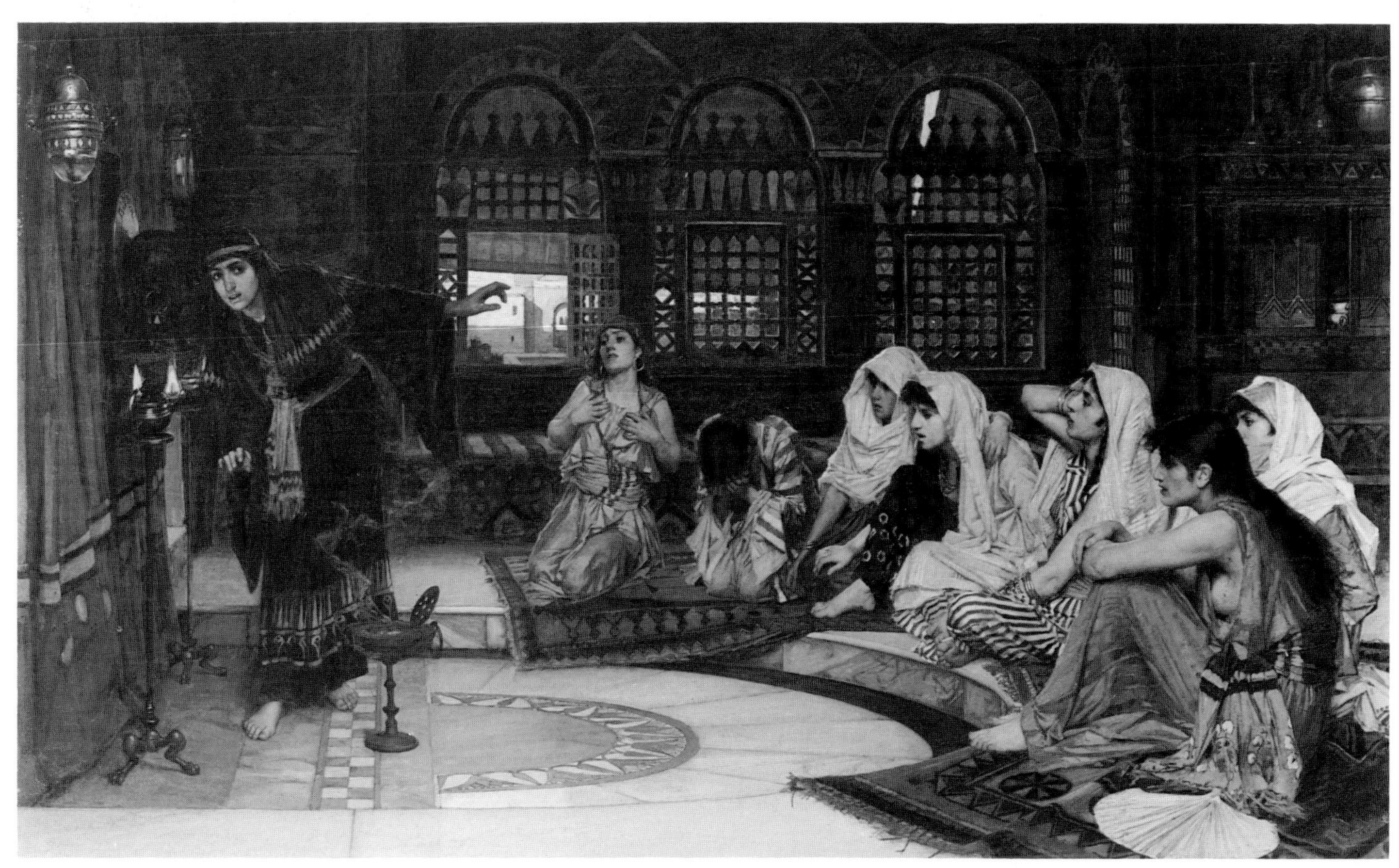

23 *Consulting the Oracle*, 1884. 47 × 78 in (119 × 198 cm). London, Tate Gallery

22 *The Artist's Wife*, *c.* 1884. 22 × 15¼ in (56 × 39 cm). Sheffield City Art Galleries

which a ring of spectators concentrate their attention upon another single figure. The 'hysteric awe' of the semicircle of women seeking the prophecies of the Teraph (a human skull), and the figure of the priestess as she 'interprets its decrees with terror', overwhelmed the critics. The *Illustrated London News* described it as one of the principal works of the year and engraved it across two pages of an extra supplement: it was bought by Sir Henry Tate and is one of the four Waterhouse pictures in the Tate Gallery.

Consulting the Oracle is also one of the earliest pictures to establish Waterhouse as a classical painter. By this I mean that he uses the classical, geometrical structures which have obtained from the architecture of the Greek temple to the altarpieces of Raphael: the vertical, the horizontal and the circle. Not for him the rushing diagonals of Rubens or the boxed-in boudoirs of Burne-Jones. In Waterhouse's pictures there is always space to breathe, and the accompanying air of serenity is derived, as here, from the regular rhythm of the window arches and the firm compass swing of the marble step. Within this structure, he knows precisely when and where to introduce the tension of the diagonal: in the inclined figure of the priestess (note her hand, carrying the message, silhouetted against the brilliant sunshine on the wall outside) and the slight slant of the disordered rug.

24 *St Eulalia*, 1885. 74¼ × 46¼ in (186 × 117.5 cm). London, Tate Gallery

In 1885, 1886 and 1887 Waterhouse exhibited only one picture per year at the Royal Academy. They comprised two major works and one which must fairly be accounted less important in spite of its popularity and its purchase under the Chantrey Bequest; the first secured his election as an Associate of the Academy. All are a testimony to the admiration of his painting in days when, as now, there was keen competition for places among non-members. In 1885, some 7,000 works were rejected out of approximately 9,000 submitted: a process accomplished in a fortnight or so and entitling the selectors, as the *Magazine of Art* sarcastically observed, 'to the warmest, the most outspoken admiration ... in a wink the aspirant was judged; was condemned to the cellars, or pronounced a painter, or held over to take his chance with the Hanging Committee, and achieve publicity if the carpenters could find him room.'

In the severely critical atmosphere of that year, when even the painting of Leighton, the President (hovering on the creation of his baronetcy), was censured for its inadequacies – 'his flesh is, as always, wax that would but cannot altogether live' – the acclaim of Waterhouse is all the more remarkable. The same reviewer wrote at length:

> Mr J.W. Waterhouse's *St Eulalia* takes a position of peculiar isolation in the year's art. ... In an age that resists the manifestations of faith and denies the miraculous, it is hard for the painter to depict supernatural phenomena without a tendency to the grotesque. Of miraculous intervention in the martyrdom of St Eulalia there was nothing but the fall of snow, which the simple faith of the early Christians conceived a heaven-sent shroud for the young saint, whose body was exposed in the Roman Forum. ... The artist's conception is full of power and

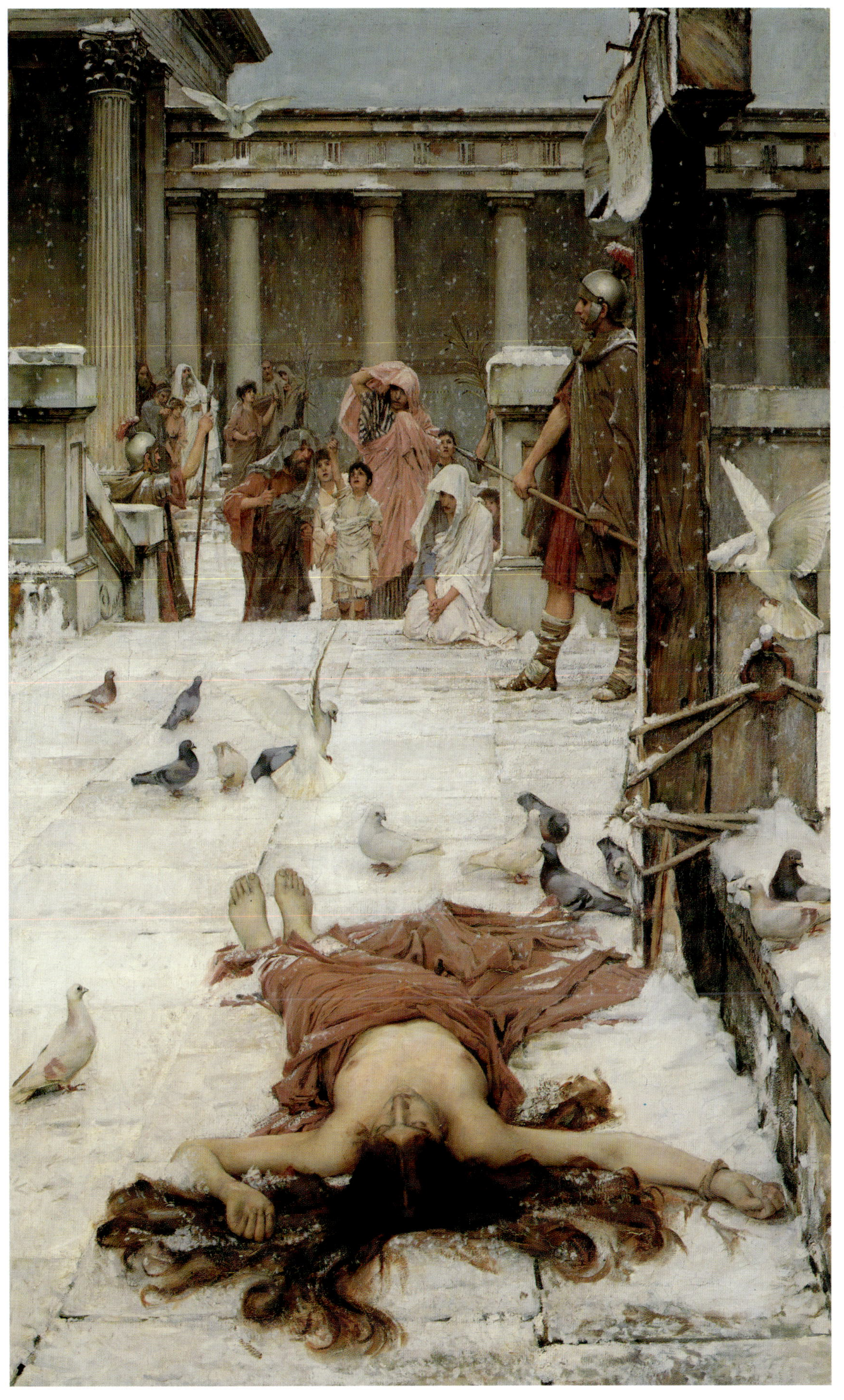

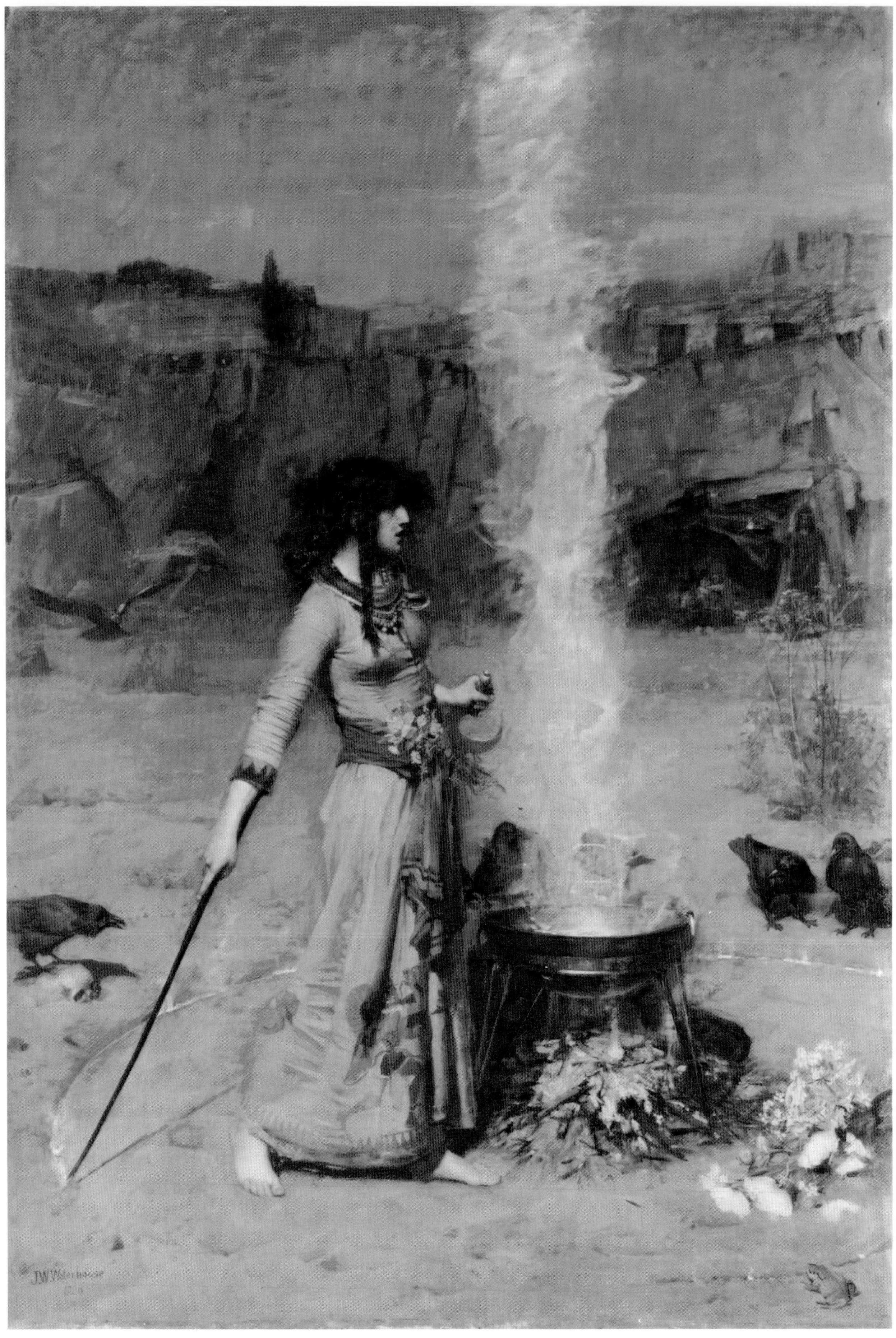
J.W.Waterhouse

> originality. Its whole force is centred in the pathetic dignity of the outstretched figure, so beautiful in its helplessness and pure serenity, so affecting in its forlorn and wintry shroud, so noble in the grace and strength of its presentment. . . . The picture abounds in evidence of care and study and thought, the outcome of which takes the shape of the potent and effective simplicity, whose direct and touching language needs no interpreter.

Victorian art criticism could be satirical and vituperative, but it always gave evidence of the writer's having examined the picture. Even if biased, its bias was arguable and generally well argued, and its satire was often laced with humour. In this case, the last sentence brings out clearly both the method and achievement of a great Victorian painter. Waterhouse's care and study and thought are perhaps discernible in the picture, but they are proved beyond doubt by earlier essays on the same theme. Four years previously, the *Art Journal* had commented on his drawing of *St Eulalia* in the Dudley Gallery exhibition as 'a ghastly and unpleasant attempt at the foreshortening of a dead body'; but this indicates in the first place his tenacious grasp of an idea to be pursued until conquered, and secondly it reiterates the fact that every one of his exhibited works had the figure as its beginning and focal point. Although he gave his full attention to the narrative, the model began to dictate the composition, and his response to the challenge of figure drawing was in the best tradition of academies since the Renaissance.

25 *The Magic Circle*, 1886. 72 × 50 in (183 × 127 cm). London, Tate Gallery

The composition of *St Eulalia* (Pl.24) is daring by any standards, leaving the centre of the canvas virtually unoccupied. Yet it succeeds beyond measure. As in the previous pictures, the single figure is the focus of attention for the group of onlookers, themselves resolved here into a central pyramid and condensed from the earlier sketch by being placed on a flight of steps leading downwards, out of sight, instead of upwards. The bulky plinth of an equestrian statue on the right is replaced by the martyr's cross, and instead of the sentry's spear pointing brusquely down at the saint's body, it is used more subtly to lead the eye down the zig-zag of ropes to the base of the composition – the outflung arms. In spite of the emphatic verticals and horizontals, the note of tension is introduced by these diagonals and echoed in the slight shift of the lower limbs. The youngest mourner points upward at the rising dove which symbolizes the departing soul, completing what Walter Armstrong in his article on the Tate collection called 'a tour de force, which not many English painters would have brought off so successfully'. It was this painting which secured Waterhouse's election as an Associate of the Royal Academy.

As time went by, Waterhouse became accustomed to work on two pictures simultaneously, one large and elaborate and the other containing only a single figure. His next Academy exhibit, *The Magic Circle* (Pl.25), fell into the latter category. In the year 1886 the Royal Academy, according to the *Magazine of Art*, was 'at its worst. It has reached its nadir.' However, 'Mr Waterhouse, in *The Magic Circle*, is still at his best – original in conception and pictorial in his results. – The

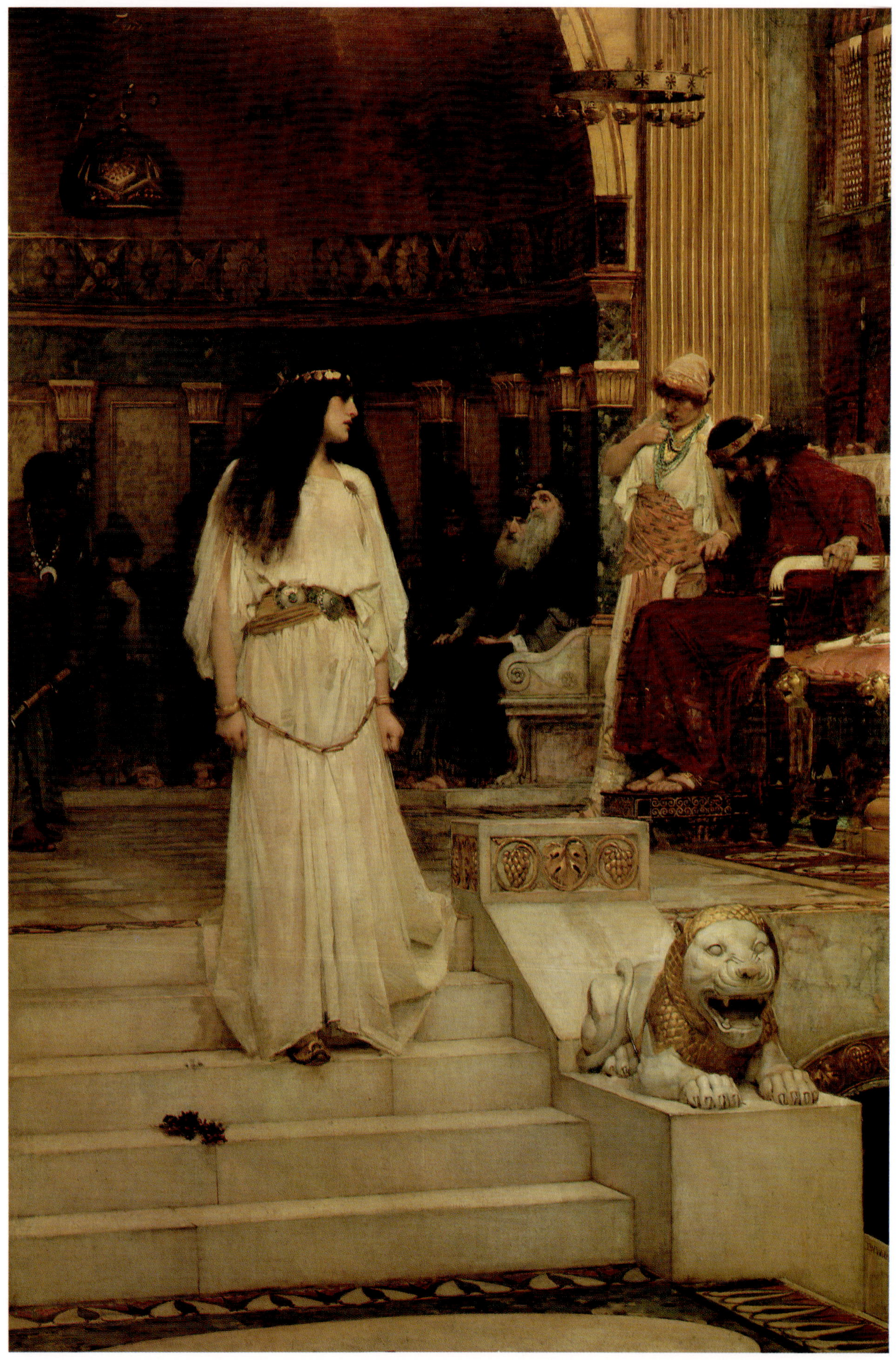

purchase [by the Chantrey Bequest for £650] ... will cause general satisfaction.' Certainly the success of the picture reflected the prevailing taste for exotic subjects; in a competition run by the *Pall Mall Gazette*, Alma-Tadema's *The Apodyterium* was voted the best picture in the Academy.

In 1887, Waterhouse compounded drama and history in the largest picture he ever painted: *Mariamne leaving the Judgement Seat of Herod* (Pl. 26). The second wife of Herod the Great, who was deeply attached to her, she is seen condemned to death by her husband in the year 24 BC during the welter of dynastic struggles in which he contrived to hold the balance between Rome and the Jews as well as between Octavian and the Senate on the one hand and Antony and Cleopatra on the other. Herod's sister Salome, who later plotted against him and Mariamne's two sons, is shown strengthening his wavering resolve with her hand on his arm. In a scene charged with the strongest emotions, Waterhouse employs all the subtleties of gesture and attitude, all the dramatic force of light and shade, in another example of the 'keyhole composition' in which we as spectators join the judges in the shadowy apse in concentrating on the tragic figure of the doomed queen. The positive and detailed geometry of the setting, and the painter's comprehensive technique, ranging from the fine veil of Mariamne's hair to the heavy impasto on the clasps of her girdle, show him at the height of his powers.

26 *Mariamne leaving the Judgement Seat of Herod*, 1887. 102 × 71 in (259 × 180 cm). London, Forbes Magazine Collection

In present-day terms, the subject is again unusual, a tribute to the artist's wide reading as well as the search for originality; and it was the outcome of mature deliberation on the historical period. He painted a *Cleopatra* about this time, and *An Herodian* which, priced at £130, must have been a picture of substance, was shown at the Royal Birmingham Society of Artists in 1881. The Herodians were religious adherents of the family of Boethus, the father of Mariamne, whose sons were raised by Herod to the High Priesthood.

The honours awarded to *Mariamne* after its appearance in the Royal Academy exhibition of 1887 were due in large measure to the efforts of its owner, Mr W.C. (later Sir Cuthbert) Quilter. With his permission it was shown two years later in the Paris Exposition Universelle, where it gained a Bronze Medal. It went to exhibitions in and around London, in Birmingham, Liverpool, Nottingham and Newcastle, and to the World's Columbian Exhibition of 1893 in Chicago. At the Brussels Exposition Internationale of 1897, it secured one of the five Gold Medals awarded by the international jury, and it figured in the Irish International Exhibition of 1907 in Dublin. Yet *Mariamne*, like the earlier *Diogenes*, signified another step in self-awareness and the end of another epoch; with it, Waterhouse retired from history painting as he had done from the cult of Alma-Tadema – at the point of his greatest success.

He was, of course, also exhibiting elsewhere of his own volition. The S.B.A. in Suffolk Street has been noted as his earliest outlet, and was followed in the 1880s by the Institute of Oil Painters – like the S.B.A., not yet 'Royal'. The Grosvenor Gallery had been opened in 1877 by Sir Coutts Lindsay and Charles Hallé. Intended as a showpiece for the Pre-Raphaelites and other 'outsiders' like the

Glasgow School, it failed to attract Waterhouse until he himself was a member of the Academy. It is worth noting that Burne-Jones, who was elected A.R.A. in the same year as Waterhouse without having actually sought the honour, exhibited at the Academy only briefly, refused to serve as a Visitor on the grounds of ill-health (having first mislaid the official notice to do so), became increasingly aggrieved at having to compete – without success – for full membership, and finally resigned. Waterhouse, on the other hand, lent his strength and support to the Royal Academy all his life and deservedly received its full honours.

In the provinces, the Birmingham Society of Artists had become 'Royal' in 1868, by the grace of Queen Victoria, the first society in the city to do so. Its list of annually elected presidents includes some of the greatest names in the Royal Academy; even P.R.A.s like Eastlake, Grant, Leighton and Millais, and the native son, Burne-Jones. In the 1870s its annual exhibitions were visited by as many as 40,000 people. There Waterhouse showed in 1886, 1888 and 1889 respectively *The Magic Circle*, *Consulting the Oracle* and *Mariamne*, all by courtesy of their new owners. As well as some smaller paintings, his drawings also were exhibited in Birmingham: *St Eulalia* in 1881, and in the Spring Exhibition *At a Greek Play*, lent in 1882 by the *Illustrated London News*, and in 1890 *The Cynic*, the property of John Aird – another glance at the ancient philosophers and probably related to the painting of *Diogenes*.

In due course, Birmingham gave way to Liverpool as Waterhouse's other main exhibition centre. The Liverpool Autumn Exhibitions of Modern Art were recognized as giving the entrée to the North of England, and their popularity was attested by the existence of the 'London' and 'Liverpool' cellars at the Walker Art Gallery, many pictures being passed on from the Summer Exhibitions of the Royal Academy. Waterhouse had first shown there in 1879 and continued to do so with some regularity until the year before his death. Esther Waterhouse sent two flower pieces to Liverpool in 1886 and 1888 and, in a succession of important paintings, *Mariamne* appeared in 1901 under its full title, lent by Sir Cuthbert Quilter, Bt.

Back in London, from 1890 onwards a secondary picture by Nino, often with only a single figure, would go to the New Gallery, which had been opened by Charles Hallé and Comyns Carr after financial losses on the Grosvenor Gallery, of which they had both been directors.

In 1888 Waterhouse exhibited at the Academy a picture which is now one of the most popular in the Tate Gallery: *The Lady of Shalott* (Pl.27). Tennyson dominated the literary scene, and Waterhouse's devotion to the poems is evidenced by his copy of Tennyson's collected works, in which every blank page is covered with pencil sketches for paintings. In this picture Waterhouse moves from history to romance; and also, for a brief period, to *plein-air* painting. Later works have outdoor settings, but they seem merely appropriate backgrounds for the figures; here is a full-scale scene from nature, surprising us by his command of it yet testifying in its way to Tennyson's own explicit imagery – so different from the unpaintable abstractions of Keats. While figure and surroundings vie for our attention, Waterhouse still carefully selects the moment within the incident to hold us in contemplation – the moment between the words: 'She loos'd the chain and down she lay.' One feels the cool of the day as the doomed girl commences her last journey, but the centre scene is held by the haunting beauty of the figure, probably in this case the artist's wife. Critical appreciation of the picture is nowhere better shown than in the retrospective article of 1909 by R.E.D. Sketchley in the *Art Journal*:

> The harmony of the willow-green, darkened with rain and closing day, of the shadowed white of the dress, the black prow, and the grey light afloat on the water, has the cool open-air unity of French naturalism. Gold and rose of the embroidered web, dipping unheeded into the green shadow of the boat, the candles, taken from the inner quiet air of some shrine to burn failingly in the drift, are imagery that paint more than the vision in the poem ... It is art which for its appreciation needs at least a capacity for realising the alliance between our thought and the romantic vision gathered in literature from Homer to Tennyson.

The actual scene is not easy to identify; it has overtones of Somerset or Devon, which the Waterhouses visited over a long period. Esther's sister Emily married the landscape painter Peregrine Feeney, who built a house at Croyde in Devon after leaving Primrose Hill Studios in 1892. The prevailing influence of Bastien-Lepage and the French *plein-airistes* was no doubt conveyed among these artists; William Logsdail wrote of his two dearest friends as being Waterhouse and Frank Bramley, one of the founders of the Newlyn School. But *plein-air* subject matter alone could not sustain the visual experience indefinitely; in the very same year Bramley himself reverted to a great human theme and, with *A Hopeless Dawn*, took the *plein-air* painter indoors again.

Waterhouse's *Ophelia* of 1889, outstretched on the grass, took one of his most frequent titles and one of his favourite themes, the desolate maiden. The fully realized landscape, clearly painted from nature, echoes that of *The Lady of Shalott*, but the single figure could hardly sum up the story, and in spite of its charm and delicacy the picture drew only muted applause from the critics. It was the air of the Mediterranean which was to draw him outdoors again, where weather was dependent on season rather than climate. The calmly beautiful paintings of *Flora* and *Arranging Flowers* need no story-telling, and *The Orange Gatherers* (Pl.28) and the superb *Alfresco Toilet at Capri* captivate us no less by the grace of the young girls than by the subtle unity of the composition.

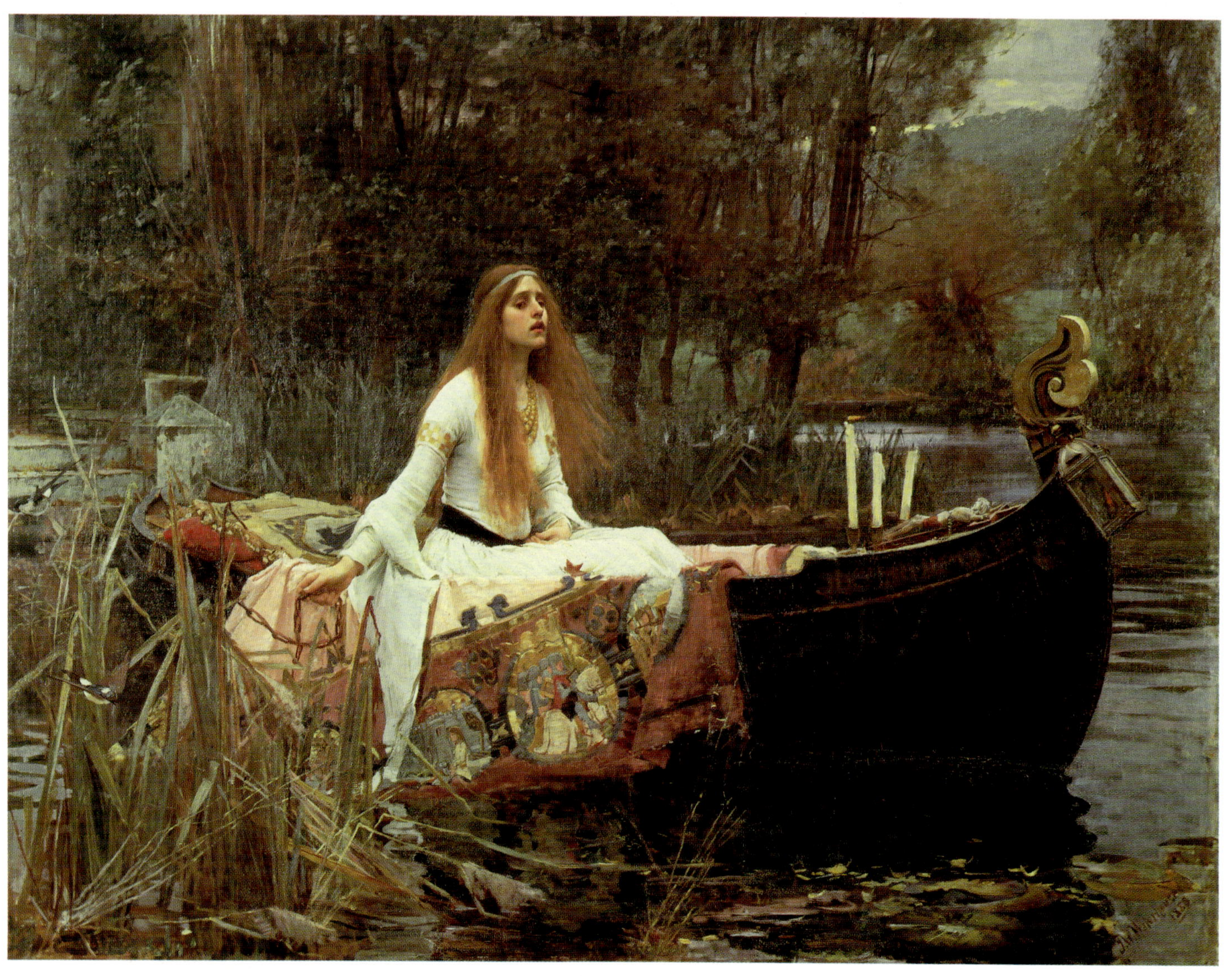

27 *The Lady of Shalott*, 1888. 60¼ × 78¾ in (153 × 200 cm). London, Tate Gallery

28 *The Orange Gatherers*, c. 1890. 45½ × 31½ in (115.6 × 80 cm). Private collection

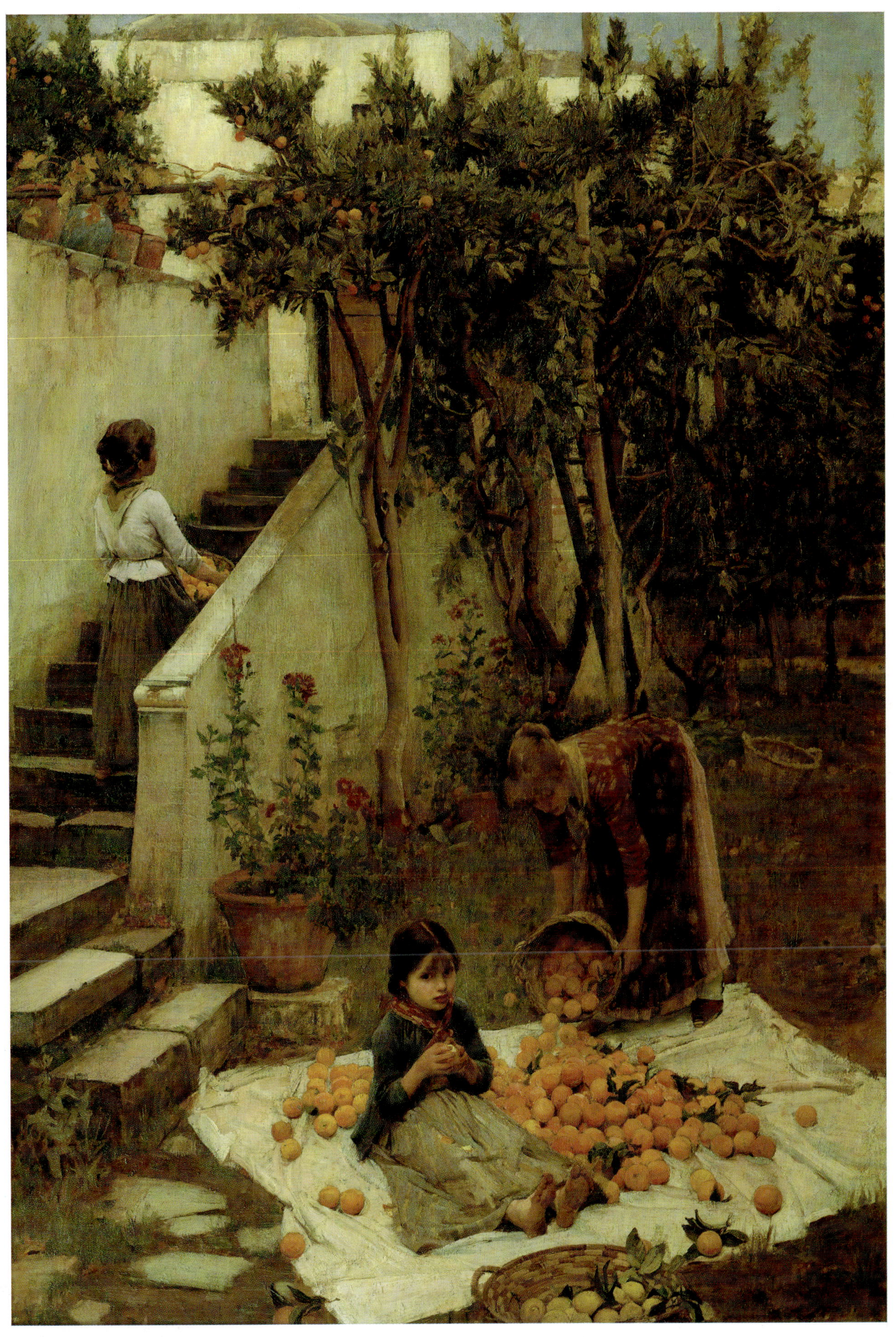

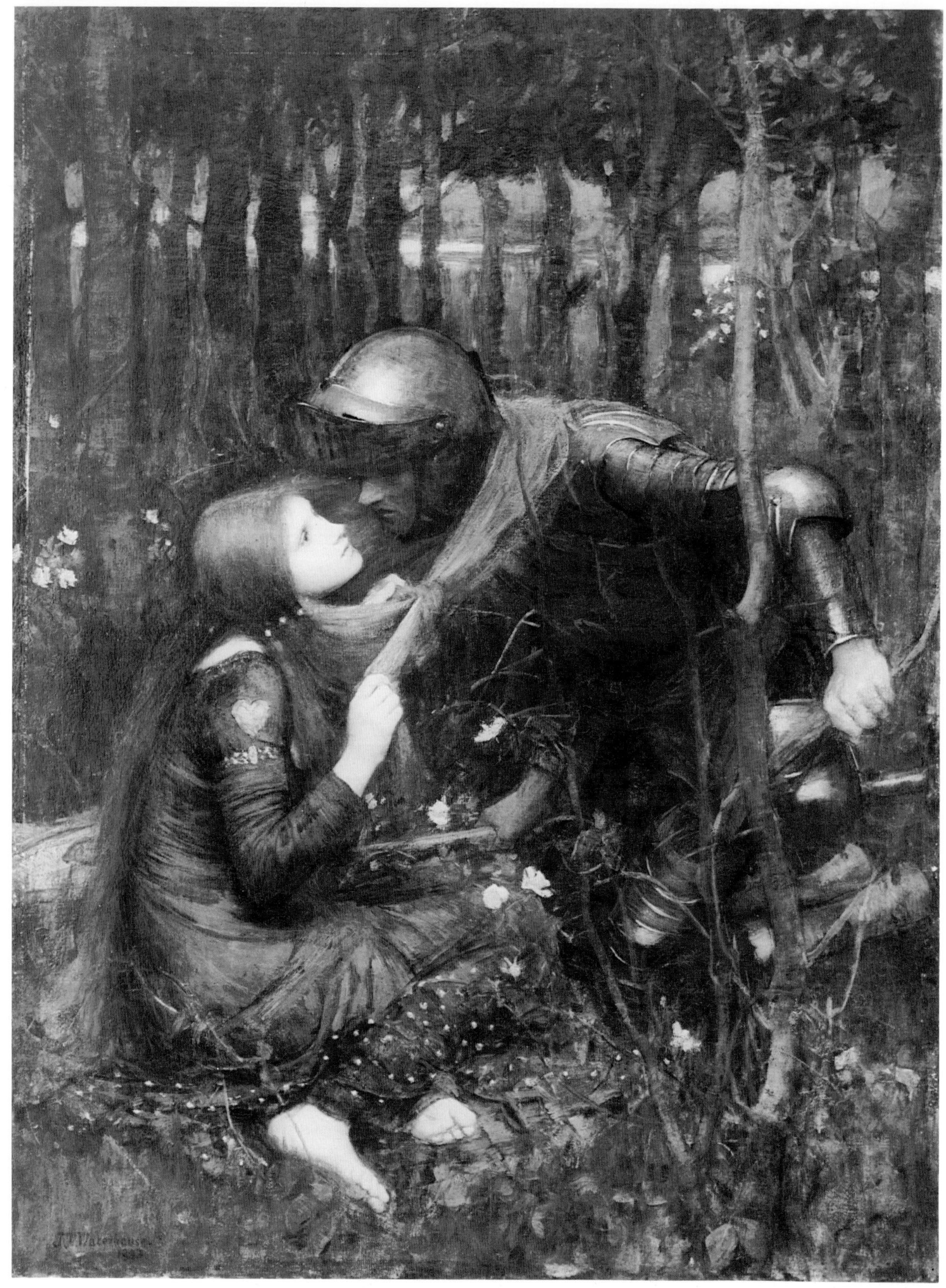

3
Return to the Legends

THE YEAR 1890 was marked by the death of Nino's father, William Waterhouse, at Boulogne on 24 January. In some ways a shadowy and paradoxical figure, he had been his son's earliest teacher and had seen him into the Royal Academy Schools; he himself exhibited paintings with evocative titles at the British Institution from 1840, and at the S.B.A. and the Royal Academy from 1846. The son of a Yorkshire weaver, his first marriage is still a mystery; his second ended in tragedy after nine years with the death of Isabella in 1857. In 1860, moving steadily upwards in the social scale, he married Frederica Mary Jane Perceval, a cousin of the Earl of Egmont. She was also a grand-daughter of Spencer Perceval, the assassinated prime minister, and one of the many beneficiaries of the country's financial compensation to Perceval's family – and their numerous and long-lived descendants. The Percevals lived in some state at Pitshanger Manor, Ealing, and Miss Frederica Elizabeth Perceval, dying at ninety-four years of age, left £15,500 for the building there of the Perceval Memorial Church of All Saints in memory of her father.

29 *La Belle Dame Sans Merci*, 1893. 44 × 32 in (112 × 81 cm). Darmstadt, Hessisches Landesmuseum

After the marriage, William Waterhouse seems virtually to have abandoned his painting practice. However, the circles in which he now moved brought him at least two important sitters: Cardinal Manning and Captain John Hanning Speke, discoverer of the source of the Nile. Speke's portrait was shown in the National Portrait Exhibition of 1868, but for some reason not photographed for the catalogue; the Cardinal's was reproduced in the *Magazine of Art* in September 1893. Unfortunately both these portraits are now lost.

Perhaps understandably, Waterhouse did not send a picture to the Royal Academy of 1890, but 1891 saw his positive reversion to the Greek legends. With his pictures still alternating between the single figure and the fully populated composition, *Ulysses and the Sirens* (Pl.30) represented the latter at the Academy, where it was received with acclamation and was selected by Hubert von Herkomer, R.A., for the National Gallery of Victoria in Melbourne. M.H. Spielmann in the *Magazine of Art* counted it 'a very startling triumph ... with a skill more consummate than even the talented artist was credited with' and even more extraordinary than the popular success of the year, Luke Fildes's *The Doctor*.

Other critics praised Waterhouse as a colourist, and as an antiquary. He had

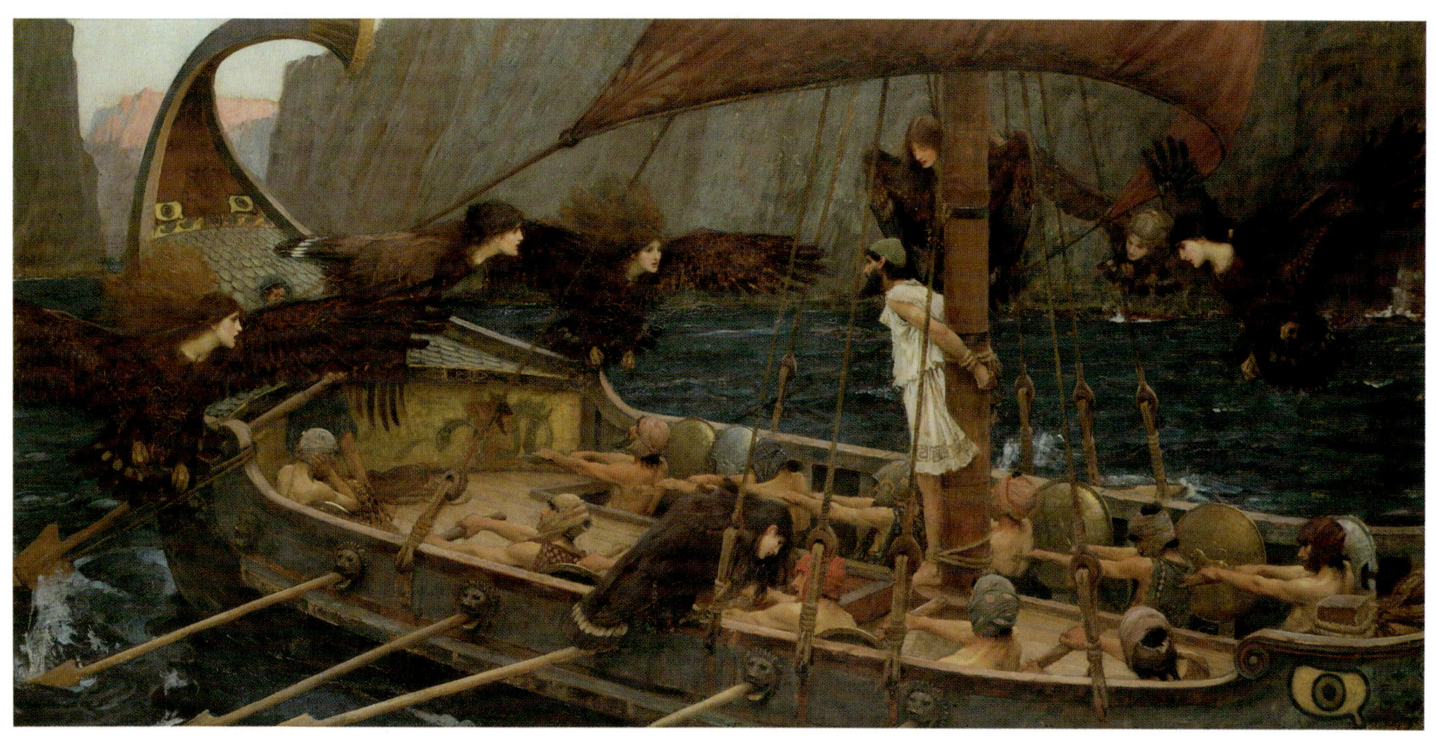

30 *Ulysses and the Sirens*, 1891. 79 × 39 in (201 × 99 cm). Melbourne, National Gallery of Victoria

31 *Circe offering the Cup to Ulysses*. 58½ × 36¼ in (149 × 92 cm). Oldham Art Gallery

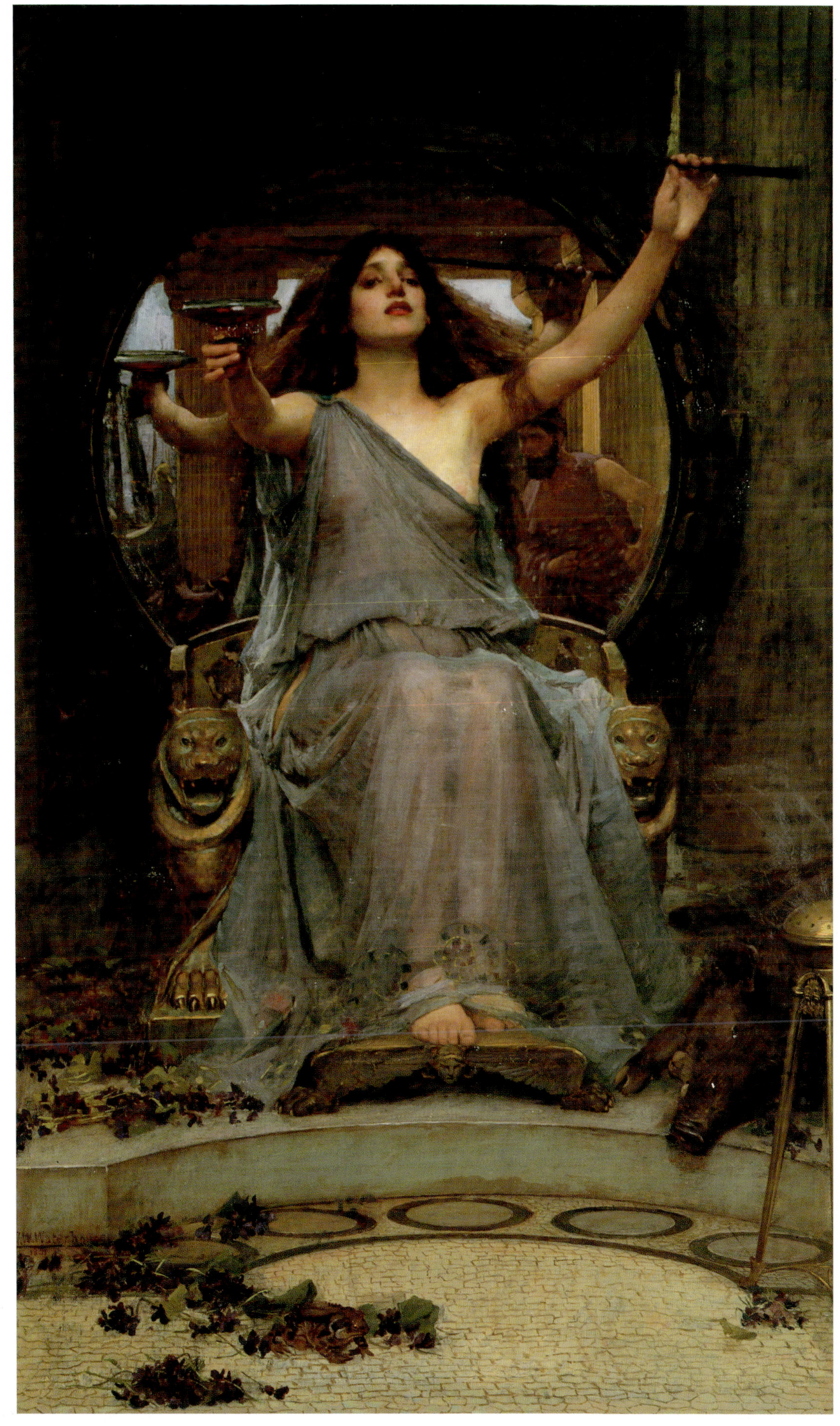

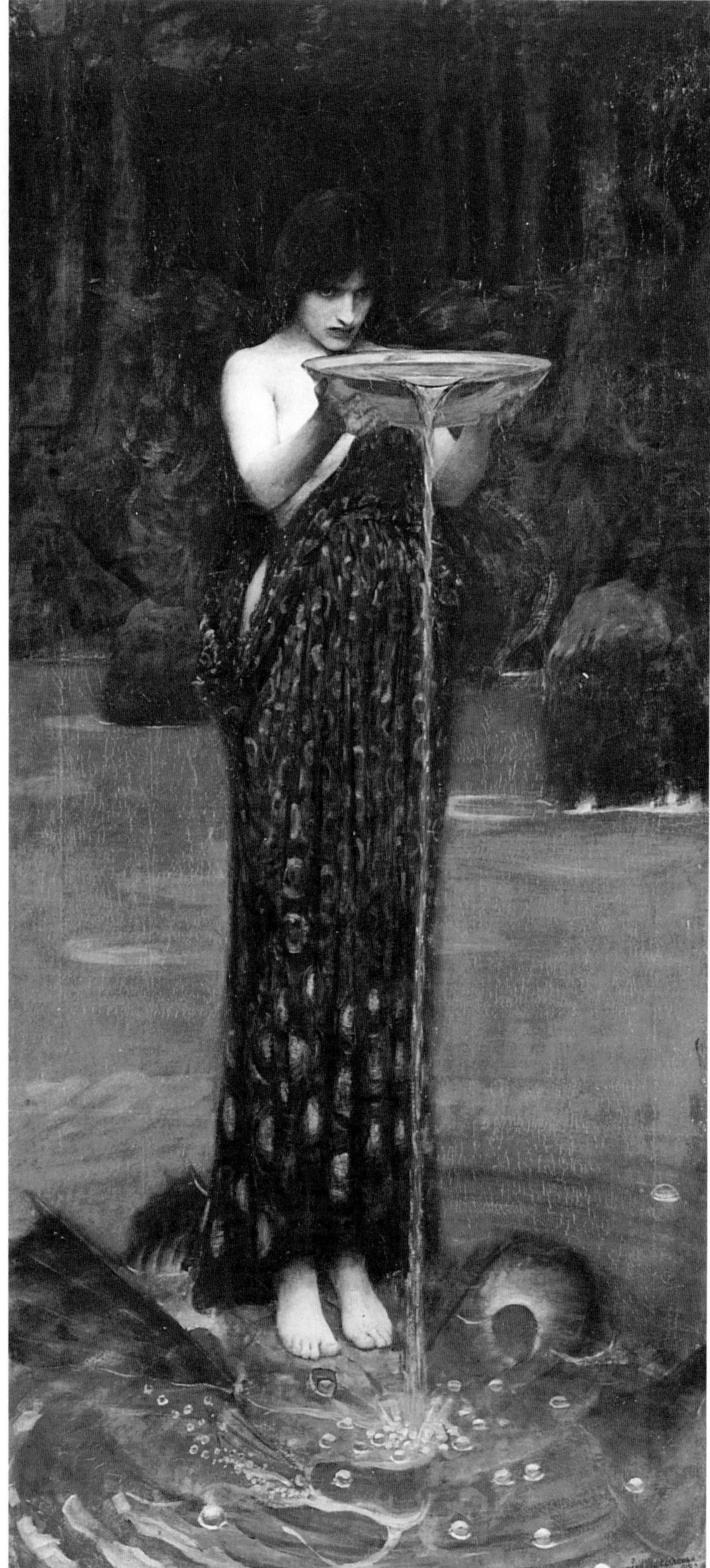

32 *Circe Invidiosa*, 1892. $70\frac{1}{2} \times 33\frac{1}{2}$ in (179 × 85 cm). Adelaide, Art Gallery of South Australia

adopted the convention in which the Sirens have the heads of beautiful women and the bodies of birds, deriving this probably from a vase in the British Museum. A leading column in the *Evening Standard* discussed the correct number of the Sirens, and a lengthy correspondence in the *Pall Mall Gazette* seriously debated details of the picture including the rigging of the ship. There seem to have been no intermediate oil studies for this painting, the composition being developed in pencil sketches in which the ship is progressively enlarged and the 'keyhole' arrangement again becomes manifest.

In the final picture, the ring of Sirens echoes the arc of the sail as they bend their beautiful but terrible eyes upon the bound figure of Ulysses. The whole effect is menacing: the only vertical line is that of the mast, the only classical shape the circle of the predatory bird-woman. All the rest is disturbance; diagonals everywhere; and, in the startling realism of paint, the high cliffs, the hurrying sea and the final frightening touch of the Siren clawed on to the gunwale, transfixing the cowering oarsman with a baleful gaze. As with all Waterhouse's paintings, the effect on the viewer is immediate, but the picture maintains its hold as the eye explores the mass of faithfully executed detail. Like Homer himself, the artist evokes a real world in which dire and sometimes supernatural events occur.

At this stage in the painter's career the innocent girls of the earlier pictures give way, if only for a time, to the *femme fatale* typified by the Sirens. This archetypal figure appeared as *Circe offering the Cup to Ulysses* (Pl.31), his other major work of 1891, exhibited at the New Gallery. The model, unknown to us by name, had a sense of theatre to balance the painter's creativity, and the single figure, framed by the serene glass but surrounded by the metamorphosed swine, combines beauty and seduction, the promise of pleasure and the barely-apprehended intimation of doom. The picture is completed by the reflections of the ship inshore, the columned entrance and the hesitant figure of Ulysses (bearing a remarkable resemblance to Waterhouse himself) as he enters the snare of the enchantress.

He was by now deeply involved in the legend of Circe. Introduced in 1891, she was probably the subject of a study of similar proportions sold in 1926 among his remaining studio works for three guineas. Another *Circe* sold at Christie's in 1948 for a few guineas may have led to the 1892 painting of *Circe Invidiosa* (Pl.32), which portrays the sorceress in the act of poisoning the sea in order to turn Scylla, her rival for the favours of the merman Glaucus, into a hideous monster. As always, Waterhouse avoids the horrific outcome, but the statuesque figure of the same beautiful model is invested with an aura of menace which has much to do with the powerful colour scheme of deep greens and blues he employed so well. The painter was again contrasted favourably with Burne-Jones, the *Magazine of Art* commenting that the *Circe*, while 'as weird as anything Mr Burne-Jones ever painted ... is far stronger in feeling and colour, and more virile and incisive in style, then we have ever had from that master.' By now the Australians had a selection committee in London, consisting of Leighton, Poynter, Herkomer and the agent-general for South Australia, Sir Arthur Blyth; purchased on their

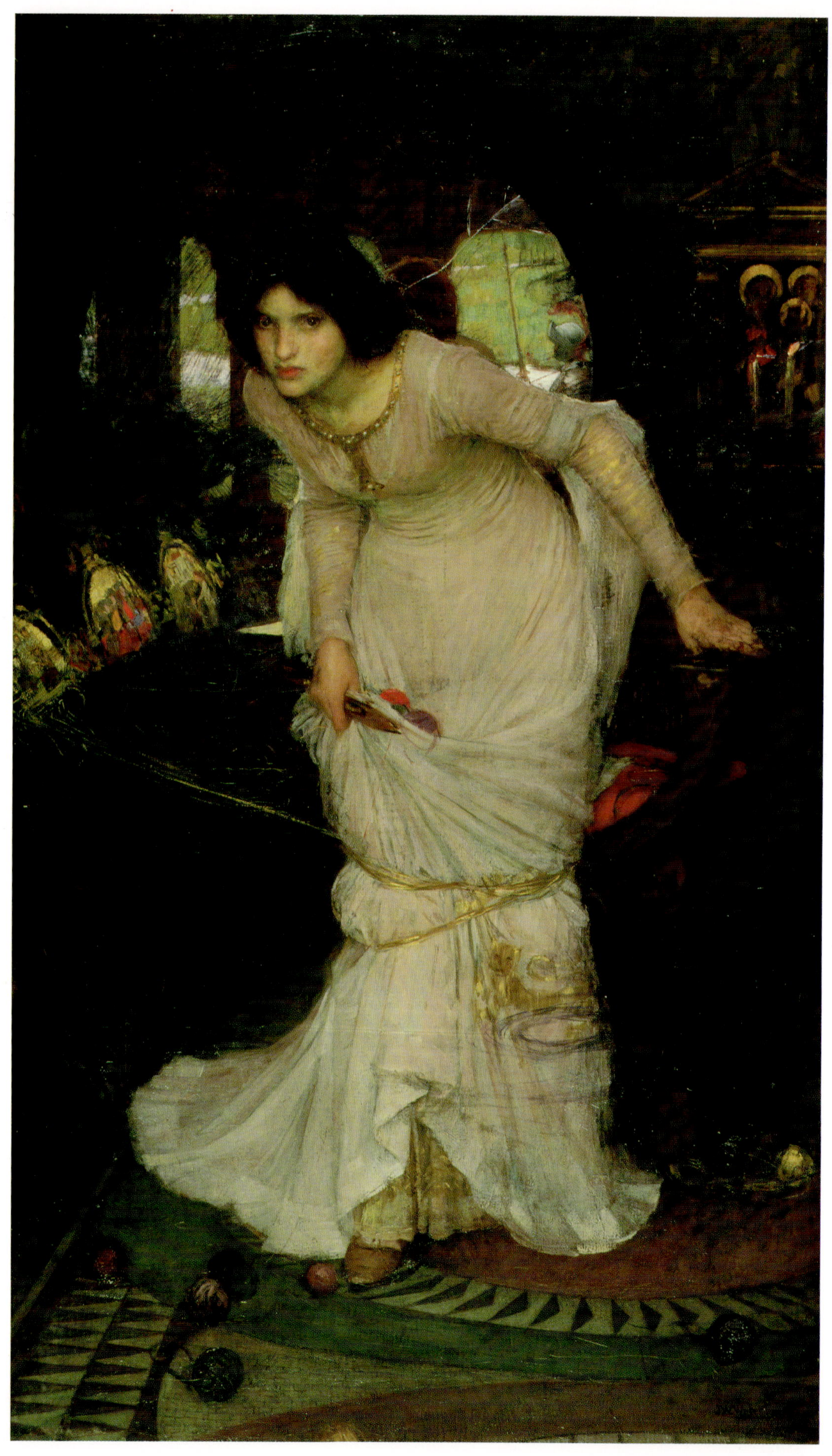

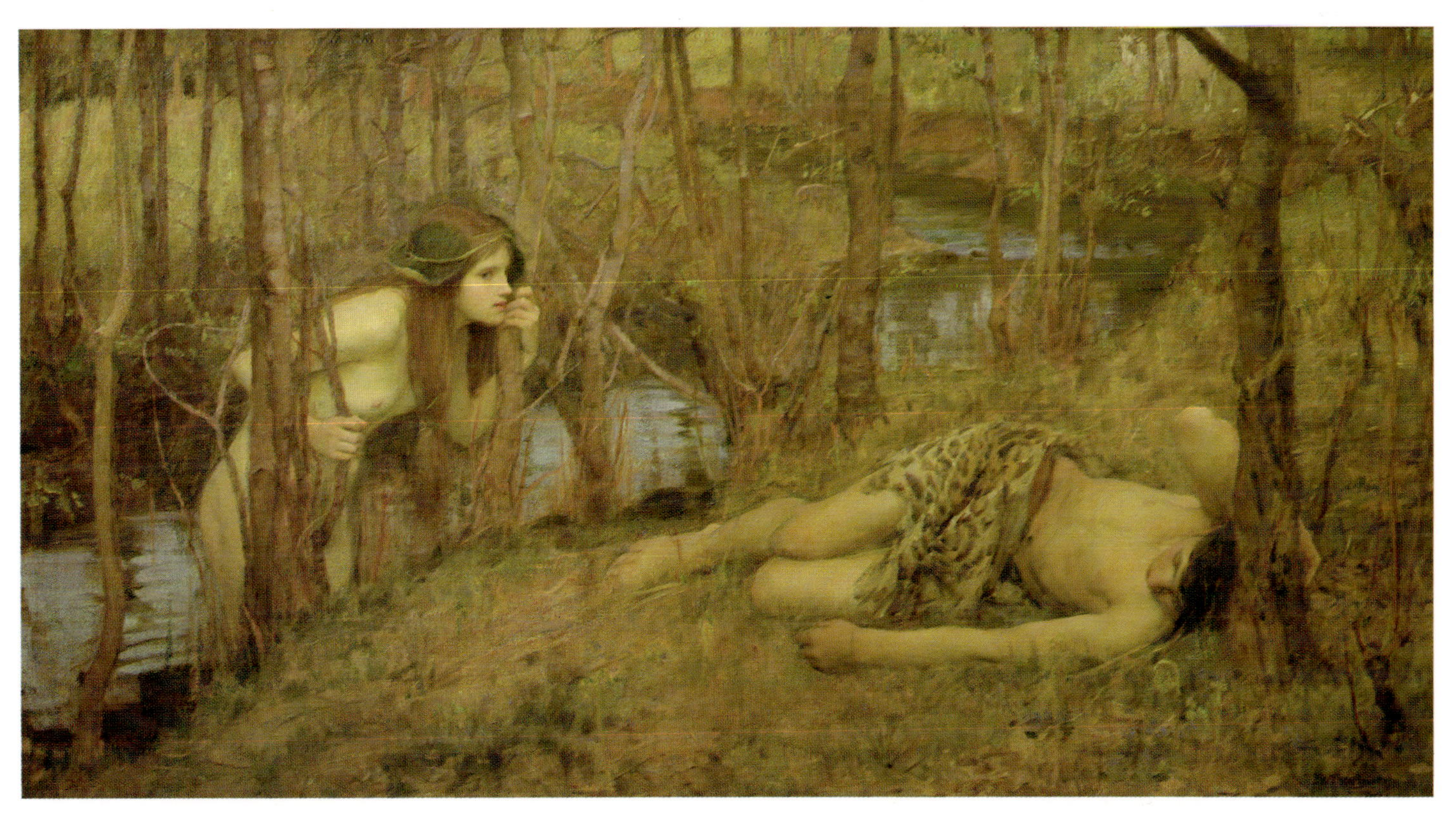

34 *A Naiad*, 1893. Private collection

33 *The Lady of Shalott*, 1894.
56 × 34 in (142 × 86 cm).
Leeds, City Art Gallery

recommendation, *Circe Invidiosa* was soon on its way to the Art Gallery of South Australia in Adelaide.

Yet even without the portrayal of the ultimate horrors, it seemed that the *femme fatale* was too much for Waterhouse. *Danaë*, exhibited in the same year, strikes a note of hope as the young mother emerges from the sea-borne chest with the infant Perseus in her arms, while *A Naiad* (Pl. 34) evinces hardly more than curiosity as she gazes at the sleeping youth. In succeeding pictures the imperious goddess gives way to the *jeune fille fatale* – young, tender, wistful, yet irresistible – drawing the hero to his destruction in an entrancingly apologetic manner.

Such a picture is *La Belle Dame sans Merci* (Pl. 29). The subject was taken from Keats's poem of the same title, which had first been published in 1820 and which inspired a number of artists over a long period, frequently as an opportunity for painting the nude. The maiden clothed, however, was recognized by the major painters as a more eloquent figure in the context of the poem. Rossetti drew her draped across the saddle-bow, with the accompaniment in his own hand of the lines:

I set her on my pacing steed,
And nothing else saw all day long,
For sideways would she bend and sing
A Fairies' song.

Keats, seeking for words as his fatal malady pressed closely upon him, committed three varying versions to paper before the publication of the poem, but the sense remained constant, and in 1903 Frank Dicksee's painting completed the stanza as the poet clearly intended, the knight striding alongside his charger while she leans from the saddle, gazing deeply into his eyes.

Waterhouse brings the couple down to earth in the mysterious wood with an erotic imagery far surpassing that of either artist. The girl crouches like a fawn, literally wearing her heart upon her sleeve, and lifting her perfect face in silent invitation to the kneeling knight she draws him down inexorably with the luxuriant noose of her hair. His full armour is emblematic of the artist's own Victorian propriety, yet here the darkened trees form a backcloth both to passion and to fear, and the shadowed countenance of the knight forebodes his inevitable doom as he grasps the lance whose rigidity betrays his desire.

The painter's newly discovered model was clearly his ideal, expressing so fully the tender beauty, the youth and vulnerability, of the heroines of the legends whose innocence was a magnet for the passions of the heroes. But as far as we know, their relationship never exceeded that of artist and model; she can be seen in the major subject pictures for many years, and appropriately takes pride of place as the mermaid in his Diploma Work.

It was, however, the dramatic personality of his other model which gave life to Waterhouse's second painting of *The Lady of Shalott* (Pl. 33). Although he was adept at the circumstantial imagery of each of his major works, it was clearly the specific incident rather than the unfolding narrative which enthralled him, and this picture moves back from that of 1888 to the climactic moment of the poem. Condemned for so long to the watery reflected image, the Lady of Shalott breaks out to life – and to death – as Sir Lancelot 'flashed into the crystal mirror', a song on his lips and the sunlight burning on his gleaming helm. It is impossible to discuss this picture without taking into consideration Holman Hunt's illustration of the same moment in the Moxon Tennyson of 1857. Waterhouse's familiarity with this must have accounted for an unusual number of preliminary sketches in which, particularly by the use of a rectangular mirror, he seems consciously to have tried to avoid duplicating the composition of the Moxon illustration – repeated in the painting which Hunt had begun in 1889 but failed to finish until 1905.

In the end, the circular mirror obviously contributed more to the composition, but the greater impact of Waterhouse's interpretation shows clearly in a comparison of the two pictures. As in other paintings, Holman Hunt is seduced by a concentration on detail which fatally weakens his narrative power. The carefully contrived tonal balance completely misses the point; it thrusts the mirror forward at the very moment when its importance has been eliminated, and at the climax of the Lady's existence she is thrown into the shadows. Hunt delivers the final blows to the text by confining her within the low embroidery frame where it must have been agony to work day after day a few inches from the floor and where she cannot possibly make the prescribed three paces through the room, and by turning her gaze neither to the mirror nor to the window, either of which would have been acceptable in the context of the poem.

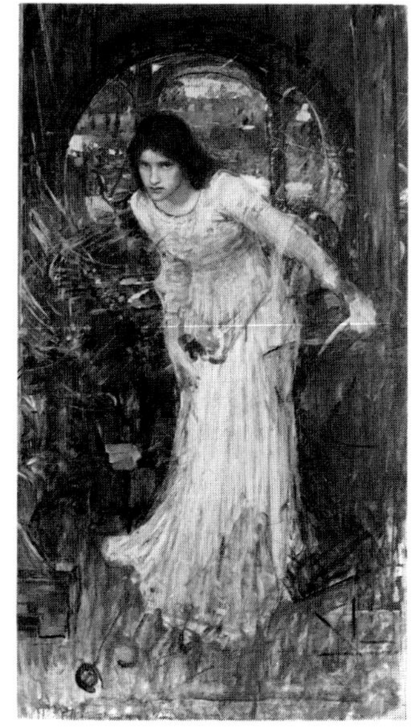

35 *The Lady of Shalott*, *c.*1894. 47½ × 27 in (120.5 × 68.3 cm). Falmouth Art Gallery

Waterhouse's painting, by contrast, has an impact as startling as the moment in the verse when 'The curse is come upon me, cried The Lady of Shalott'. The figure of the girl is the centre of our attention. The passing knight is visible in the mirror; we take his place in the window and she looks into our eyes. We could not be more directly involved in the action. All the accessories confirm the imagery of the poem. As she whirls from the mirror and from the loom, rising from her chair to rush towards the window, the golden threads encircle her knees – the subtle touch by which the painter actually enforces the moment of stillness upon which the picture dwells eternally. As in the earlier masterpiece, *Consulting the Oracle*, the circles of classicism are evident: the roundels of the tapestry and the tiled floor, the semi-circle of the chair, the mirror itself. Once these essentials were decided, the excitement of the subject became evident in the sparkling brushwork of the final study in oils (Pl.35).

At the end of 1894, after the exhibition of this picture, a contemporary critic could say that Waterhouse had

> 'a place which he shares with no one else. He has the reputation of being an innovator of judicious and well-balanced views; he is, with justice, given by the popular voice a position among the most capable of his profession; he is well established upon the ladder of official recognition ... one of the rarest types of modern artists ... who, having had a past, has still left a future.'

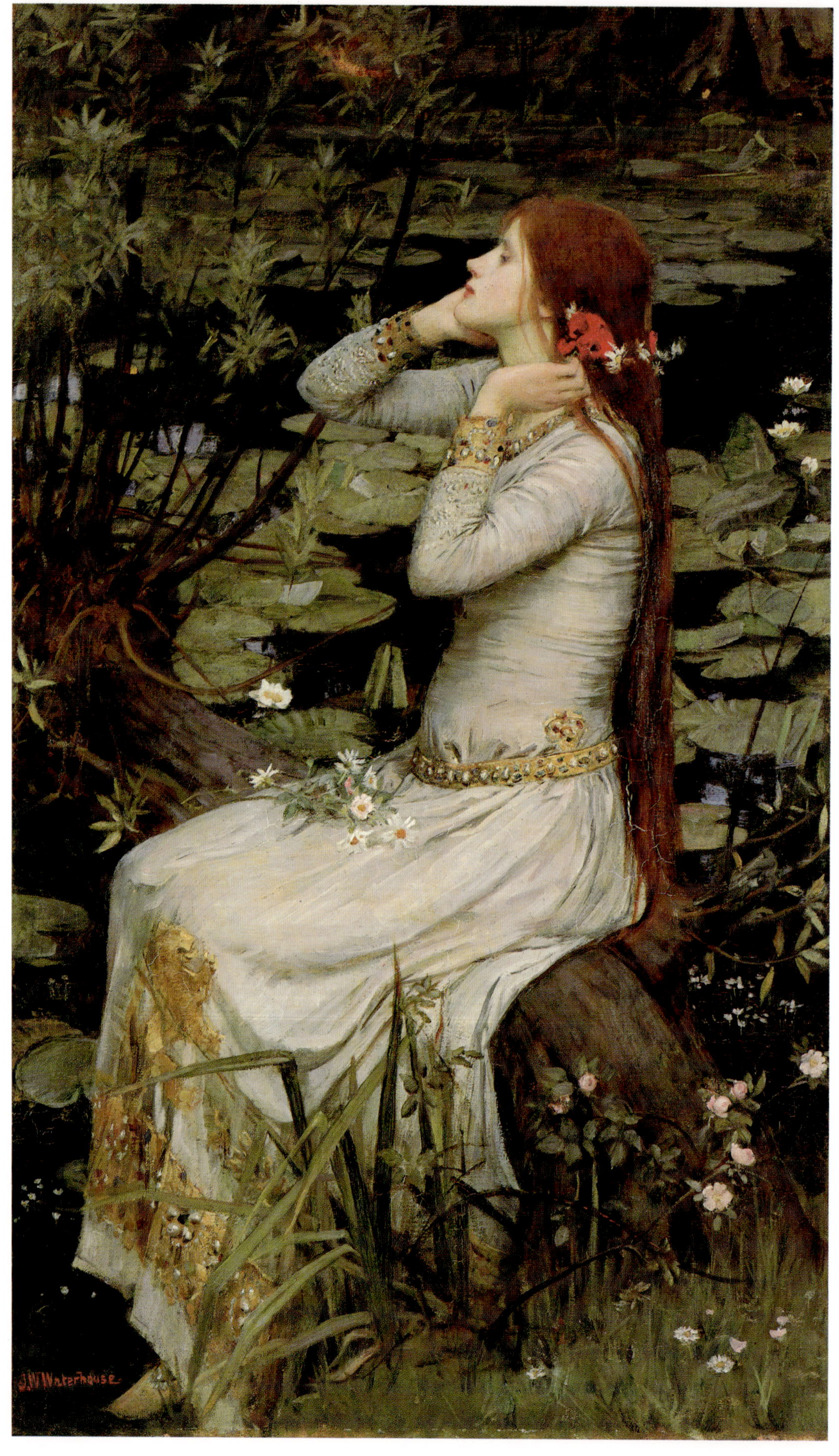
J.W. Waterhouse

4
A Royal Academician

A HUNDRED YEARS ago, the elections of the Royal Academy formed an annual event of public interest, but with the proliferation of art societies and exhibitions, the Academy's position has become less commanding and the public's occupation with art matters is more diffused. However, the progress of the artist from Associate to full Academician, depending at each stage on the votes of eminent practitioners, has always been a topic of intense interest within the Academy itself, and we can gain a fresh insight into Academic careers by scrutinizing the results of past elections. There have been brilliant students in the Royal Academy Schools who never even achieved the Associateship; while the time elapsing between Associate and full Membership can testify not merely to natural talent and consistent achievement but to fashionable taste and even personal acceptability.

36 *Ophelia*, 1894. 49 × 29 in (124.5 × 73.5 cm). Courtesy Christie's

Waterhouse had participated in this competitive but unpredictable exercise at appropriate intervals. His election to Associateship in 1885 with forty-one votes was followed immediately by a separate accolade: the purchase of *St Eulalia* under the Chantrey Bequest. In 1893 he was proposed for full Membership. The other candidates included G.H. Boughton, an Associate since 1879 and the painter of a wide variety of subjects from landscapes to over-pretty women in a technique stigmatized by Ruskin as that of a converted crossing-sweeper. Waterhouse, at forty-four years of age, was classified by the critics as one of our younger artists, and he was much the youngest of this particular group. Boughton was already sixty and had to wait another three years for his R.A., while the architect G.F. Bodley was sixty-seven and had been a pupil of Sir George Gilbert Scott before Waterhouse was born. Even the personable Valentine Cameron Prinsep, versatile follower in turn of Watts, the Pre-Raphaelites and Leighton, and the model for Taffy in du Maurier's novel *Trilby*, was eleven years older than Waterhouse; the landscapist B.W. Leader and the marine painter Henry Moore were both sixty-two. On 4 May there were two other vacancies, filled by Henry Woods, painter of Venetian genre, and Scots landscapist John MacWhirter, after Associateships of eleven and fourteen years respectively. Nino had done well to stand in such company, and may not have been too disappointed when in the third ballot of the evening Moore was elected.

In the following year Waterhouse again improved his position, this time losing to

Prinsep in the final ballot, but in July 1895 the *Magazine of Art* was able to report his election as full Academician amid little excitement: 'His promotion was rightly considered a certainty.' As usual, the new member was obliged to deposit a Diploma Work before receiving his Diploma of membership and the Sovereign's approval and adding his signature to the vellum roll of Royal Academicians, which consequently shows members in order of their reception by the Assembly and not necessarily of their election.

Letters in the Academy's archives show Poynter and Dicksee as being among R.A.s who were late sending in, and Waterhouse was still apologizing to the Secretary and Council in 1900. However, a substitute work was acceptable in the meantime, and after a delay of six months he submitted an *Ophelia*, probably the one exhibited in 1894 at the New Gallery and in the Liverpool Autumn Exhibition (Pl.36). This charming picture, eloquent in pose and gesture, was reproduced in the *Magazine of Art* in 1895 and in the *Art Journal* and *The Master Painters of Britain* in 1909, and was for twenty years in the celebrated collection of Mr George McCulloch. The same young model appeared in *The Shrine* (Pl.37) in 1895.

While his Diploma picture proper remained incomplete, Waterhouse produced a fresh series of which the most important is *St Cecilia* (Pl.38). It was bought by George McCulloch before it left the painter's studio and eighteen years later, when the McCulloch collection was dispersed, sold for the large sum of 2,300 guineas to Mr (later Sir) Brodie Henderson – the earliest of many Waterhouse paintings acquired by the family of Lord Faringdon.

This is not a devotional picture, though some Victorians might have regarded it as such; Waterhouse was not a 'religious' painter in the iconographical sense. Tennyson again encouraged him into the company of the nymphs: the verse in 'The Palace of Art' where 'on a terrace by the sea/Slept St Cecily' is the only one of the multitude of references in the poem in which the ambience is wholly feminine. It provided Nino with the image also projected by Rossetti in the Moxon edition, although he eschewed the erotic overtones implicit in Rossetti's swooning saint as 'an Angel kiss'd her'.

In Waterhouse's painting, costume and setting blend the medieval and the classical. The treatment is by definition Renaissance; Cecilia, martyred in the second or third century, was not recognized in art as the patron saint of music until the fifteenth century, and her particular attribute, the portative pipe organ, had in fact disappeared from actual use by the sixteenth. The shape and decoration of the little free-standing organ, flanked by the angels with their bowed instruments, are certainly reminiscent of Rossetti's earlier illustration, but Waterhouse's research is, as usual, more exact. What might appear to be an excessive perspective of the organ pipes indicates that the pipes of the portative organ traditionally become shorter from left to right, moving from bass to treble like the strings of a piano.

Rejecting the Pre-Raphaelite in favour of the classical, the composition, drawing us out from the level terrace between the massed trees and across the harbour to the high horizon, is in unmistakable homage to Leighton, who was to die in the

January following the picture's exhibition. However, the details of costume, flowers and embroidery, down to the well-researched emblems of the saint including the roses and lilies carved on the classic chair, are Waterhouse's own. The linking device of flowering branches is familiar but always delights the eye, and a carpet unites the three figures just as an earlier one sealed the gap between the emperor Honorius and his tame birds.

Waterhouse was now firmly established in the ranks of the Royal Academy and in favour with both critics and public, but this did not cause his output to falter, either in quantity or – more importantly – in quality. Current work in the studios of celebrated artists was always noted in the art journals, and *The Studio* in March 1896 mentioned Waterhouse as being busy with *Hylas and the Nymphs* (Pl.42), 'one of the best examples of his later manner which he has as yet produced', and followed with a lyrical description of the picture, which must by then have been well advanced. Probably not completed in time for the Royal Academy of that year, it was purchased from the artist for £800 by Manchester Art Gallery, where it has been a source of pleasure ever since. It was shown immediately in the Manchester Autumn Exhibition and in the Royal Academy in 1897, and has been the most widely and regularly exhibited of his works, from the Paris Exhibition of 1900 to the Arts Council's Great Victorian Pictures of 1978. Its place in twentieth-century idealism was evidenced in the 1970s by its publication as a popular print and the use of an imitative photograph to advertise a toilet preparation.

None of this was achieved without his chosen models, as the charcoal studies (Pl.39) and the oil sketch (Pl.40) indicate. Apart from these studies for the paintings, Waterhouse left a large number of superb drawings of heads, and this constant practice suggests that the personality of the model was one of his major sources of inspiration (Pl.41). To a public by now accustomed to the pseudo-realities of film and television, the words of a critic describing *Hylas and the Nymphs* in 1896 seem oddly prophetic: 'It carries conviction to the extent of seeming something of a vague memory rather than the creation of an age alien to that associated with the subject.'

Pandora (Pl.43), which appeared in the Academy exhibition of 1896 and went on to Liverpool, ushered in the kneeling pose of the model which inspired more than one painting in the artist. The following year he showed at the New Gallery the haunting picture of *Mariana in the South* (Pl.47). Poynter had dealt with Tennyson's desolate maiden in his *Mariana* of 1851, but his symbolism was forced and his damsel's attitude conveys only an aching back – hinted at by Ruskin in his review when he wrote: 'If the painter had painted Mariana at work in an unmoated grange, instead of idle in a moated one, it had been more to the purpose.' In contrast, Waterhouse's lovely girl conveys all the heartfelt message of the lines: 'Low on her knees herself she cast', 'And on the liquid mirror glow'd/The clear perfection of her face'.

The full-scale study for the picture (Pl.48) shows how he brought the 'Old letters, breathing of her worth' into a simplified harmony with the figure, and emphasizes the sensitivity which he developed over the years in successive

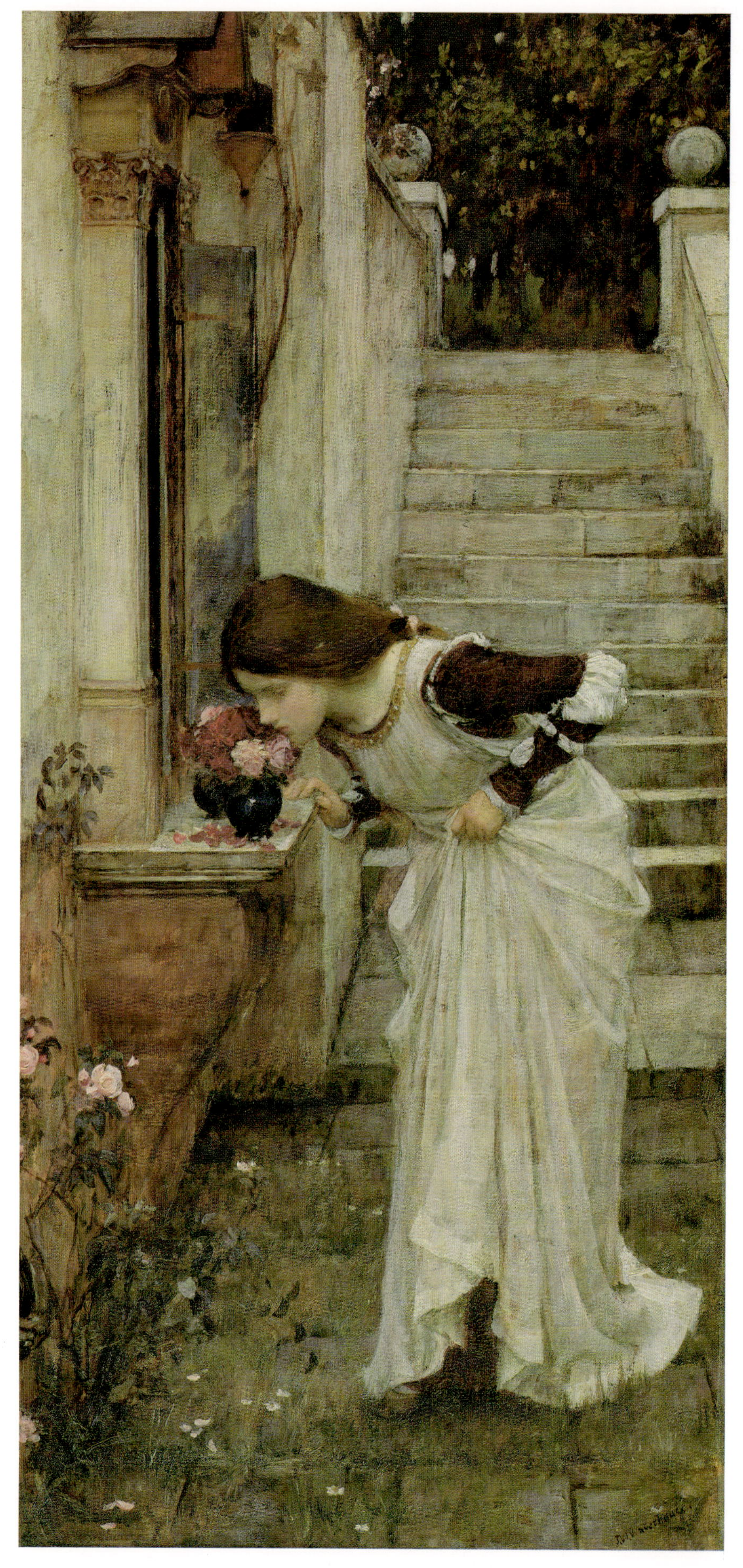

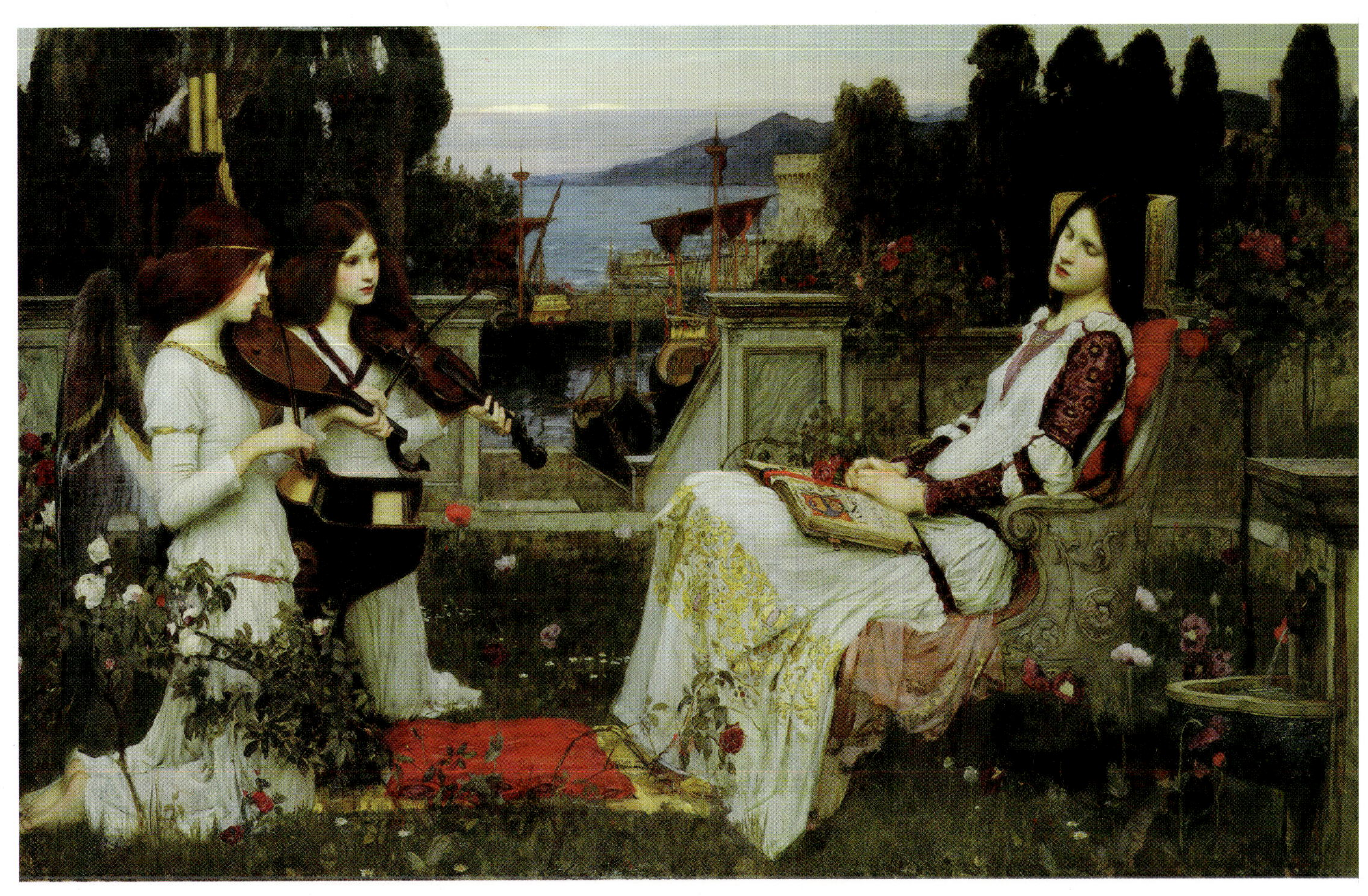

38 *St Cecilia*, 1895.
46 × 77 in (117 × 196 cm).
Courtesy Sotheby's

37 *The Shrine*, 1895.
Private collection

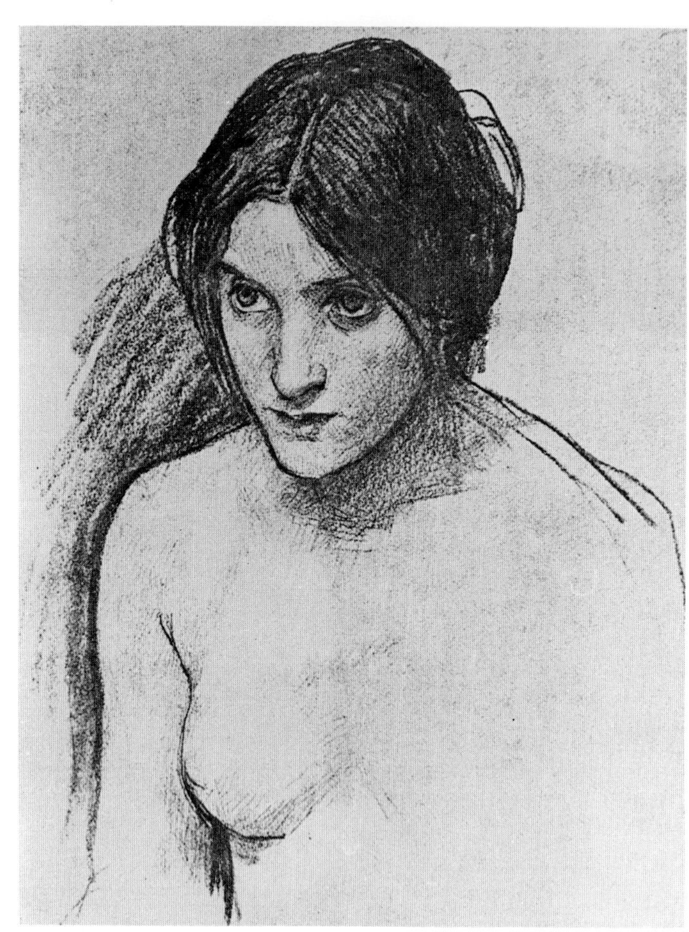

39 Study for *Hylas and the Nymphs*, *c.* 1896. Charcoal. Location unknown

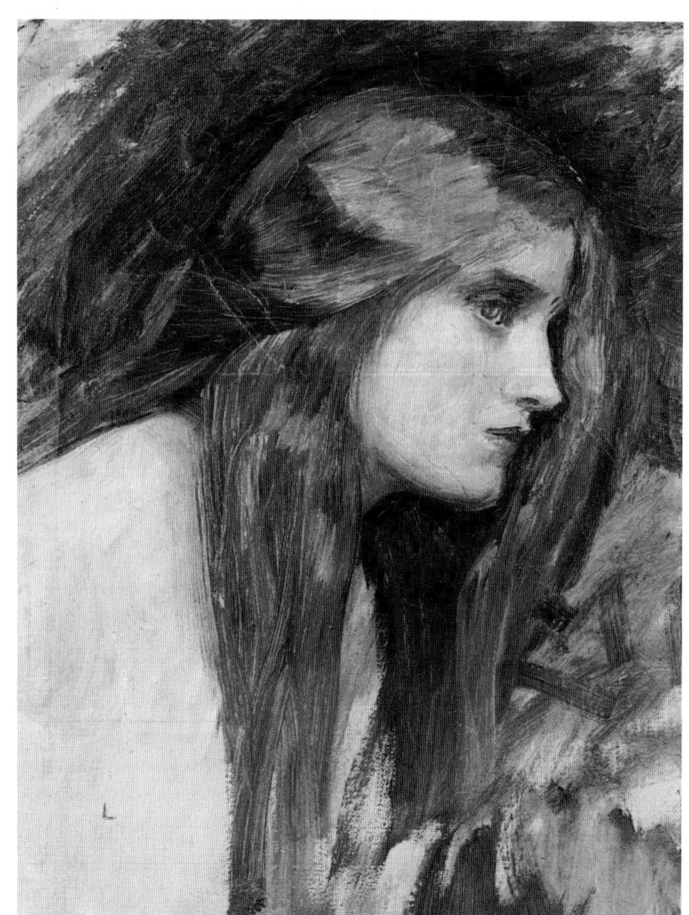

40 Study for *Hylas and the Nymphs*, *c.* 1896. 14 × 12 in (38 × 30.5 cm). Courtesy Sotheby's

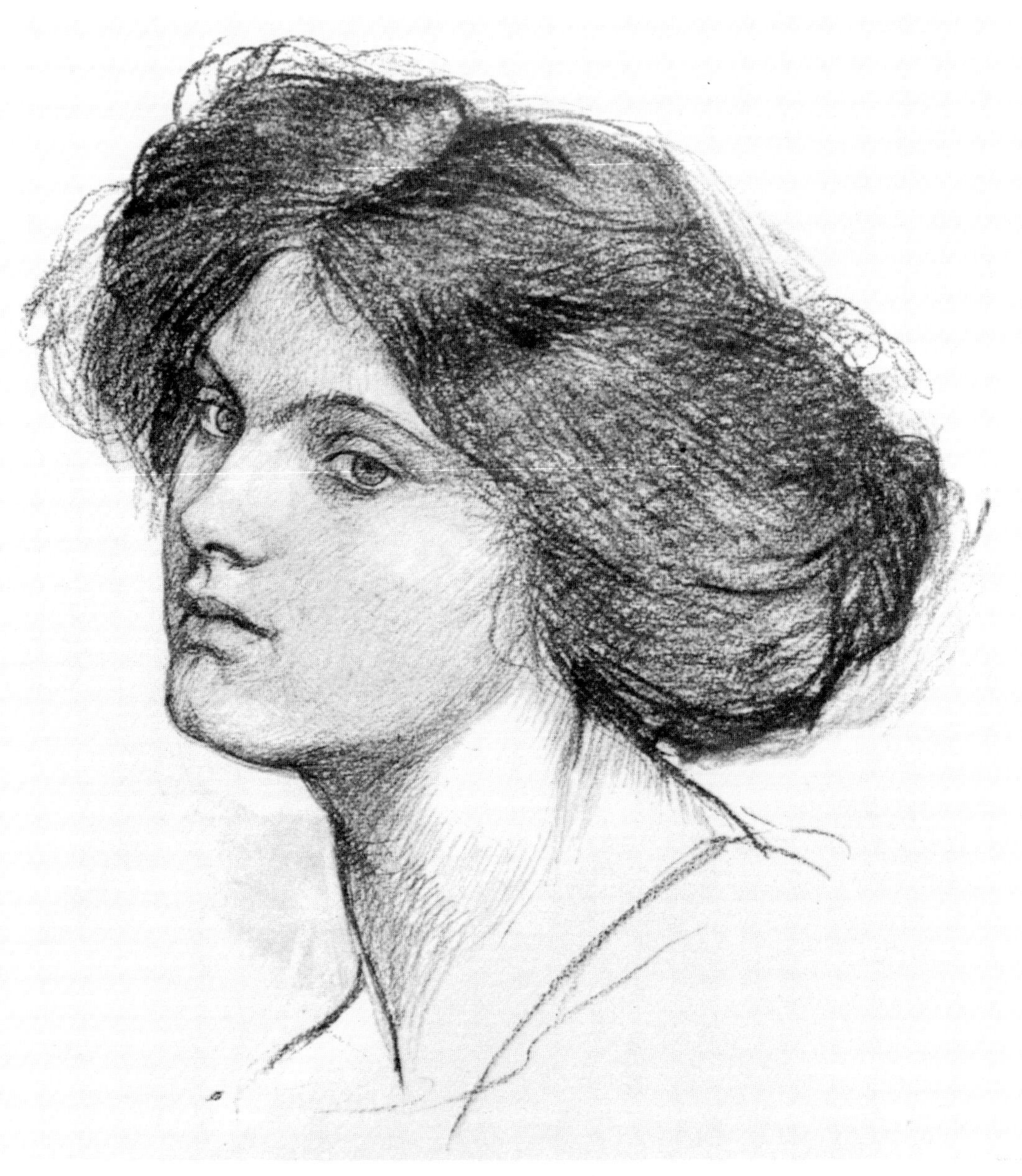

41 *Head of a Girl*, *c.*1889.
Pencil. Location unknown

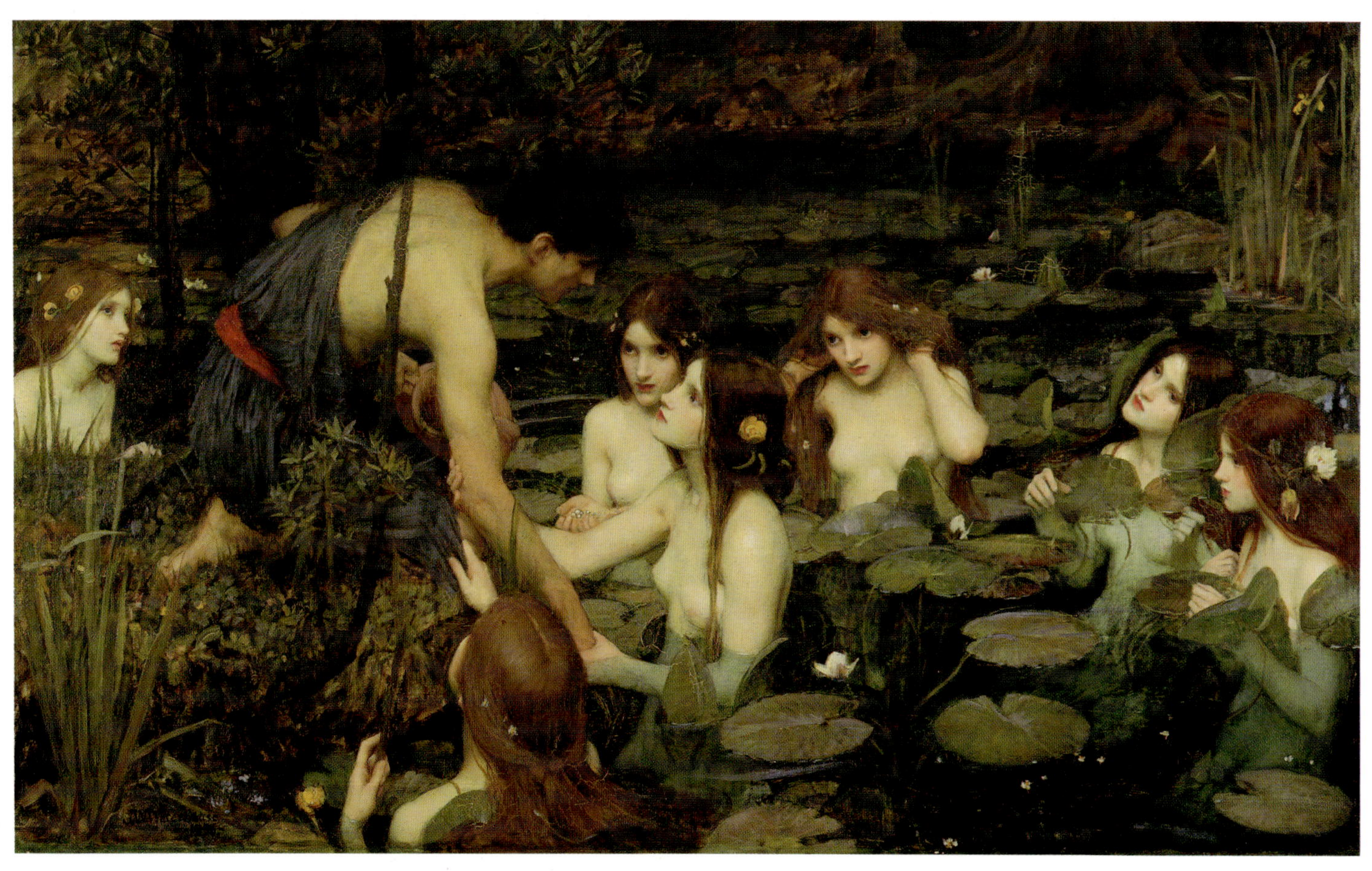

42 *Hylas and the Nymphs*, 1896. 38½ × 64 in (98 × 163 cm). Manchester City Art Gallery

43 *Pandora*, 1896. 60 × 36 in (152 × 91 cm). Private collection

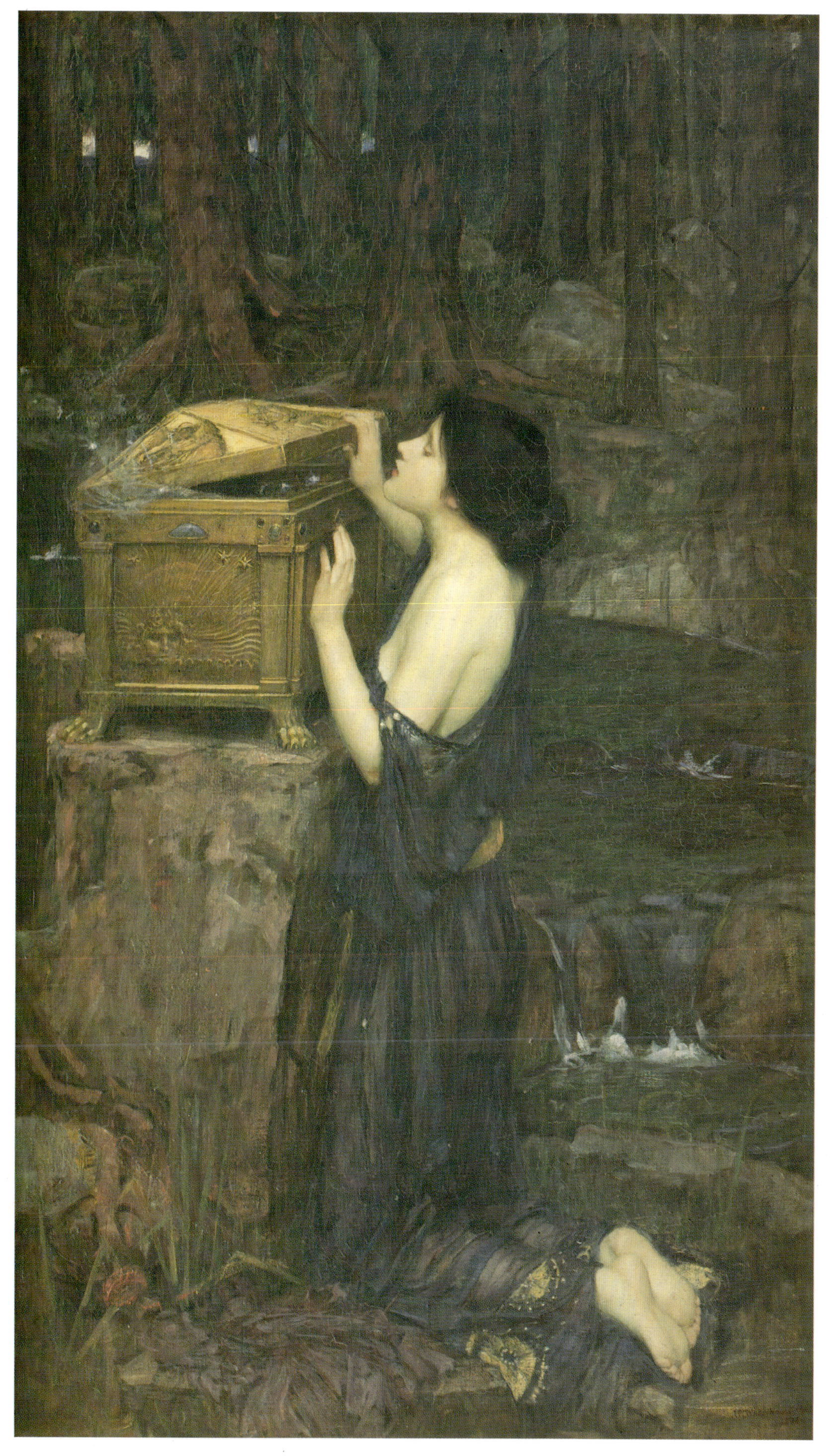

paintings, not only to an expressive pose of the figure but to a gentle and appropriate gesture. The attitude of the girl, moving back the heavy weight of her hair, is that of the nymph in *Hylas* and of the 1894 *Ophelia*. It shows Waterhouse's self-taught ability to retain an image in the mind, together with the fluency in painting which enabled him to carry a picture forward through a large-scale oil study with very little variation from the original idea.

This is also demonstrated in his 1898 group picture *Flora and the Zephyrs*, where the final work differs only sightly from the full-size oil study. In the latter, amid a profusion of constructive brush-strokes, he dwelt upon the painting of heads and hands, as if to testify again to the overpowering presence of the young models in the studio. At this time Waterhouse's women were always girls, as Lord Leighton's girls were always full-grown women, but his admiration for the late P.R.A.'s work is shown again in *Ariadne* (Pl.45), where the fragile figure of the Cretan princess reclines in a horizontal setting as reminiscent of Leighton as that of *St Cecilia*.

44 *Juliet*, 1898. 27½ × 18¼ in (70 × 46.3 cm). Private collection

A call upon idealism can bring out the best in the painter. In 1899 the Boer War had begun in South Africa, and in the spring of 1900 330 artists donated works to the Artists' War Fund in support of the British troops. After being exhibited in the London Guildhall, the pictures were auctioned by Christie's, who waived the £12,000 profit in favour of the Fund. *Destiny* (Pl.46) was painted by Waterhouse especially for the cause, as shown by his own inscription 'Artists' War Fund' above his signature, and was selected by *The Studio* as one of the most noteworthy in the exhibition. The girl drinking a libation to the departing heroes was a favourite model for the rest of his career; statuesque in her beauty, she casts a sympathetic gaze towards the ships already under sail. Waterhouse's setting is typical of his origins – Italianate and geometrical: the circles of the mirror and its stand are repeated in the arches of the tiled loggia and the front of the lectern.

His second picture of that year, exhibited at Agnew's and sold by them to Mr (later Sir) Ernest Moon, reverted to Tennyson, whose explicit imagery once more sufficed the artist. The theme of *The Lady Clare* is the familiar one of the desolate maiden; in this case, having unwittingly deceived her betrothed as to her real identity, she goes accompanied by his gift of the lily-white doe to offer him his freedom. An unusual feature of the painting is that it recalls the subject of a much earlier study in oils discovered by the writer beneath another canvas – one of the studies for the *Springtime* series of about 1913. The subject is out of place in the series of classical myths pursued by Waterhouse between 1896 and 1912, and it is tempting to wonder whether the picture resulted from a sudden impulse or an enquiry to Agnew's by Ernest Moon, who was later to acquire two more Waterhouses. Certainly the composition of the final work is precisely the same as that of the study (which, incidentally, is half as large again), and this may suggest a painting produced to order on the basis of an earlier concept.

By the end of the century, it could be truly said that Waterhouse had reached the peak of his achievement. In the studio at Primrose Hill, his art had matured and his

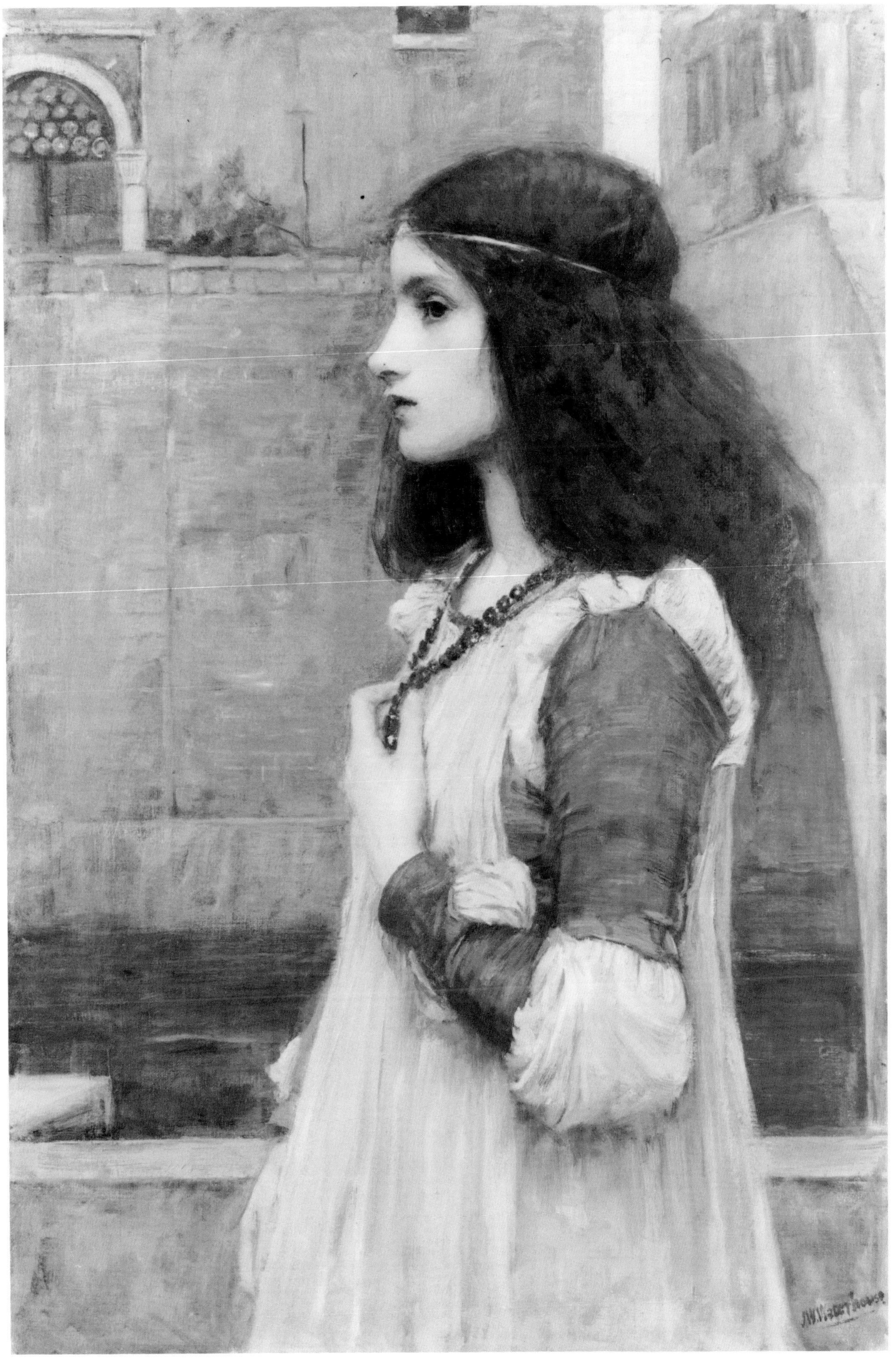

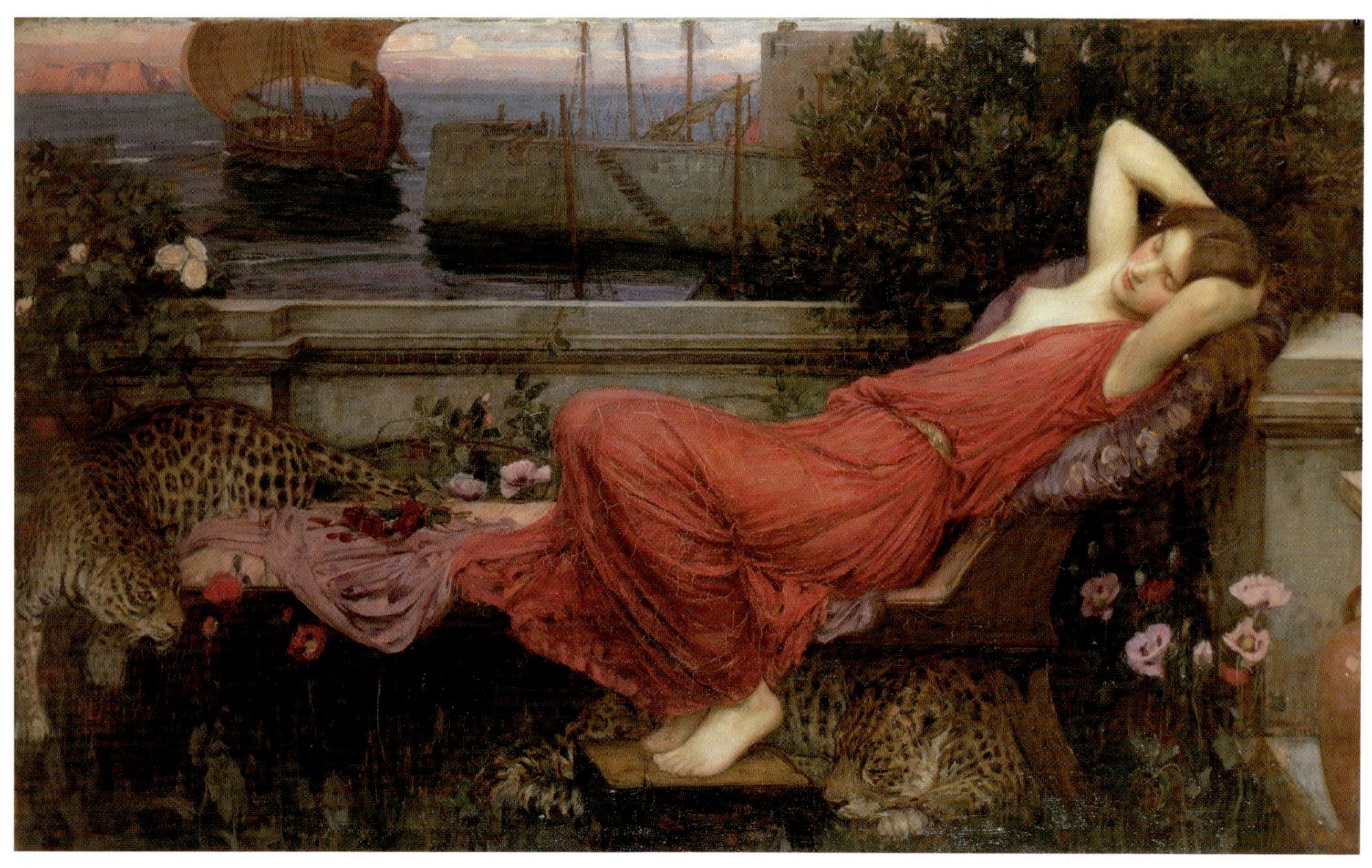

45 *Ariadne*, 1898.
36 × 59½ in (91 × 151 cm).
Private collection

46 *Destiny*, 1900.
27 × 21½ in (68.5 × 55 cm).
Burnley, Towneley Hall Art Gallery

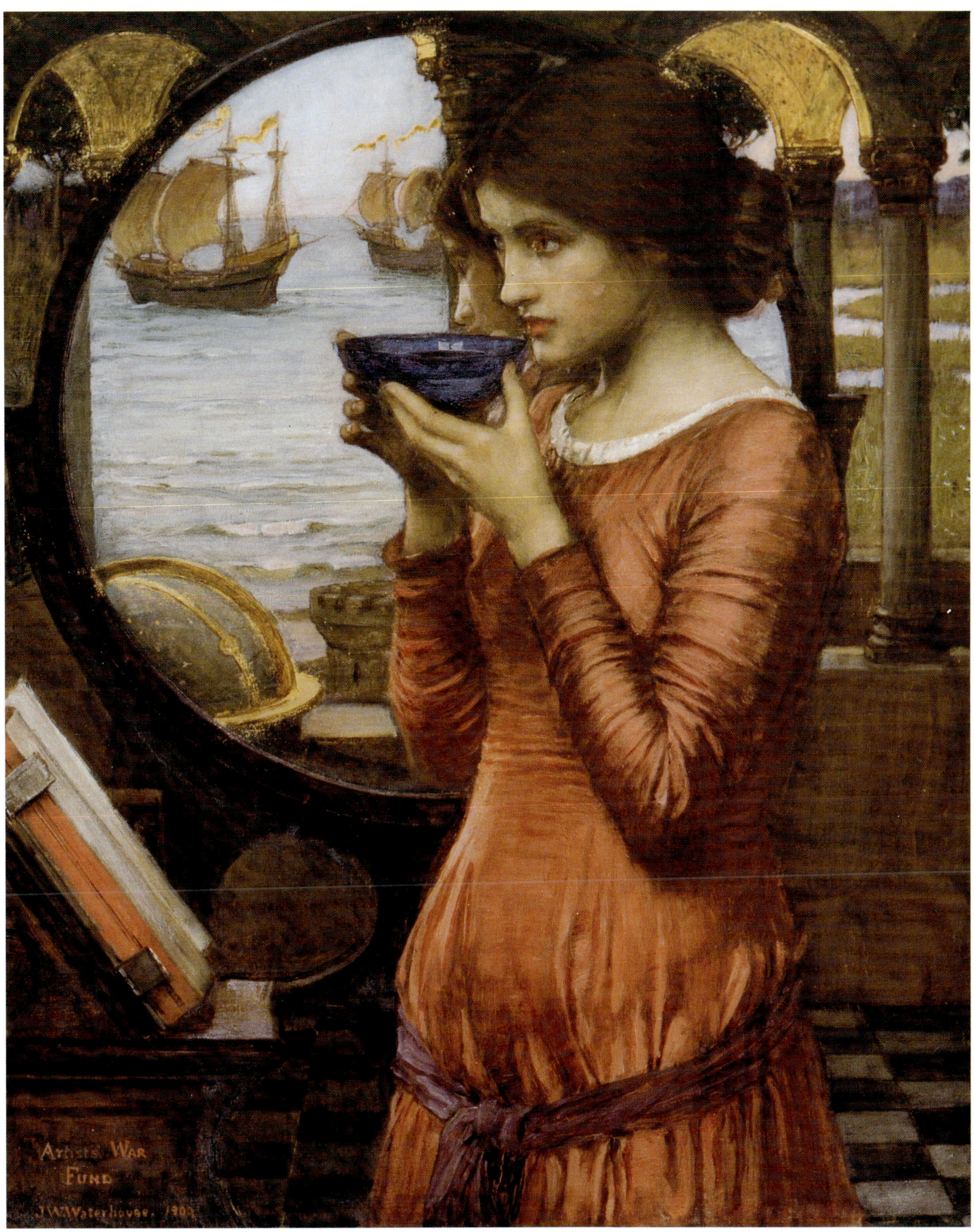
Artists' War
Fund
J.W. Waterhouse.

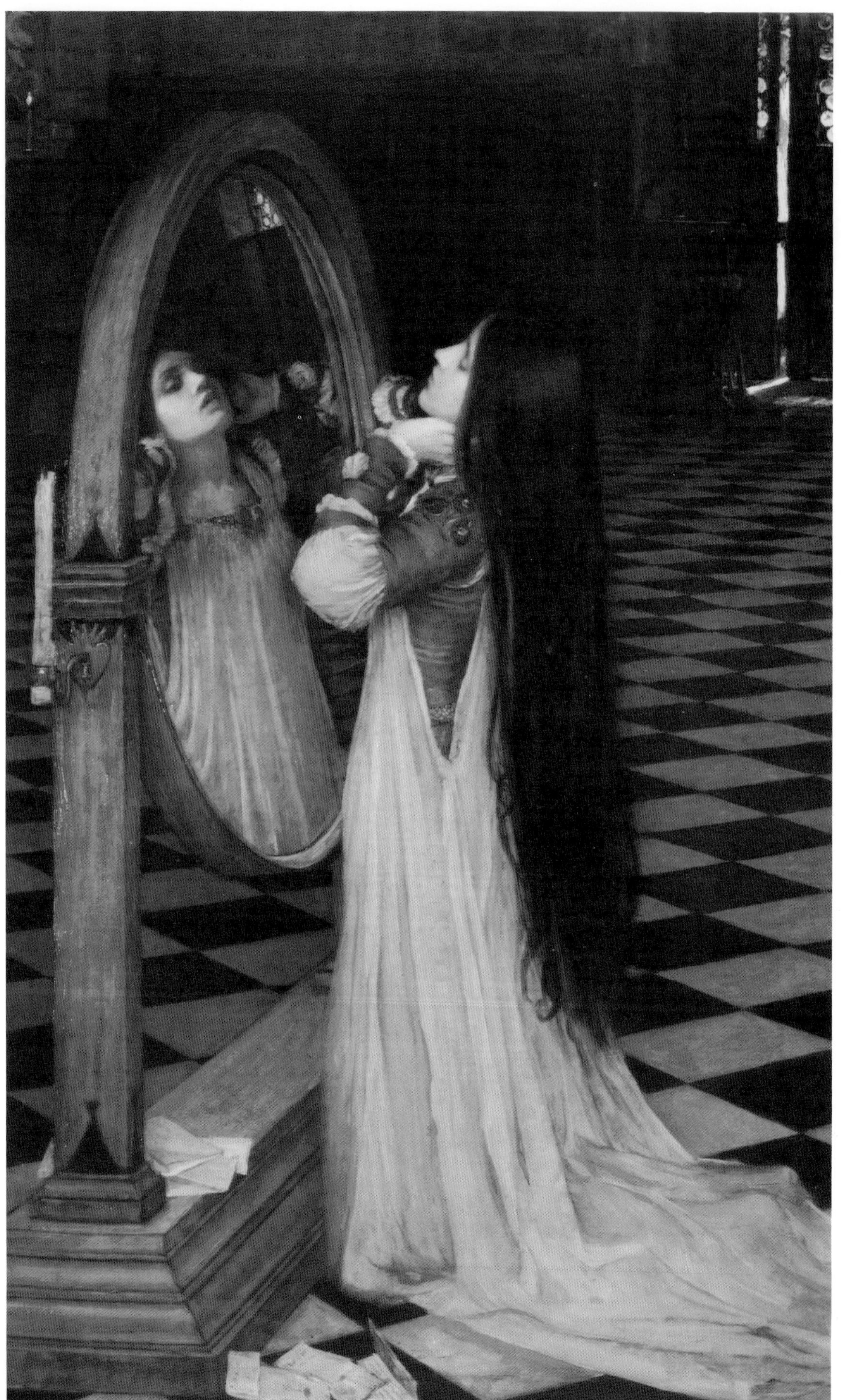

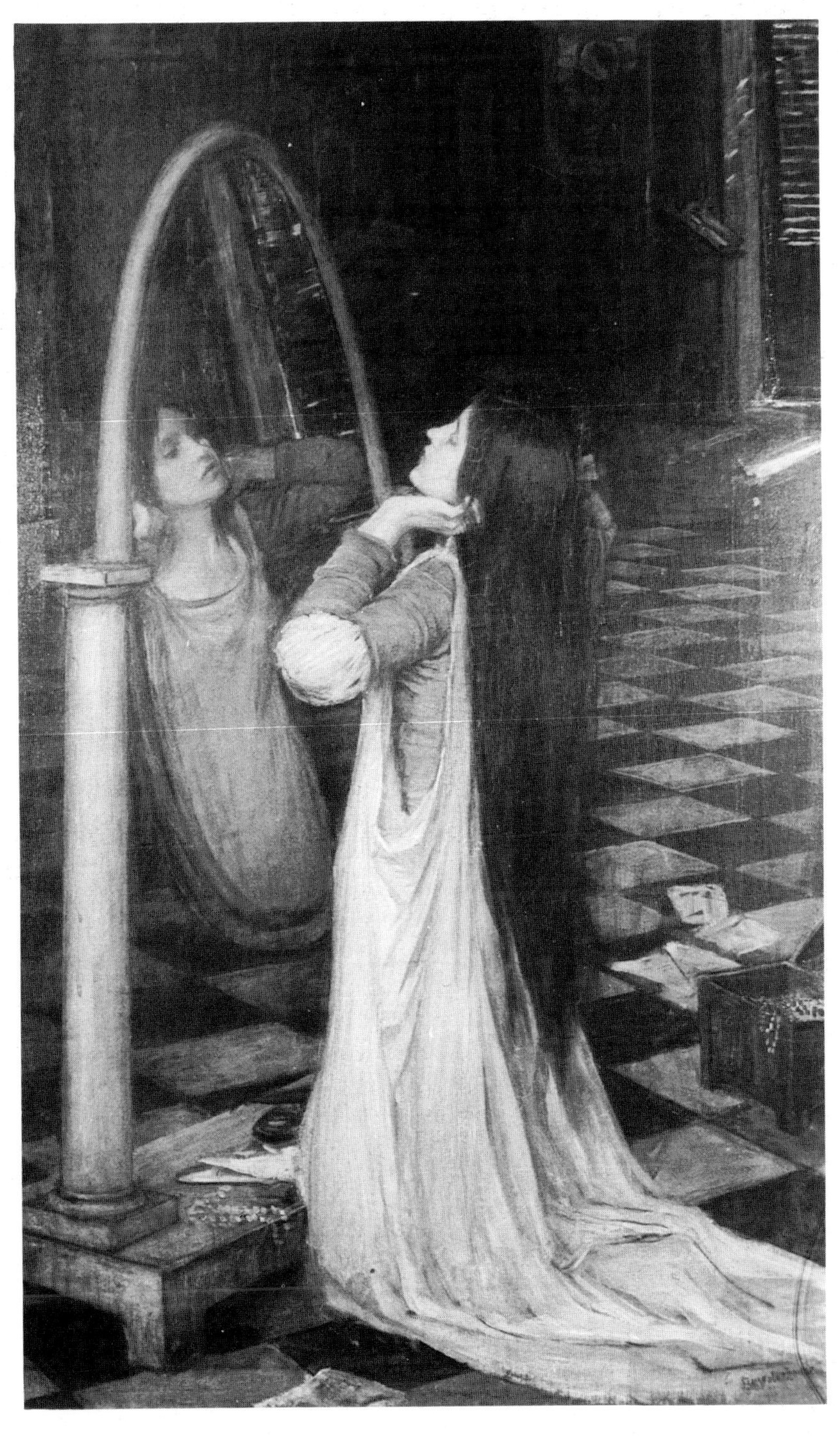

48 Study for *Mariana in the South*, *c.* 1897. 51½ × 32 in (131 × 81 cm). London, Fulham Public Library

47 *Mariana in the South*, 1897. 45 × 29 in (114 × 74 cm). Courtesy Christie's

finest works had been produced. He was universally admired as an artist and his Academic honours were complete. True to his somewhat retiring nature he seems never to have desired the Presidency, although there are not unexpected rumours of his being urged towards it.

As time went by, the deeply-researched subjects of history became less compulsive, but the ever-present mood of romance was reinforced by his continued readings of Tennyson and Shakespeare (Pl.44) in addition to the legends. His health was not perfect in these years, and illness had kept him from the Hanging Committee of the Academy in 1897. Alternating at the easel between one large composition and several single figures inspired by the model, his pictures became in a sense more optimistic, more comforting by their simple escapism. Pensive, wistful ('they are all of them wistful', said one critic) but seldom melancholy, the nymphs inhabit gardens, pick flowers, dream and hope in their Renaissance interiors. *The Awakening of Adonis* of 1900 was in a similar vein to *Flora and the Zephyrs*, though the number of pencil sketches for it indicates a greater difficulty in finalizing the composition. The little putti seen here in the oil sketch (Pl.49), though charming enough in themselves, are superfluous to the action.

Yet his creative invention was still strong and, though he had every excuse to relax his efforts, there were fine paintings still to come in a new studio and a new century.

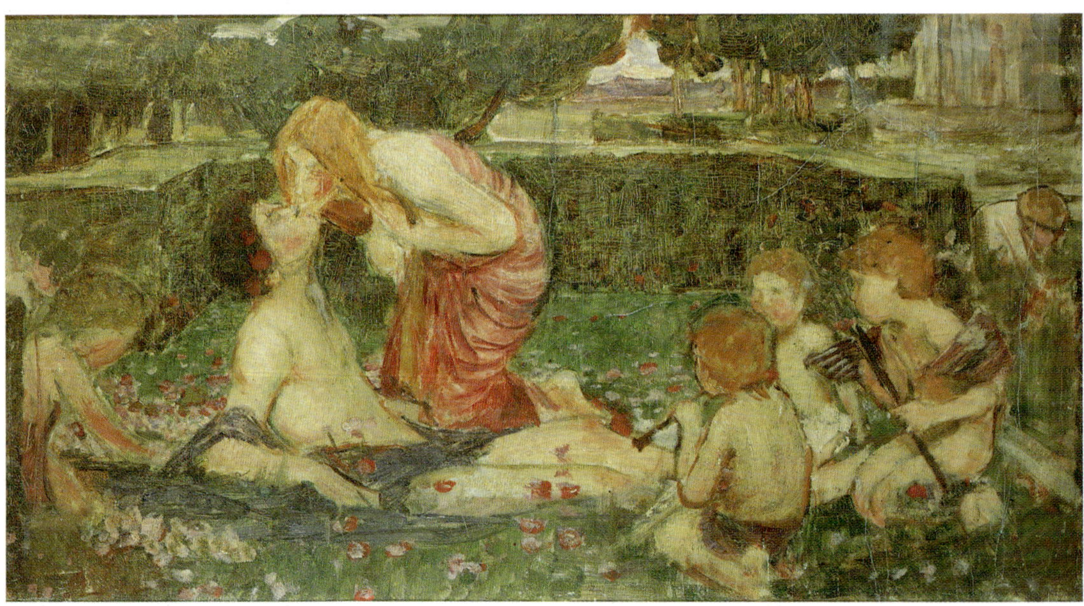

49 Study for *The Awakening of Adonis*, *c*, 1900.
13½ × 26½ in (34 × 67 cm).
Courtesy Sotheby's

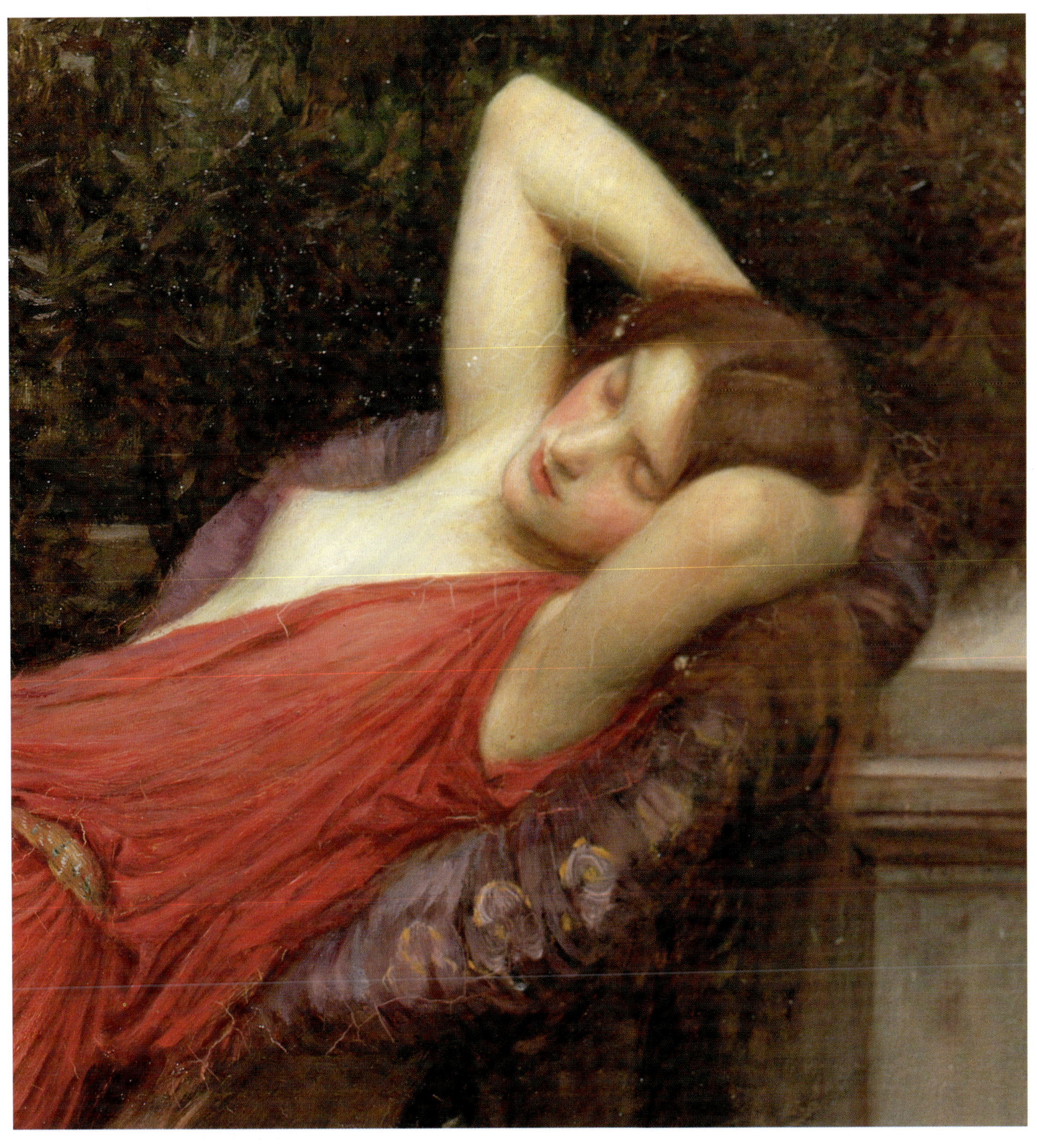

50 Detail from *Ariadne* (Pl.45)

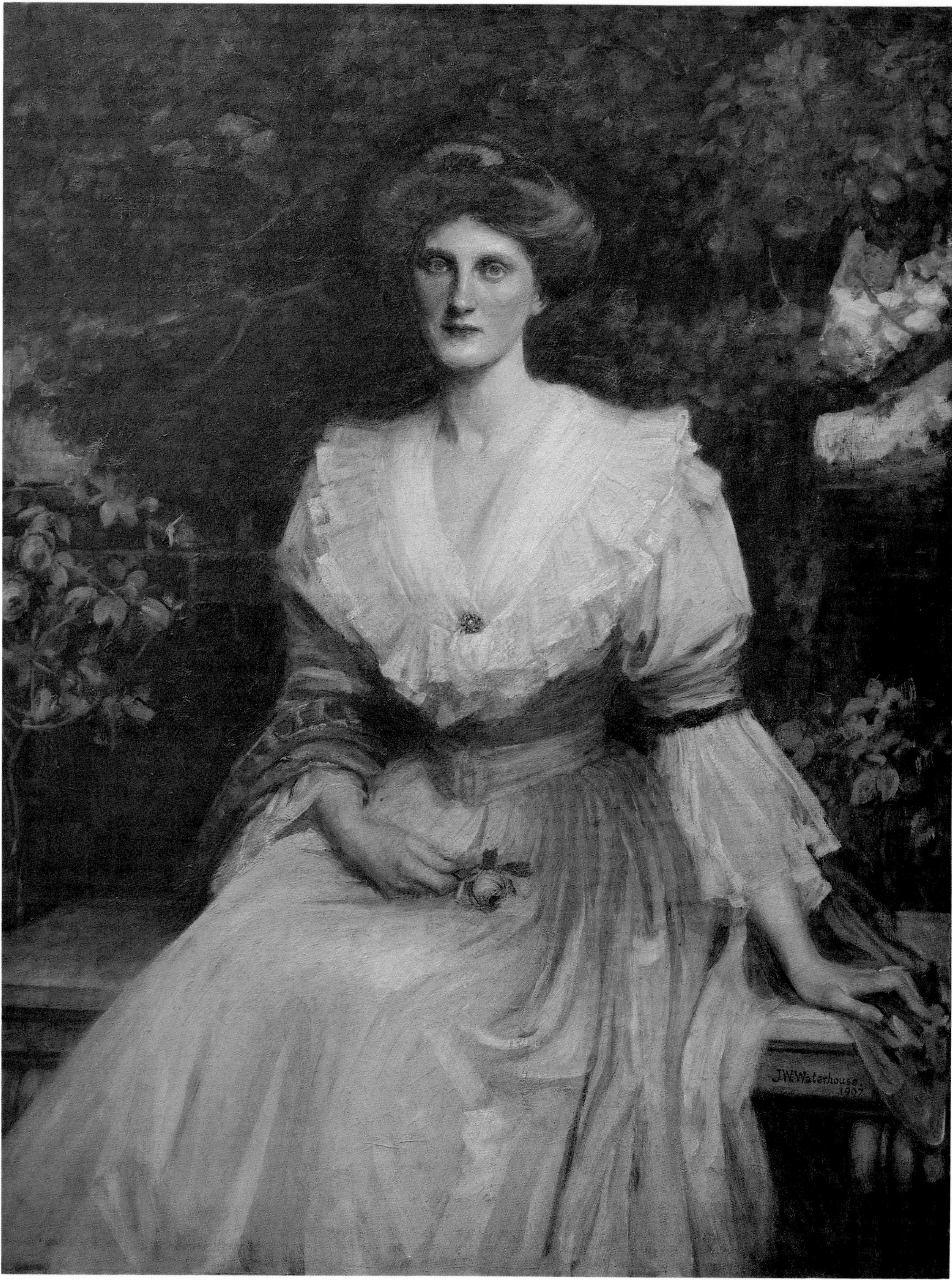
J.W. Waterhouse
1907

5
St John's Wood

WHAT PROMPTED the move away from Primrose Hill Studios? Nino and Esther had lived there for seventeen years, and the studio had been adequate for his greatest paintings. Some of their neighbours had certainly moved on, and the intimate friendships of the earlier years may have seemed less easy to maintain. Though they had no children and Esther does not seem to have wanted any, perhaps as a housewife she required more space. Perhaps they both felt that his status as an Academician deserved a more imposing residence in a more fashionable area.

51 *Lady Violet Henderson*, 1907. 50 × 40 in (127 × 101.5 cm). The Lord Faringdon

In the years following the foundation of the Royal Academy, artists had congregated in Marylebone. Newman Street, on the eastern boundary of the parish, was virtually occupied by them, and Benjamin West, the second President of the Academy, lived at No. 14 for forty-five years until his death in 1820. But as the neighbourhood became more and more popular, the most eminent artists began to move west and north, to Lisson Grove and up to St John's Wood, where Edwin Landseer bought a small cottage in 1824 for £100, opposite what is now Lord's Cricket Ground.

Henry Samuel Eyre had purchased the St John's Wood estate in 1794 from the Earl of Chesterfield, and the speculative builders who developed the area on the basis of the plans prepared by his descendants had done so with a good deal of taste. In contrast to the continuous terraces and imposing squares in the rest of fast-expanding London, St John's Wood provided large detached or semi-detached houses with spacious gardens which offered both privacy and proximity to a community of like minds drawn together by art and by music. In the summer, the gardens saw lively social gatherings and resounded to the click of croquet mallets; in the winter, private concerts employed the most celebrated musicians of the day. Billiards was in tremendous vogue among the gentlemen after its modern history began about 1800. Landseer had replaced his cottage with a house in which equivalent space was allotted to the studio and the billiard room.

In the 1860s the cheerful fellowship of the St John's Wood Clique – future Royal Academicians P.H. Calderon, W.F. Yeames (already Associates), Henry Stacy Marks, G.D. Leslie, Frederick Walker, G.A. Storey, J.E. Hodgson, and their founder David Wynfield (who died without attaining membership of the Academy) –

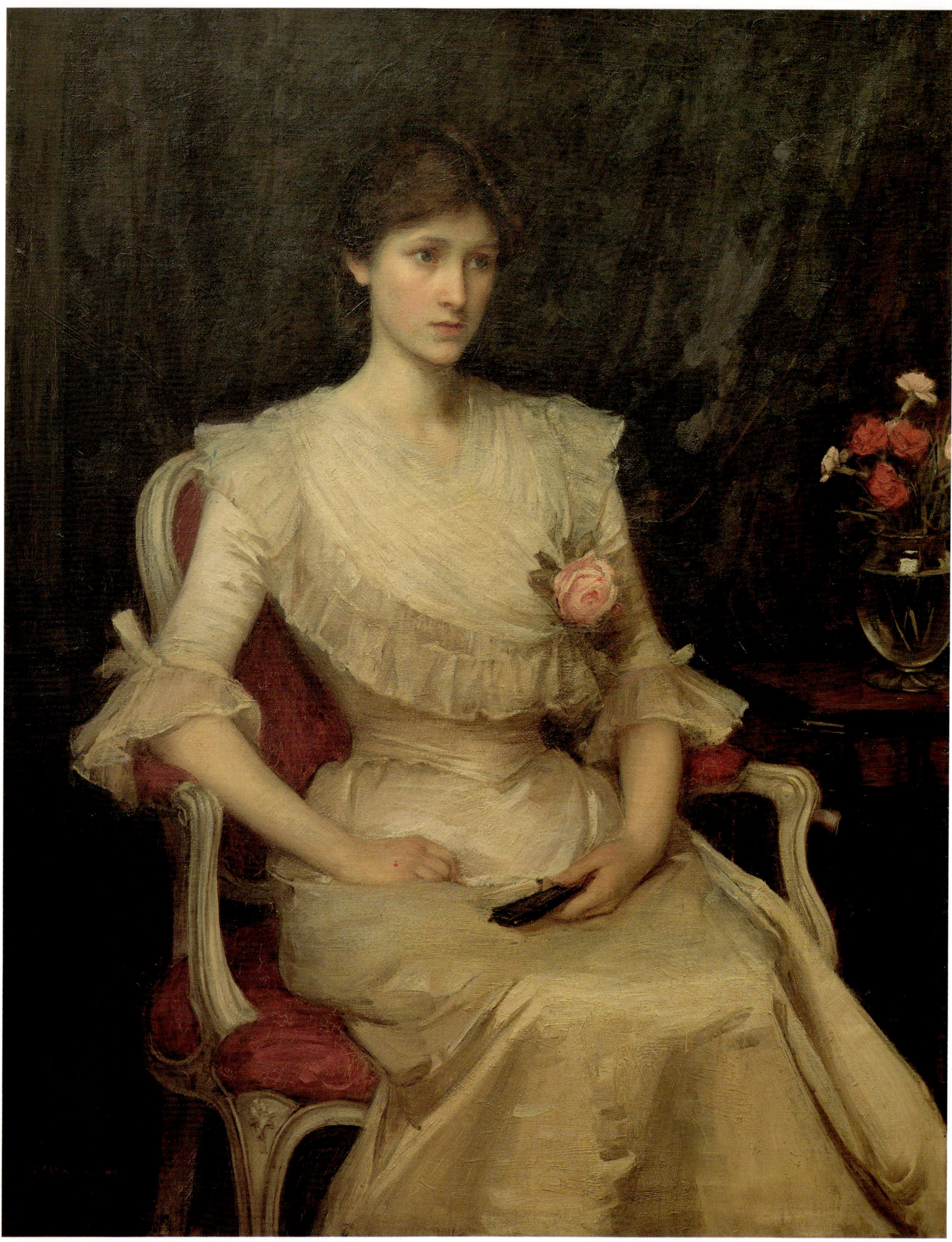

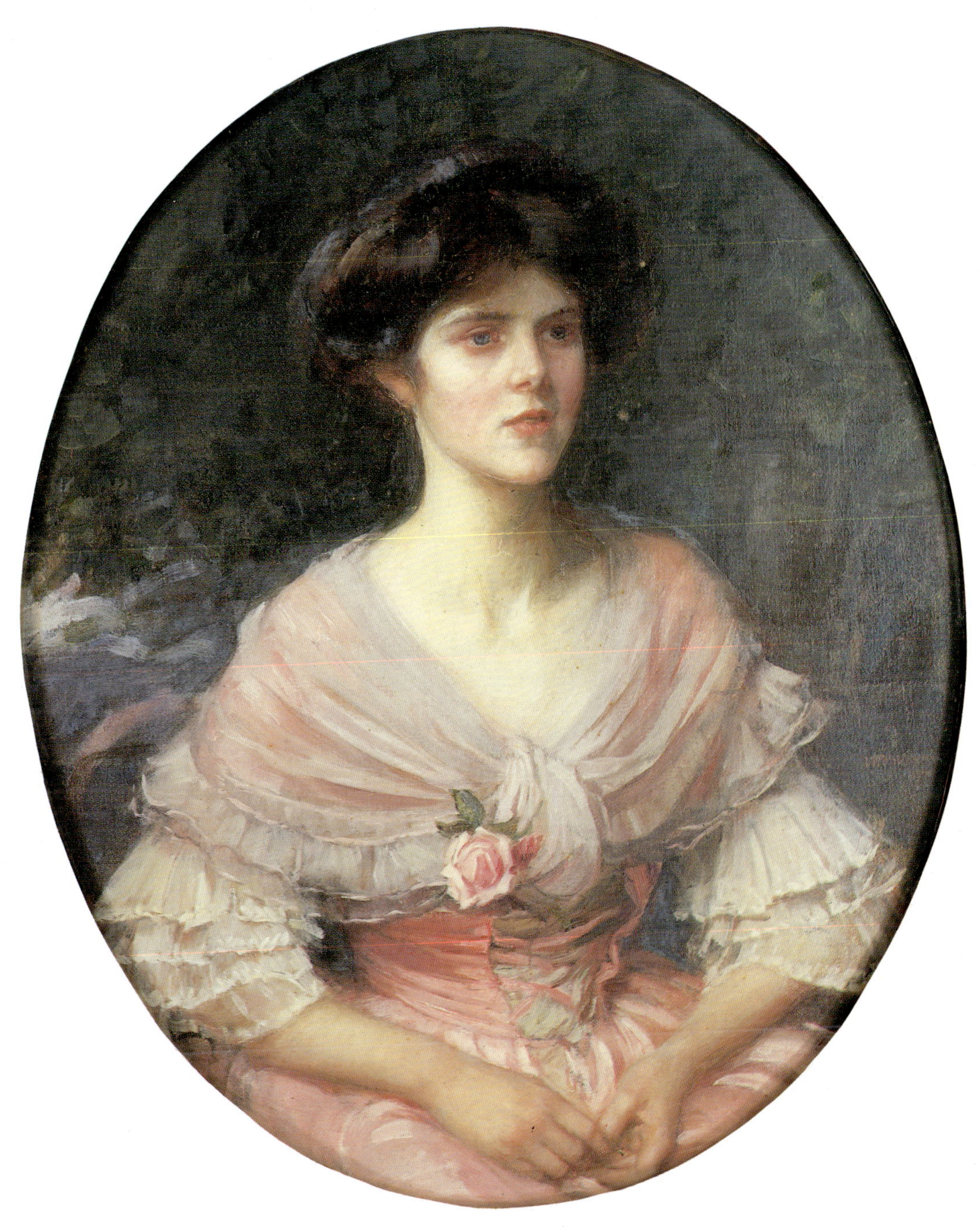

53 *Mrs A.P. Henderson*, 1908. 30 × 25 in (76 × 63.5 cm). Courtesy Sotheby's

52 *Miss Margaret Henderson*, 1900. 49¾ × 38¾ in (125 × 97 cm). The Lord Faringdon

played billiards at Calderon's, met weekly at each other's houses to draw, paint and criticize a subject set for the evening, and organized uproarious expeditions into what was then the countryside of Neasden and Watford. By the late 1880s the Clique had disintegrated as its members died (Walker in 1875, Wynfield in 1887), progressed (Calderon became Keeper of the Royal Academy), or simply moved; in the end only Marks remained, dying in 1898.

But there were still many friends to be found in St John's Wood in 1901 when the Waterhouses moved into No. 10 Hall Road. Formerly the home of the sculptor Harry Bates, its studio was understandably in the basement, with a conveniently large exit into the garden. The Greiffenhagens had left Primrose Hill Studios in 1895 for No. 12 Loudoun Road, and Maurice Greiffenhagen immediately put Nino up for membership of the St John's Wood Art Club among former fellow-students Ernest Waterlow, Arthur Hacker and C.W. Wyllie. Other members included Yeend King, R.B.A., R.I., painter of rustic genre; the landscape painter and illustrator from Leicester, John Fulleylove, R.I.; and later on Alma-Tadema, Clausen, Dicksee, Goetze and Arthur Rackham – the latter having meanwhile occupied the Waterhouses' first home at No. 3 Primrose Hill Studios. Waterhouse also joined Clausen and George Frampton (R.A. the following year and knighted in 1908) on the Honorary Advisory Council of the St John's Wood Art School, which he had already been visiting monthly since 1892 to criticize the students' work.

The social round included 'Picture Sunday' or 'Show Sunday', when shortly before the sending in of pictures to the Royal Academy Summer Exhibition the artists' studios would be thrown open to patrons and friends to the accompaniment of music and refreshments. Stacy Marks mourned the degeneration of these occasions from small friendly encounters, including a dealer or two, to invasions of unknown and generally uninterested spectators who were not above pilfering small objects from their hosts; but perhaps one must allow for his irrepressible sense of humour. The daughter of portrait and genre painter Walter Urwick recalled years of these 'very smart affairs' when 'children used to hand the cakes round, dressed up in their best clothes and behaving beautifully, and all sorts of well-known and distinguished people came. ... Our house had fifteen rooms and it all led through from ante-room to gallery to studio and out into the garden.'

In *Punch* of 9 April 1887, George du Maurier's drawing *Picture Sunday* had a penetrating caption which showed how the rising artist sought desperately to attract the influential critic to these occasions. Though sales may have been comparatively few, as Marks commented, patronage resulted – especially in the form of the hundreds of portrait commissions emanating from artists' studios in the latter years of the century. It is a tribute to Waterhouse that he did not give himself up to this lucrative trade, maintaining his quiet preoccupation with the imaginative work which had made his reputation. In spite of his many drawings of heads, his portraits in oils are few and far between. All the known ones are feminine, and the sitters are generally the daughters or wives of friends or patrons. Occasionally he was struck by a certain aspect of beauty like the waist-length hair of Roma Catriona

Macfarlane, daughter of the minister of the Church of Scotland at Kingussie in Inverness. Then aged about ten, she was walking with her mother when the artist approached them for permission to paint her, and the portrait was excellently received in the 1914 Academy.

The cult of the red-haired girl owes a great deal to the Pre-Raphaelites, as Stacy Marks noted in one of his humorous songs about 'a P.R.B., one of the chosen clique', beginning 'No vulgar daily life for me' and ending:

> But that which most delights me is a woman with red hair,
> Which cheers the young Pre-Raphaelite all of the present time.
> [*Spoken with emphasis*] She must have *red* hair.

Waterhouse himself was not above changing the colour of the model's hair, as in the 1888 *Lady of Shalott*, for which his wife is said to have sat, or later in *The Sorceress* (Pl. 78), for which the oil study shows a dark brunette (Pl. 77).

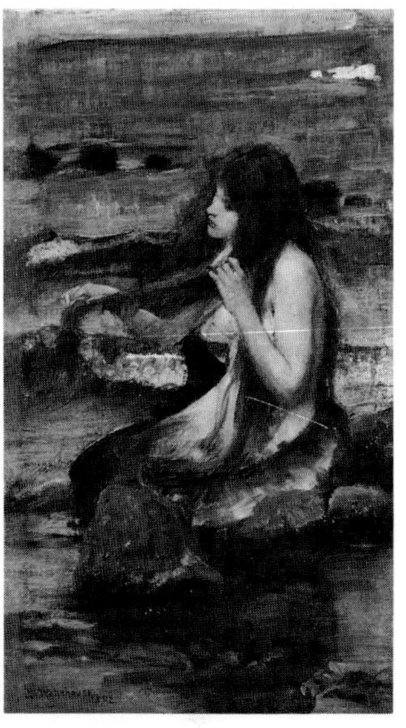

54 *The Mermaid*, 1892. 12½ × 7 in (31.75 × 17.75 cm). Whitford & Hughes

The patronage of the Henderson family was perhaps the most important of Waterhouse's career. The key figures were the financier and connoisseur Alexander Henderson, later the first Baron Faringdon, and his brothers Mr H.W. Henderson and Mr (later Sir) Brodie Henderson. The Faringdon Collection at Buscot Park includes early Italian and Spanish paintings, fine pictures by Reynolds, Lawrence, Gainsborough and Honthorst, and nineteenth-century works by Leighton, Landseer, Watts, Millais, Rossetti and Ford Madox Brown, with Burne-Jones's *Briar Rose* series magnificently ensconced around the walls of the Saloon.

Comparison with Burne-Jones seems inevitable throughout Waterhouse's career and in later criticism, and always redounds to Nino's advantage. In 1892 the *Magazine of Art* devoted a lengthy article to Alexander Henderson's collection, and in spite of the tenor of admiration throughout, Walter Shaw-Sparrow's final note on Burne-Jones encapsulates his negative qualities: 'To me the work of this painter appears as great art lost in a mass of affectations, which seem merely to strive after an effete ideal. No figure really lives. The female form is pared of its graces, of its fulnesses, of its riches. Yet it escapes being divine.' The Hendersons' subsequent encounter with Waterhouse's pictures, their classic compositions peopled with warmly human figures acting out the legends, fulfilled the needs of the connoisseur and his relations to the extent that between them they eventually owned over fifty Waterhouse paintings. They prevailed upon him to undertake the rare portraits of Alexander Henderson's daughter Margaret and his daughter-in-law Lady Violet Henderson (Pls. 51 and 52), both at Buscot, and the brilliantly vital *Mrs A.P. Henderson* (Pl. 53).

Waterhouse's genuine friendship with the family is evidenced by his letter from Hall Road, to 'My dear Aline' (the daughter of Mr H.W. Henderson, Sir Alexander's younger brother and one of Nino's earliest patrons) enclosing 'the promised drawing', his 'belated wedding present'. She was twenty and Nino sixty-two, and the lapse of time between her wedding on 15 February 1911 and the letter

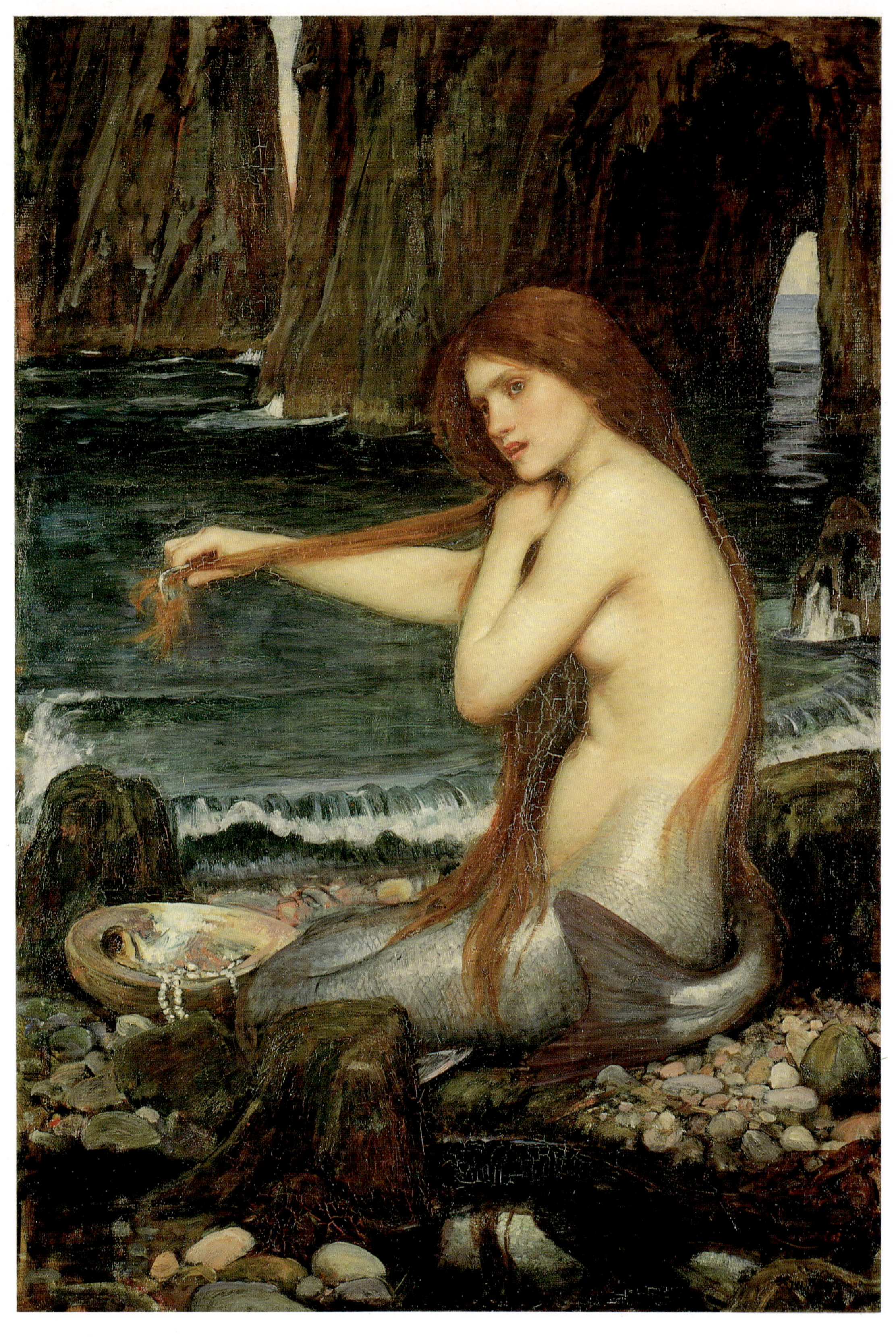

55 *A Mermaid*, 1901.
$38\frac{1}{2} \times 26\frac{1}{4}$ in (98×67 cm).
London, Royal Academy of Arts

56 *The Siren*, *c.* 1900.
32×21 in (81×53 cm).
Courtesy Sotheby's

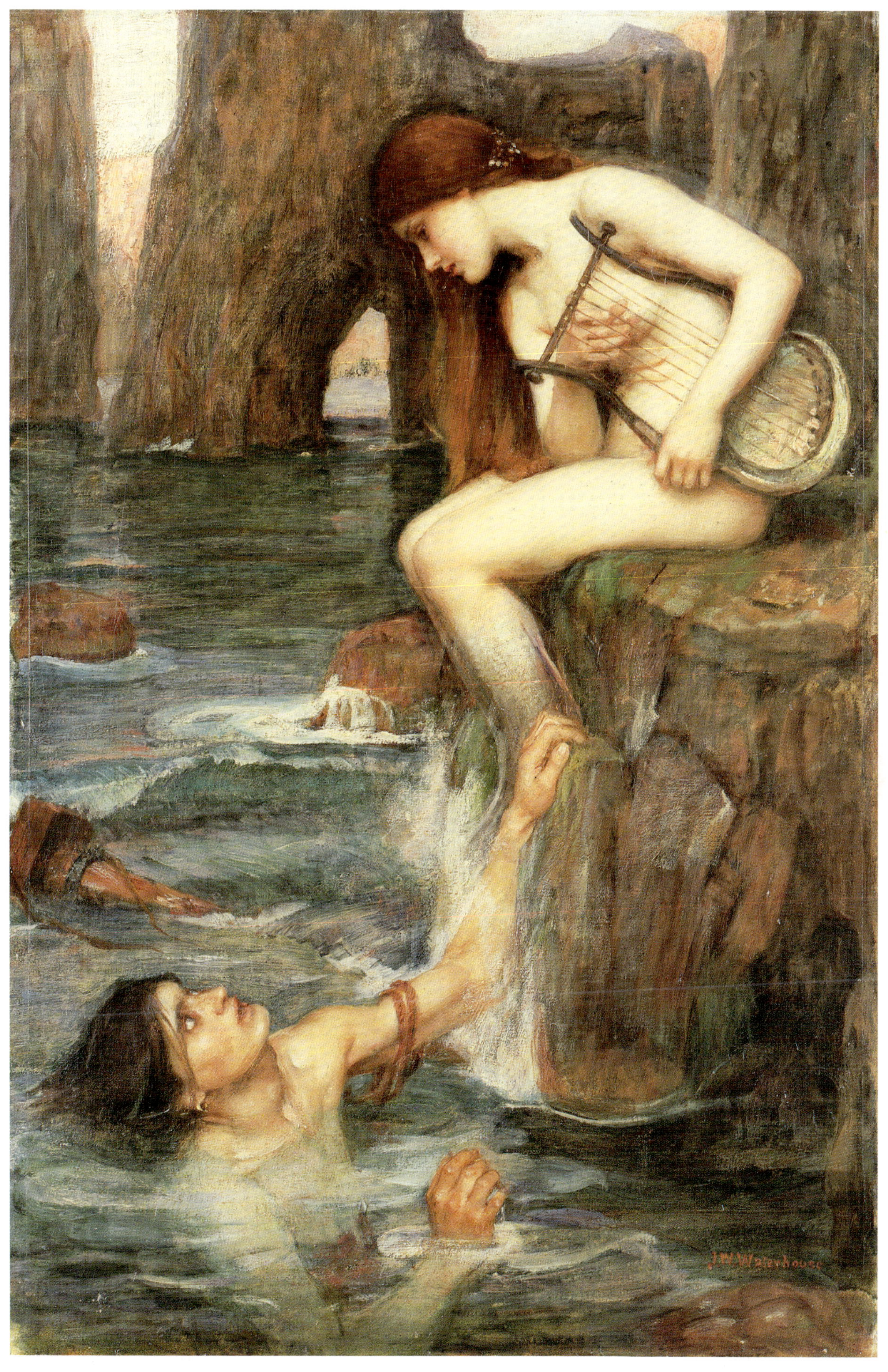

dated 13 June seemed characteristic of the other-worldly nature of the artist, who was said to have arrived a day late for a garden party at Buckingham Palace.

But Waterhouse's creativity never lapsed. Belated though it was, his Diploma picture finally arrived at the Academy in time for the Summer Exhibition of 1901. Foreshadowed as far back as 1892 in an oil study from life (Pl.54), *A Mermaid* (Pl.55) is one of his most delicate conceptions, and understandably he had lingered long in bringing it to perfection. It has a timeless quality based on its classic composition – a square within a rectangle. The mermaid combs her hair while the small waves turn endlessly behind her on the sea-margin and the massive rocks. As always, Waterhouse is able to capture the natural moment of stillness; the comb pressed to the end of the auburn tress, the parted lips and dreaming eyes speaking of thoughts far away. The beauty of the favourite model seems independent of the mermaid's coiled tail. The *Art Journal* was moved to a positively lyrical note:

> But the conception is charged with romance, the line with rhythm. The wistful-sad look of this fair mermaid, seated in her rock-bound home, combing the dull-red hair ere she studs it with pearls that lie in the iridescent shell, is potent in suggestion. It tells of human longings never to be satisfied ... The chill of the sea lies ever on her heart; the endless murmur of waters is a poor substitute for the sound of human voices; never can this beautiful creature, troubled with emotion, experience on the one hand unawakened repose, on the other the joys of womanhood.

Again the Burne-Jones comparison leaps to mind. From his coldly intricate designs to Waterhouse's living legends is a vital step which no one would willingly retrace.

There is no menace in *A Mermaid*, only the beauty of the unattainable – perhaps the perpetual key to Waterhouse's creative imagination. Even in *The Siren* (Pl.56), painted about the same time (for which he had made pencil sketches on the fly-leaves of his copy of Shelley's poems), the mermaid, herself in the grip of unaccountable impulses, gazes regretfully at the drowning sailor she has drawn to his doom. There are indeed no happy endings for the men in Waterhouse's paintings: there was a part of himself in which desire was for ever unsatisfied, and which helps to account for the continuity of his pictorial invention.

Beside *A Mermaid* in the 1901 Academy hung another painting destined for the Faringdon collection: *Nymphs finding the Head of Orpheus* (Pl.57). There is no more masterly work in the whole of Waterhouse's *oeuvre* than this gloss on the story of Orpheus. After the loss of his wife Eurydice, the body of the legendary musician was dismembered by infuriated Bacchantes, flung into the River Hebrus and floated down to the sea where sympathetic nymphs recovered the head, its long hair entwined in the still vibrant lyre.

The subject was not new, and other artists such as Gustave Moreau had attempted it in their own manner. But this is Waterhouse's own creation. Typically, he chose not to show the horrific aspects of the legend. Tension is present in that moment of stillness when the two nymphs glance down to see the disembodied head floating in the pool where they are about to draw their water, but it is, as the *Art Journal* said, 'a theme of wonder'. Compassion is written upon both their faces, and one can almost hear the soft intake of breath as the girl on the right raises a hand to her throat in a wholly natural gesture of dismay. The colour is subdued; even more emphatic in this case is the composition, brought once again to perfection through a series of studies, among which the half-finished work in oils (Pl.60) is itself a work of infinite charm. The softness of flesh and the gentle articulation of the limbs form part of a firm rectangular structure in which the downward gaze of the nymphs is stopped by the horizontal of the lyre and the drifting head. The eye of the spectator is constantly enticed around the perimeter by cunning alternations of light and dark – face, garment, arm, head – assisted by the curves of the bodies and the placing of the saplings (another compositional device of the painter, seen before but always purposefully employed).

The rock-bound pool was to be used again as a setting for the figure, and the paintings which follow are mainly variations upon familiar themes. Single figures are placed in rocky, lightly wooded landscapes or in richly furnished interiors. True to the painter's origins, both costumes and interiors have the flavour of the Italian Renaissance: the verticals and horizontals of the compositions continue to hold together a series of circles rather than the pointed arches of the Gothic. *The Crystal Ball*, *The Missal*, both exhibited in the 1902 Academy, and later *The Love Philtre* are all examples of this particular genre which began with *Destiny* in 1900.

The model is portrayed out of doors in 1903 as *Psyche opening the Golden Box* (Pl.61) and in the following year as *Psyche entering Cupid's Garden* (Pl.62). 'Mr Waterhouse is always painting Psyche,' said the *Standard*. 'Psyche – not Venus, not Minerva, not Diana – is the personage he understands and cares for.' This was not an adverse criticism: there is no doubt about Waterhouse's standing at this time, and reviews of the 1903 Royal Academy Exhibition were unanimous in their praise of *Psyche opening the Golden Box*. 'Classic work', said M.H. Spielmann, editor of the *Magazine of Art*, 'the most complete and delightful of his contributions'. A.L. Baldry in the *Art Journal* dismissed Alma-Tadema's *Silver Favourites* as 'so like many of his other arrangements that it hardly calls for description', but the *Psyche* was 'almost inexplicably attractive ... a work of extraordinary power'. Returning in *The Studio* to this 'exquisite picture', Baldry wrote that 'Mr Waterhouse, indeed, has not often before touched so high a level, admirable artist as he always is.'

These reactions to the painting of a single figure and a simple incident make *Psyche opening the Golden Box* worthy of closer consideration. Waterhouse's creativity was continually inspired by his models and, as in this case, many of his paintings were preceded by full-scale oil studies in which the face and figure were carried virtually to completion. Moreover, because the figure was always human, sensitive, and never a mere stereotype, his repetition of certain visual themes never impairs our emotional response to the picture.

The opening of the box therefore evokes a comparison with the 1896 *Pandora*,

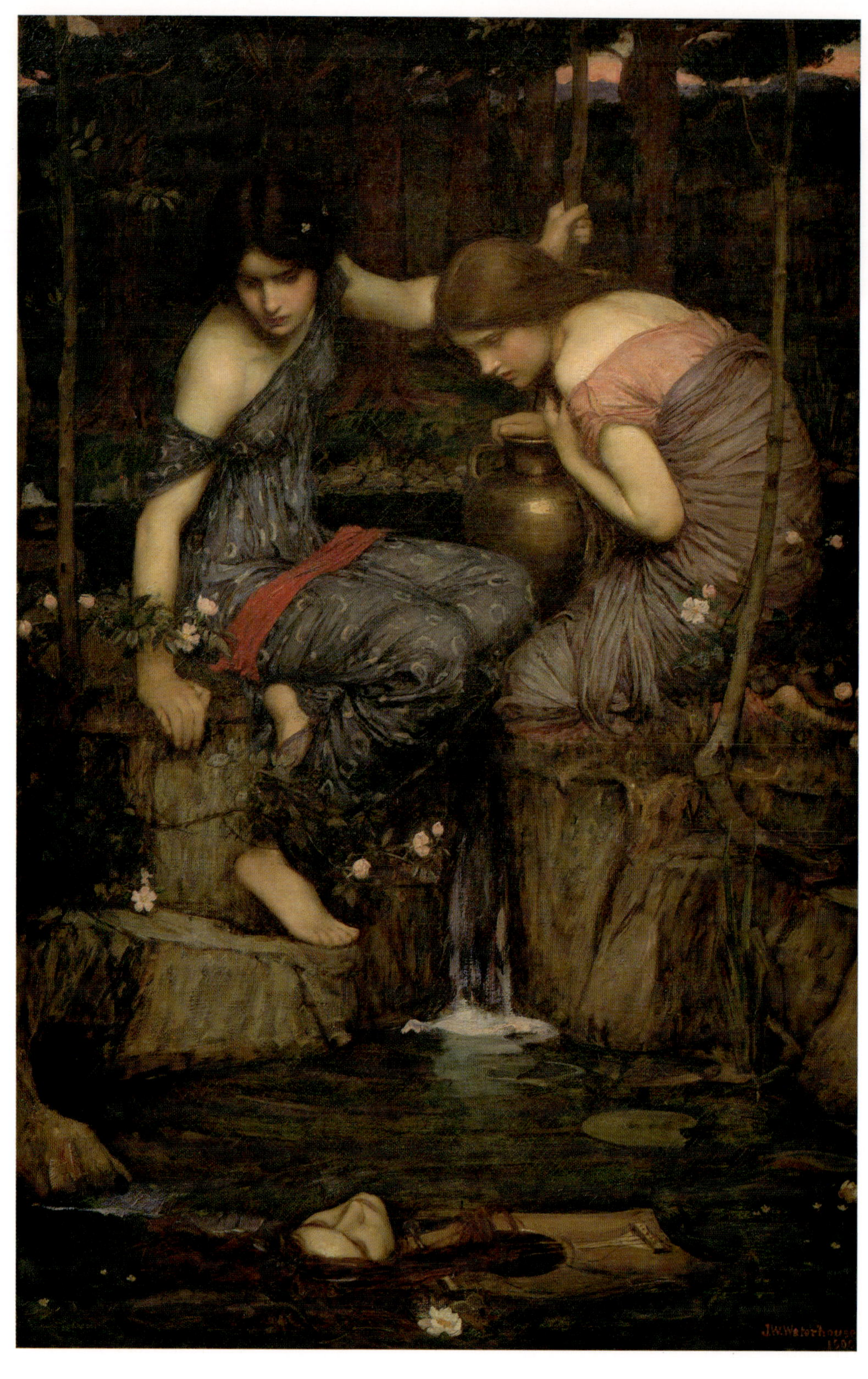

57 *Nymphs finding the Head of Orpheus*, 1900.
58½ × 39 in (149 × 99 cm).
Private collection

58 Detail from *Nymphs finding the Head of Orpheus* (Pl. 57)

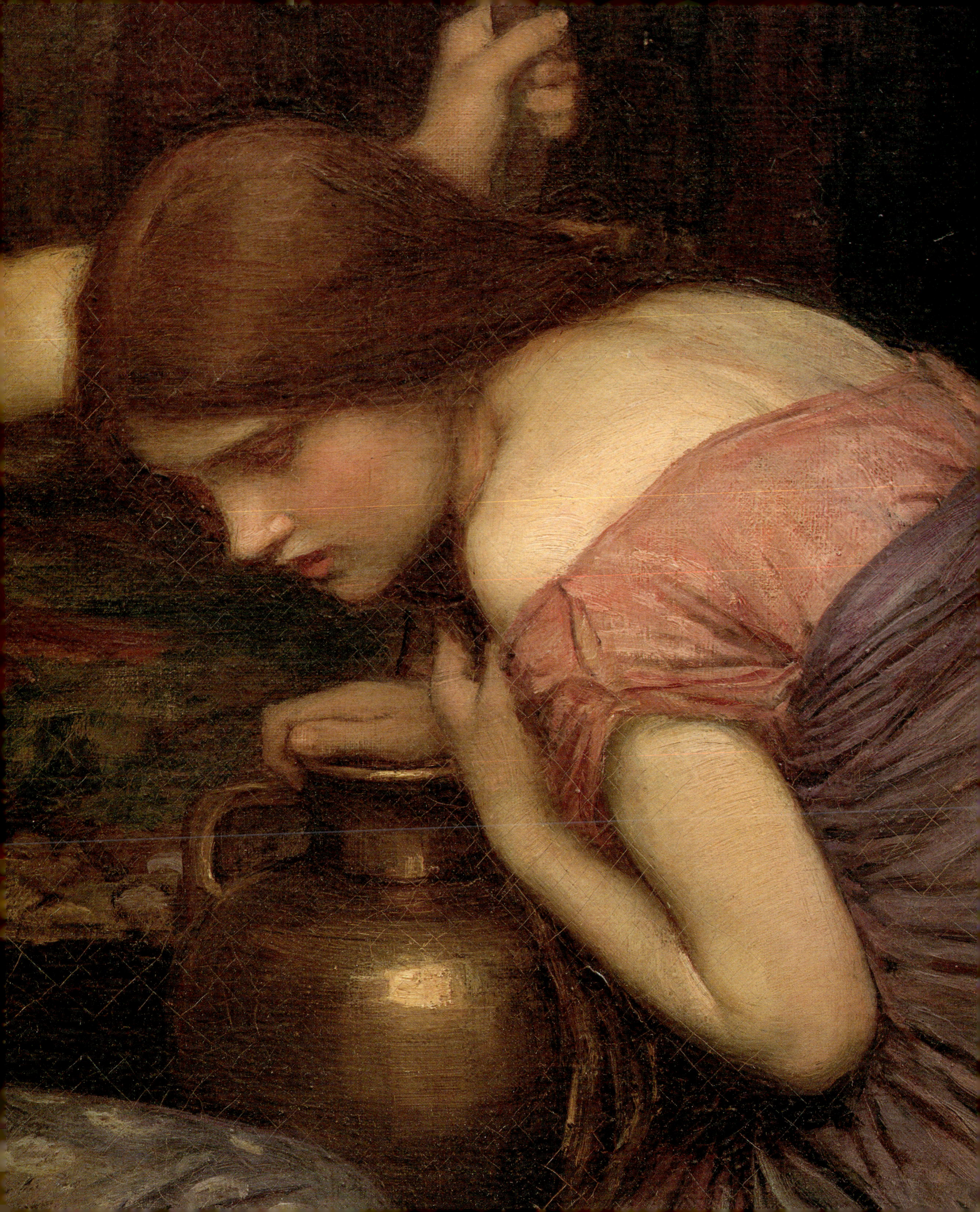

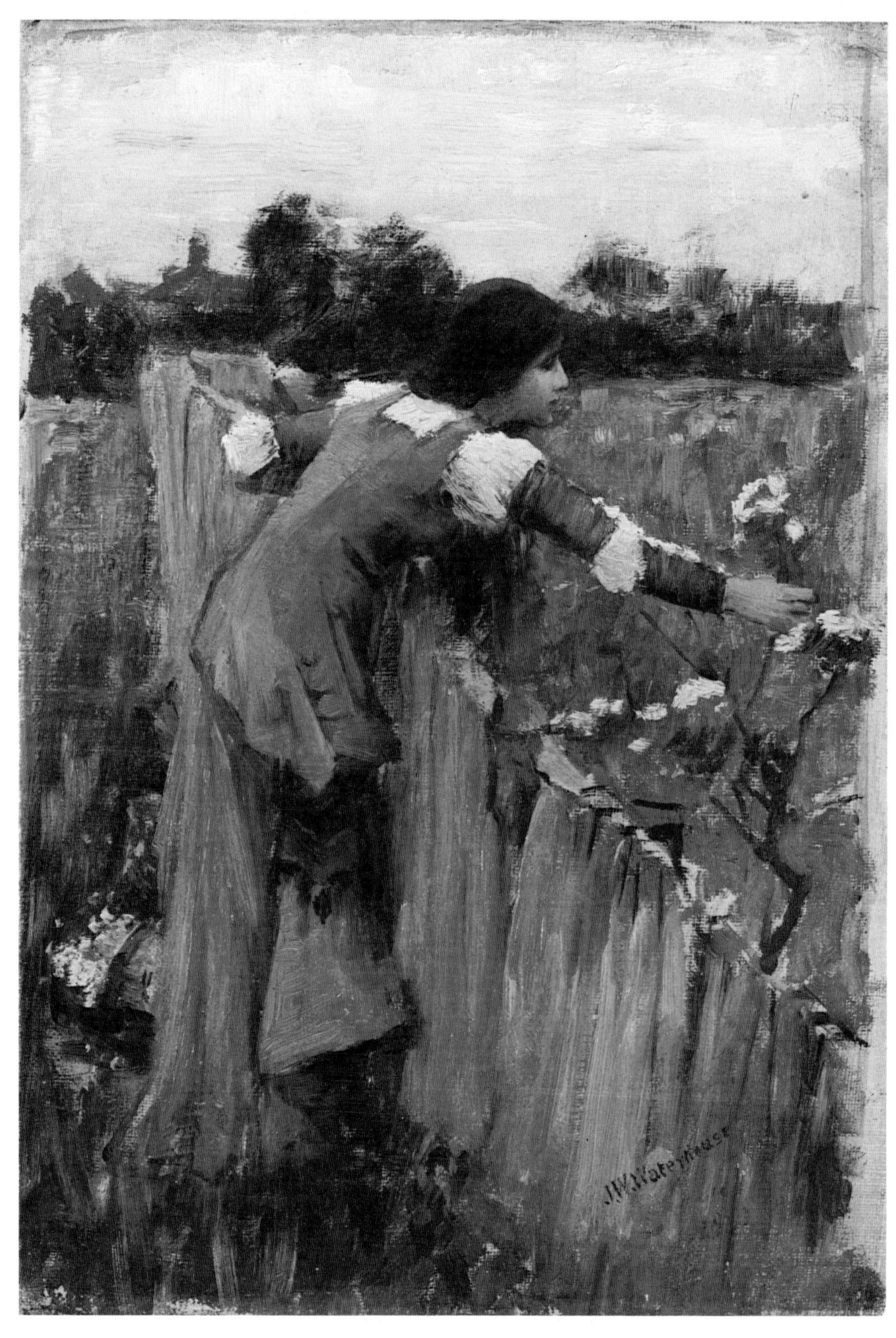

59 Study for *The Flower Picker*. Private collection

and the rocky setting and seated pose occur in *The Charmer*, *The Necklace* and the 1909 *Lamia*. However, Waterhouse distinguished each legend by his careful attention to the artefacts. Pandora's box is rather large, and it is difficult to imagine her carrying it. Presumably she had some attendants when she was sent by Zeus to become the bride of Epimetheus, the brother of Prometheus, against whom, as the giver of fire to mankind, all the evils contained in the box were directed by the gods who had created her. So Pandora's box typifies the gift which is really a curse, like the gold of Midas, and Waterhouse's designs upon it, including the classical head on the near end and the figures on the lid, are worthy of study.

Psyche shares Pandora's curiosity, but her problems are of a more individual nature. Her name literally means the breath of life, but since she also personifies the soul, finding its immortality after many trials, the psyche itself has been appropriated by modern science as its equivalent. In the legend, she is a maiden so lovely as to arouse the envy of Venus, who sends Cupid to couple her with the vilest of mortals in revenge for her beauty. Cupid falls in love with her himself, takes her to his palace, and visits her only by night, forbidding her to seek his identity. However, when she disobeys and lights a lamp to gaze on him, a drop of hot oil falls from it and awakens Cupid. He leaves her in anger, the palace vanishes, and in the hope of winning him back she undertakes a series of perilous or apparently impossible tasks set by Venus. One of these is to bring back the box from Proserpine in Hades.

Waterhouse's knowledge of the legends was such that, without over-dramatizing, he always contrived to include the details which identified them. Therefore he placed Psyche's lamp at the left, its flame symbolizing the eternal love which would eventually reunite her with Cupid and secure her a place with him on Olympus. The box, unlike Pandora's, contained only the spirit of sleep, and the embossed decoration on the end shows a pair of owls, recognized attributes of Hypnos (Sleep), whose mother was Night and whose brother Death. Waterhouse had already shown his awareness of this myth in 1874 by his first Royal Academy exhibit, *Sleep and his Half-Brother Death*. Finally, one can only remark again upon the perfect posing of the model, the delicacy with which she holds and opens the box, and the apprehension with which she ventures to look within it.

Psyche was abandoned like Ariadne and cruelly treated before achieving happiness and immortality, but Echo simply pined away for love of Narcissus until nothing but her voice remained, and Waterhouse treated this theme in his large picture of 1903, *Echo and Narcissus* (Pl.63). The wooded landscape is familiar, and in another well-considered composition the meandering stream separates the Psyche-model posed as Echo from her inaccessible and wholly self-absorbed beloved. The *Art Journal* called it 'one of the best examples of imaginative art which can be found in the Academy': it too went on to the Liverpool Autumn Exhibition, and was acquired in December for the Walker Art Gallery, whose records show the perennial appeal of unrequited love by its continual reproduction, not only in *The Studio* and the *Art Journal* but in a wide range of magazines,

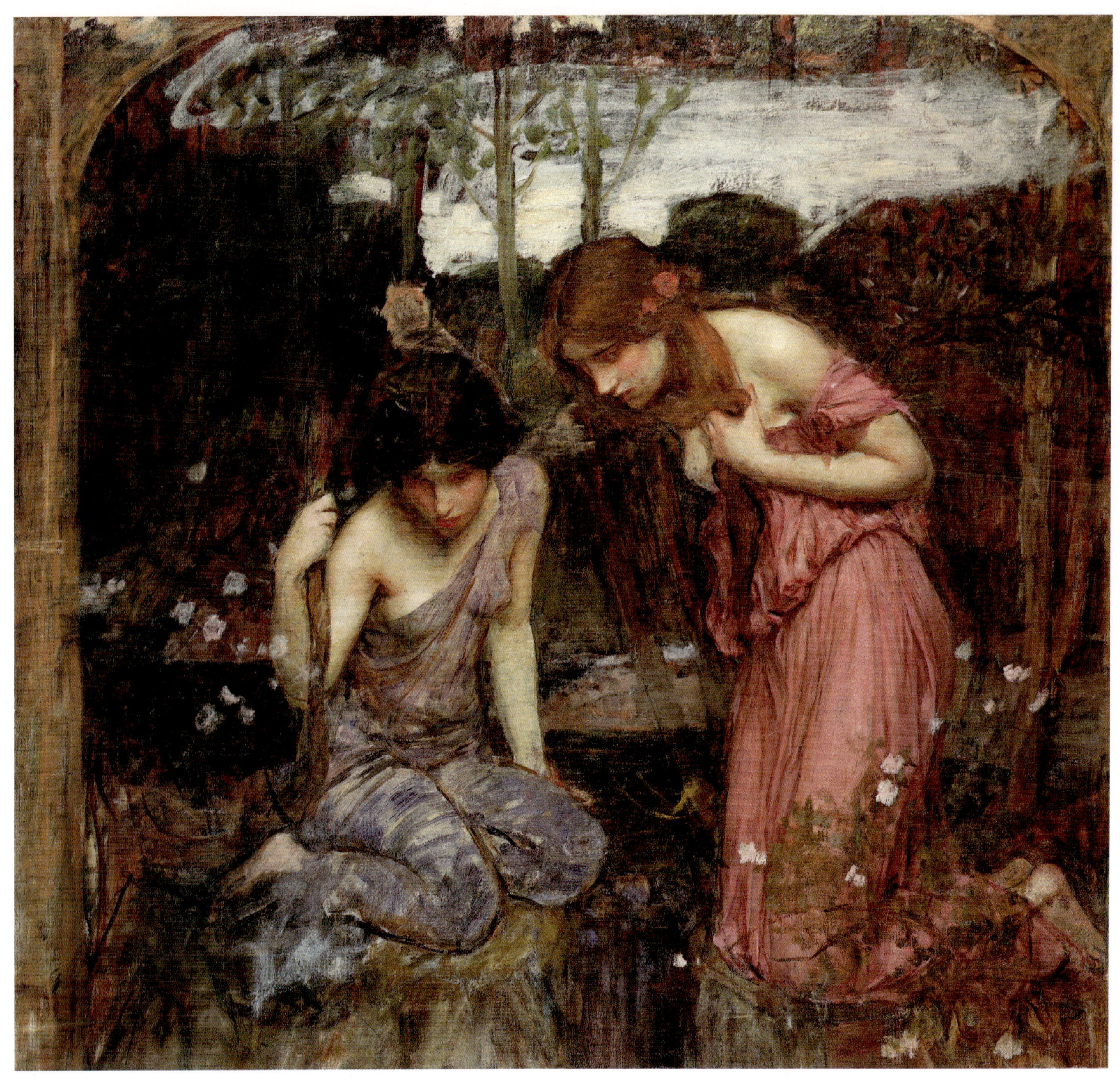

60 Study for *Nymphs finding the Head of Orpheus*, *c.* 1900. 38¼ × 41 in (97 × 104 cm). Courtesy Sotheby's

61 *Psyche opening the Golden Box*, 1903. 46 × 29 in (117 × 74 cm). Private collection

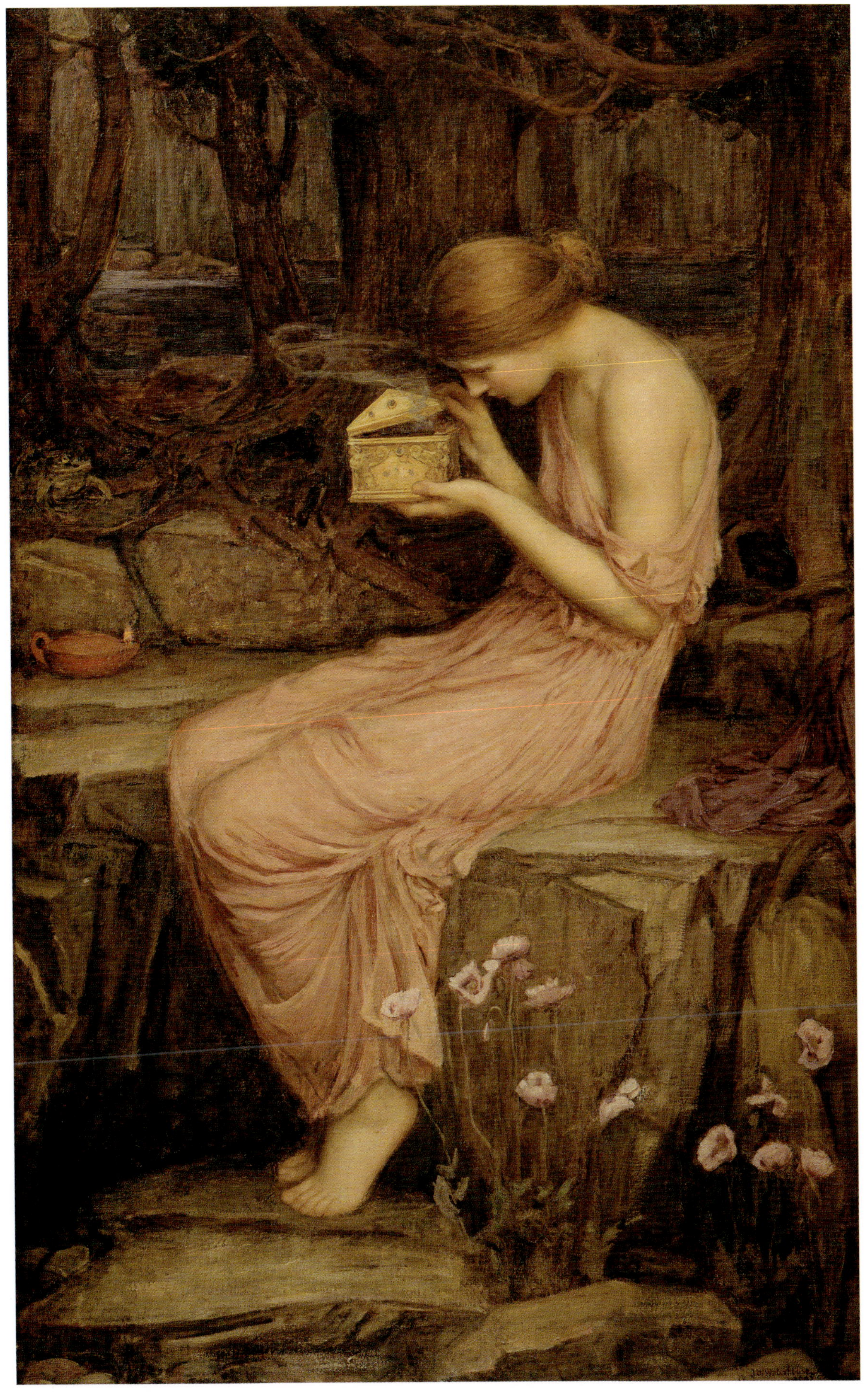

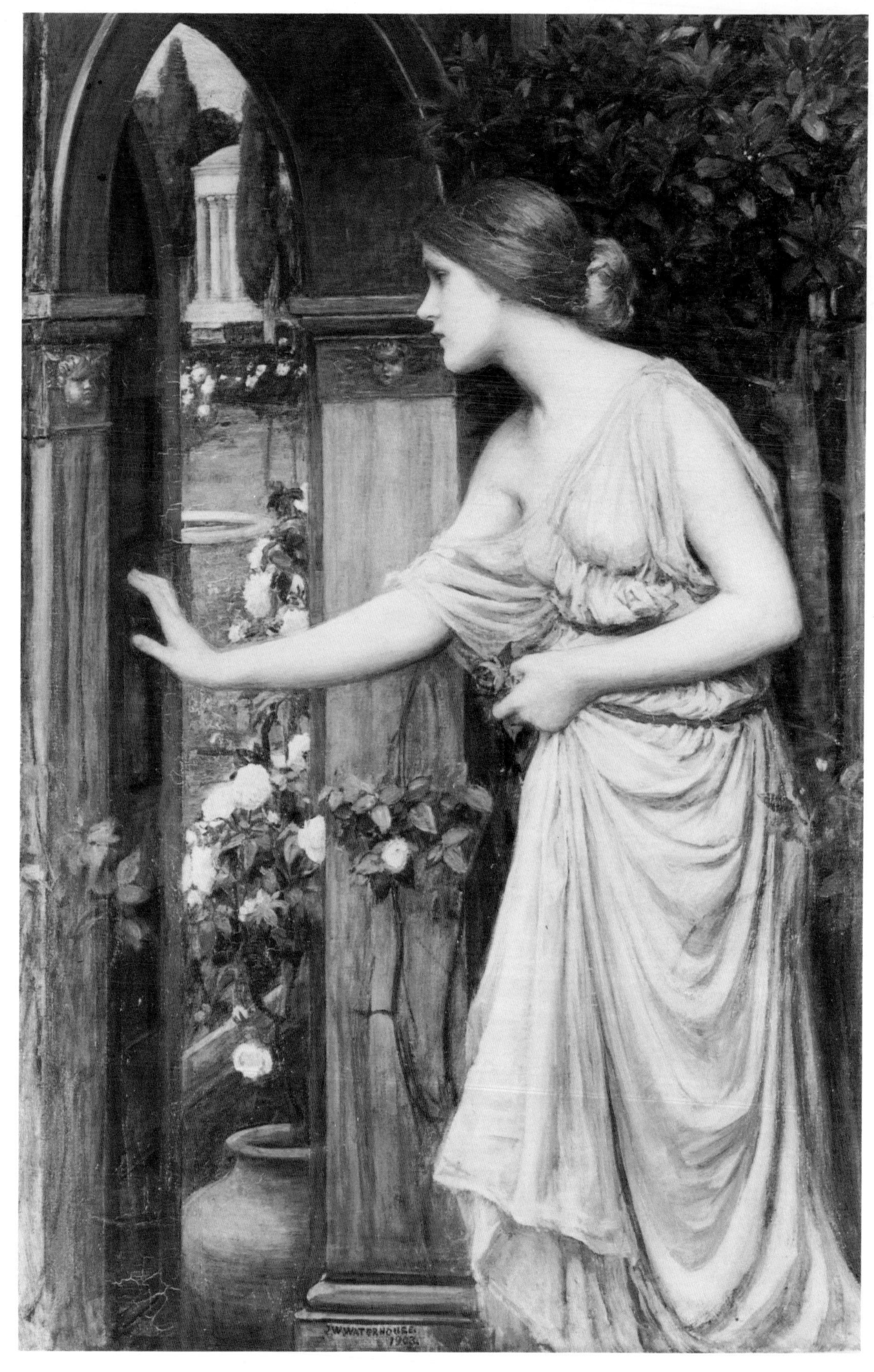

62 *Psyche entering Cupid's Garden*, 1904. 43 × 28 in. (109 × 71 cm). Preston, Harris Museum & Art Gallery

encyclopedias, postcards, calendars and eductional publications.

Over the next few years legend alternated with literature, the former always predominating, and the larger group pictures gave way to the meaningful juxtaposition of two figures, repeatedly the couples of the legends: *Phyllis and Demophoön*, *Jason and Medea* (Pls.64 and 65) and *Apollo and Daphne* (Pl.66).

Perhaps the most moving work of this period is the 1905 *Lamia*. This demon of mythology fascinated its victims in the form of a beautiful girl before devouring them as a monstrous serpent. As retold by Keats, the imagery is frightening, fantastic and almost impossible to render in paint, but Waterhouse, true to his romantic nature, goes no further than the initial seduction. The touch of hand and arm, and the long gaze exchanged, recall *Hylas and the Nymphs*, and in the wooded setting he used so often, the snakeskin girdling the temptress is sufficient to indicate the transformation to come. The pleading girl and the armoured knight play the same roles as in *La Belle Dame Sans Merci*: the painter replays his major emotional theme, conveying to us once more both the intense attraction of the beautiful young model and the inevitable barrier to fulfilment.

The Hendersons continued their acquisitions, including in 1909 the portrait of Mrs A.P. Henderson (Pl.53), who was to die so tragically young in 1913. In 1911 her husband, Major the Hon. Alex P. Henderson, second son of Lord Faringdon, bought both *The Charmer* and *Listening to my Sweet Pipings*. Another charming and rare portrait of the period is that of *Miss Betty Pollock*, painted in 1911 and shown at the Academy and in the Liverpool Autumn Exhibition the following year. Here the introduction of patron to artist is still obscure. It may have come about through Esther Waterhouse, and perhaps it was through her intercession that the painter placed the youthful figure of the girl in front of a lily-strewn pool clearly recalling that in *Hylas and the Nymphs* and the 1894 *Ophelia*.

In 1902 an important picture, *Windflowers* (Pl.67), had ushered in a new theme, that of girls in flowing costume gathering flowers in a more open landscape, and this was pursued at intervals for some ten years. The lost paintings *March Winds* and *Boreas* probably relate to it, and we see it in the later *Springtime* series. Charming works such as *Vanity* (Pl.68), show Waterhouse's love of flowers, and the studies for these pictures, like *Camellias* (Pl.71) and that for *Gather Ye Rosebuds* (Pl.69) are often equally attractive. Throughout his career the compositional studies in oils carry the girls' heads virtually to completion, as in *The Rose Bower* (Pl.70) and *Maidens Picking Flowers by a Stream* (Pl.74).

But the creatures of legend always returned, always feminine: *Thisbe*, with her ear to the wall (Frontispiece); another image of the beautiful demon *Lamia*, encircled by her snake skin, for which *The Necklace* (Pl.73) clearly demonstrates the original composition; *Circe*, her name on the back of the canvas of *The Sorceress* (Pl.78). The kneeling pose was renewed in *Isabella and the Pot of Basil* – again, the girl bereft of her lover, and another contemporary subject dealt with less evocatively by Holman Hunt.

Not that all this work meant total seclusion. The social round continued and

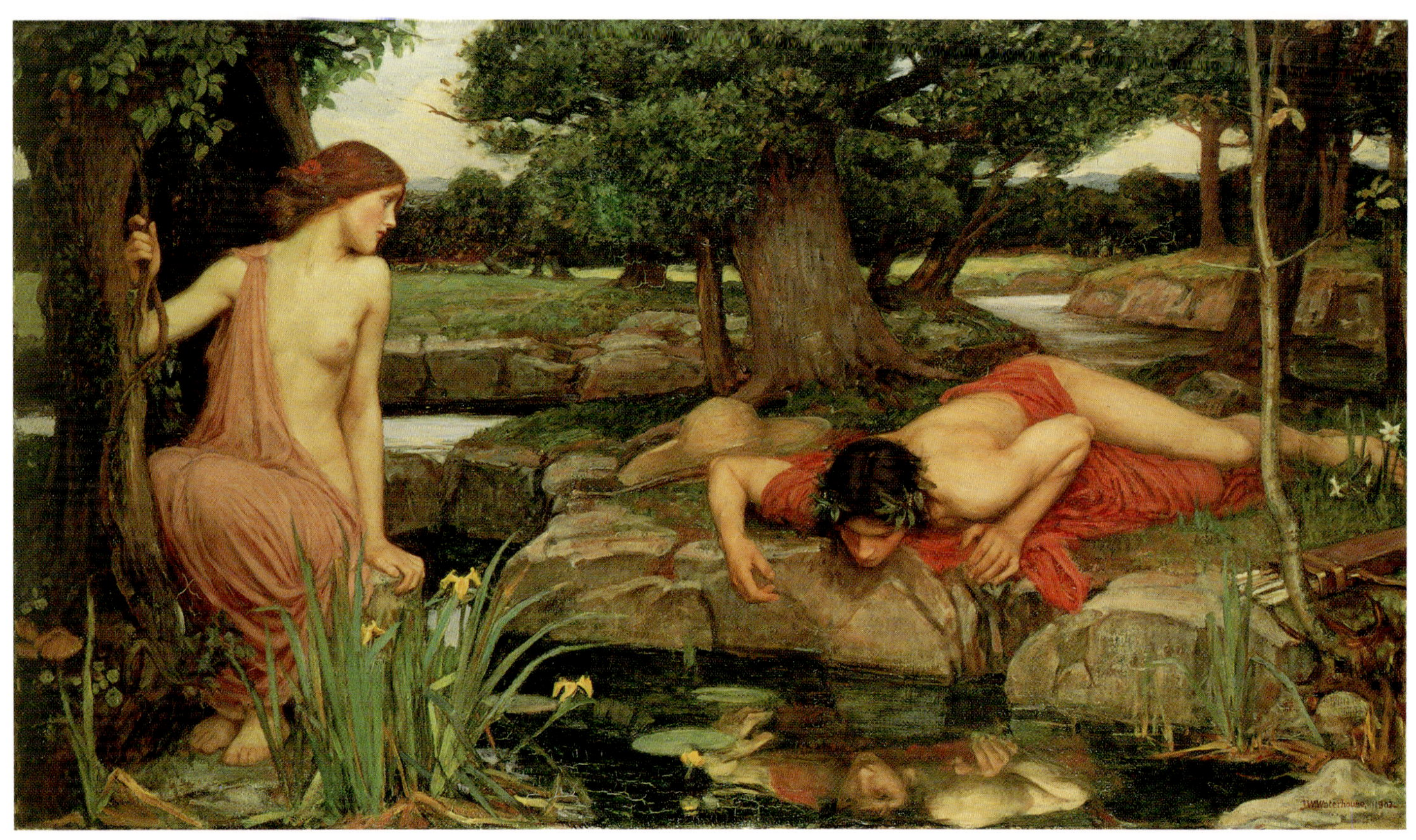

63 *Echo and Narcissus*, 1903. 43 × 74½ in (109 × 189 cm). Liverpool, Walker Art Gallery

64 Study for *Jason and Medea*, *c.* 1907. 36 × 24 in (91.5 × 61 cm). J. Nicholson, Beverly Hills, CA

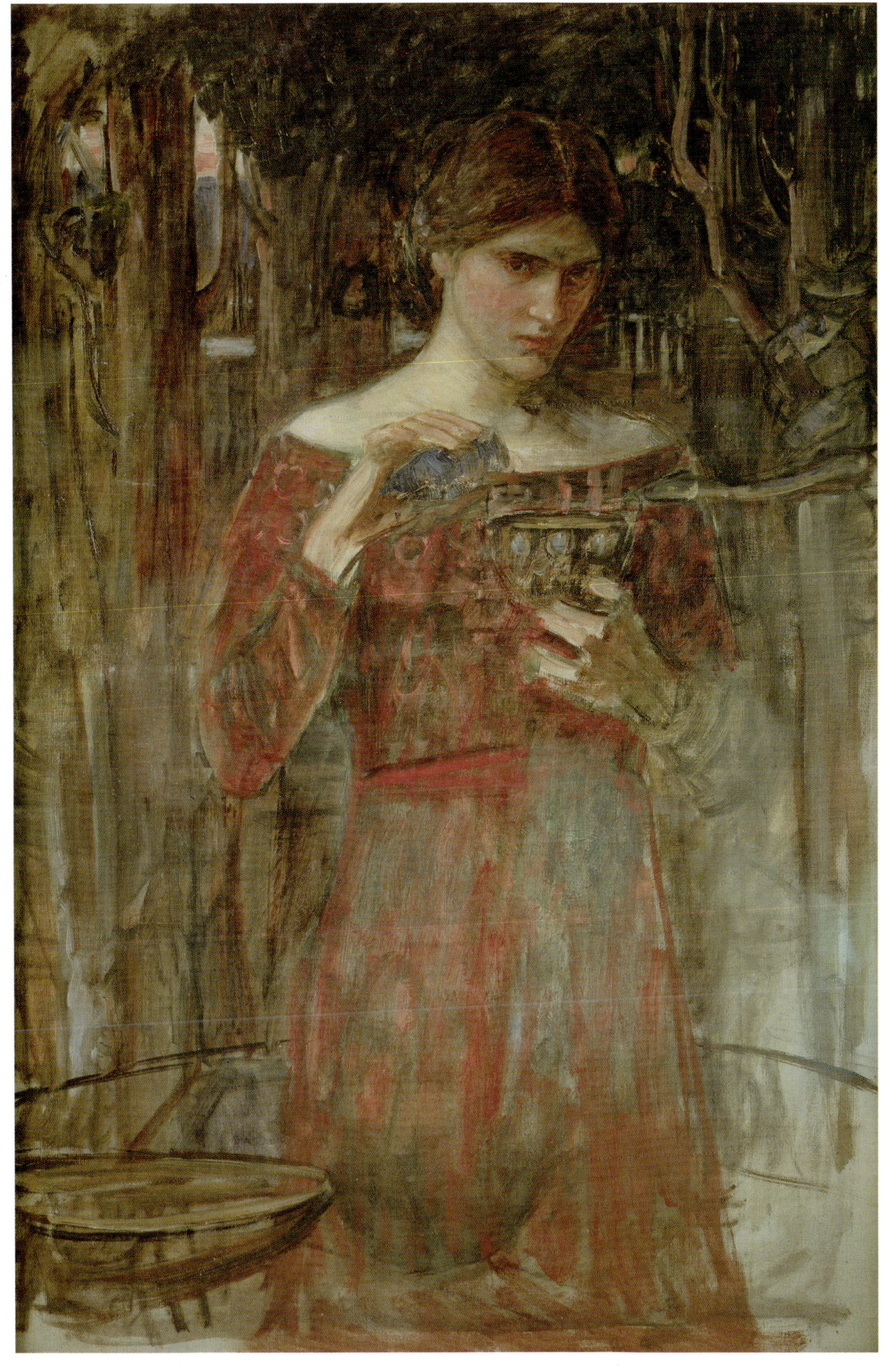

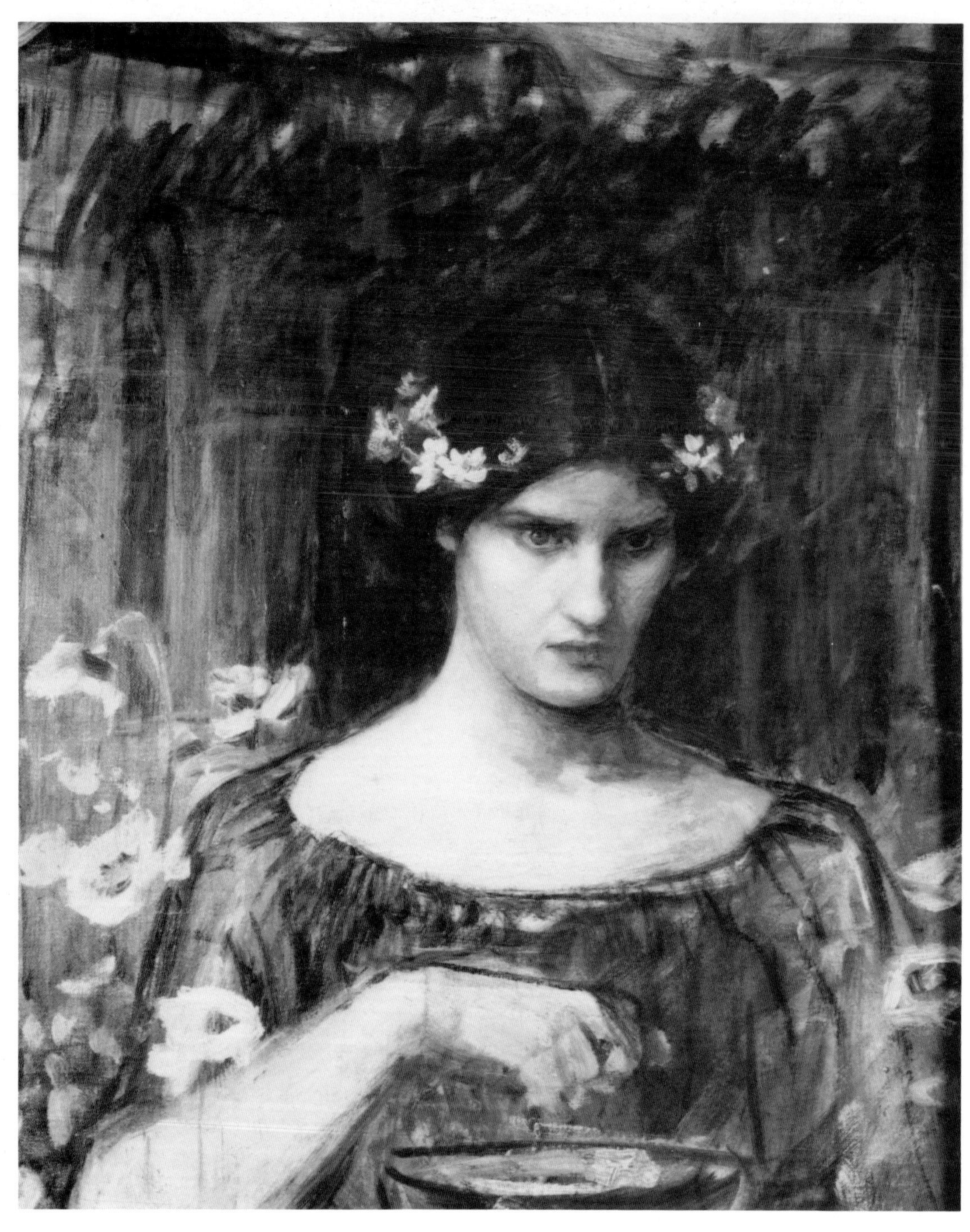

65 Study for *Jason and Medea*, *c.*1907. 24 × 21 in (61 × 53 cm). Courtesy Sotheby's

66 *Apollo and Daphne*, 1908. 57 × 44 in (145 × 112 cm). The Lord Lambton

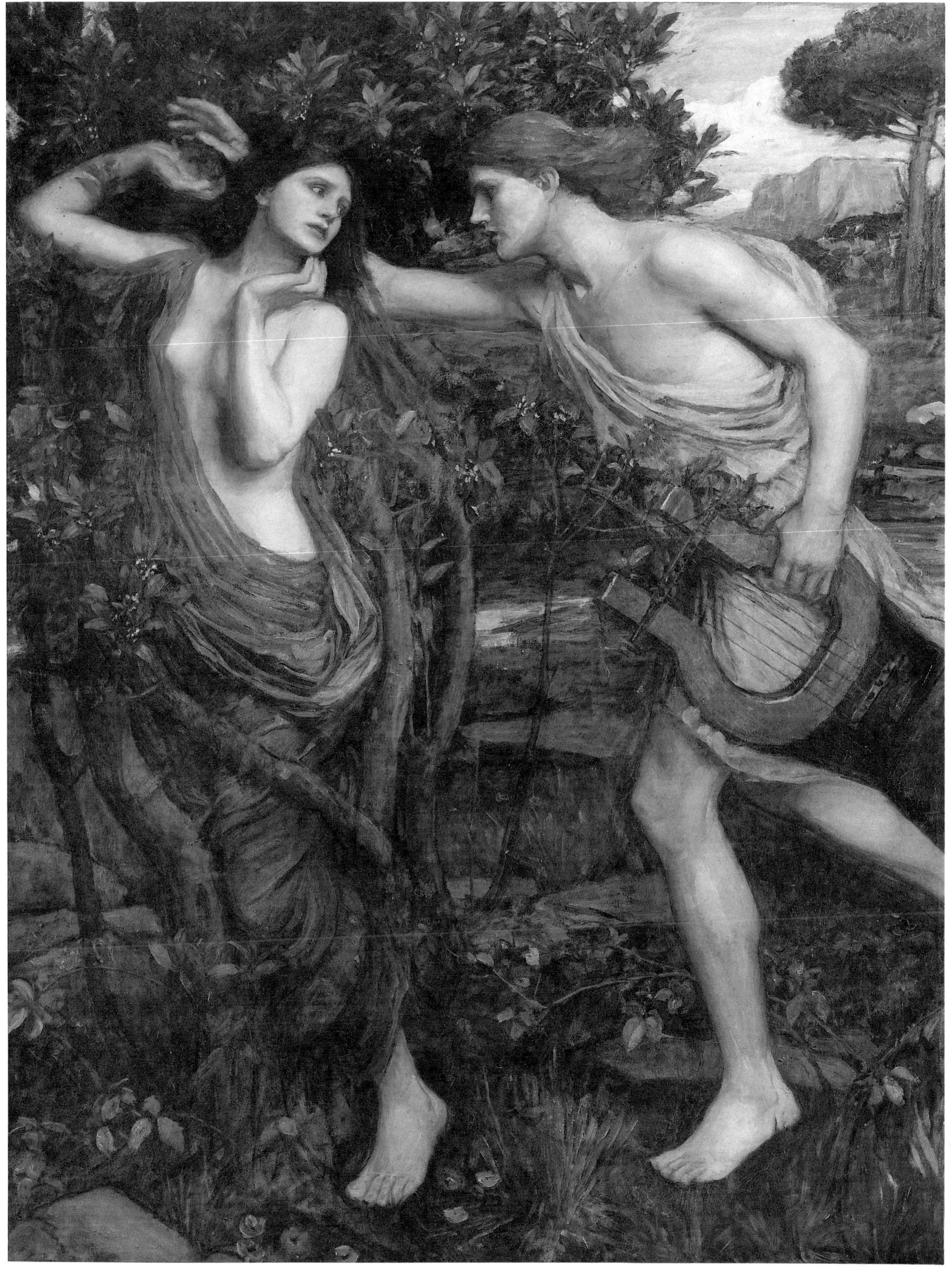

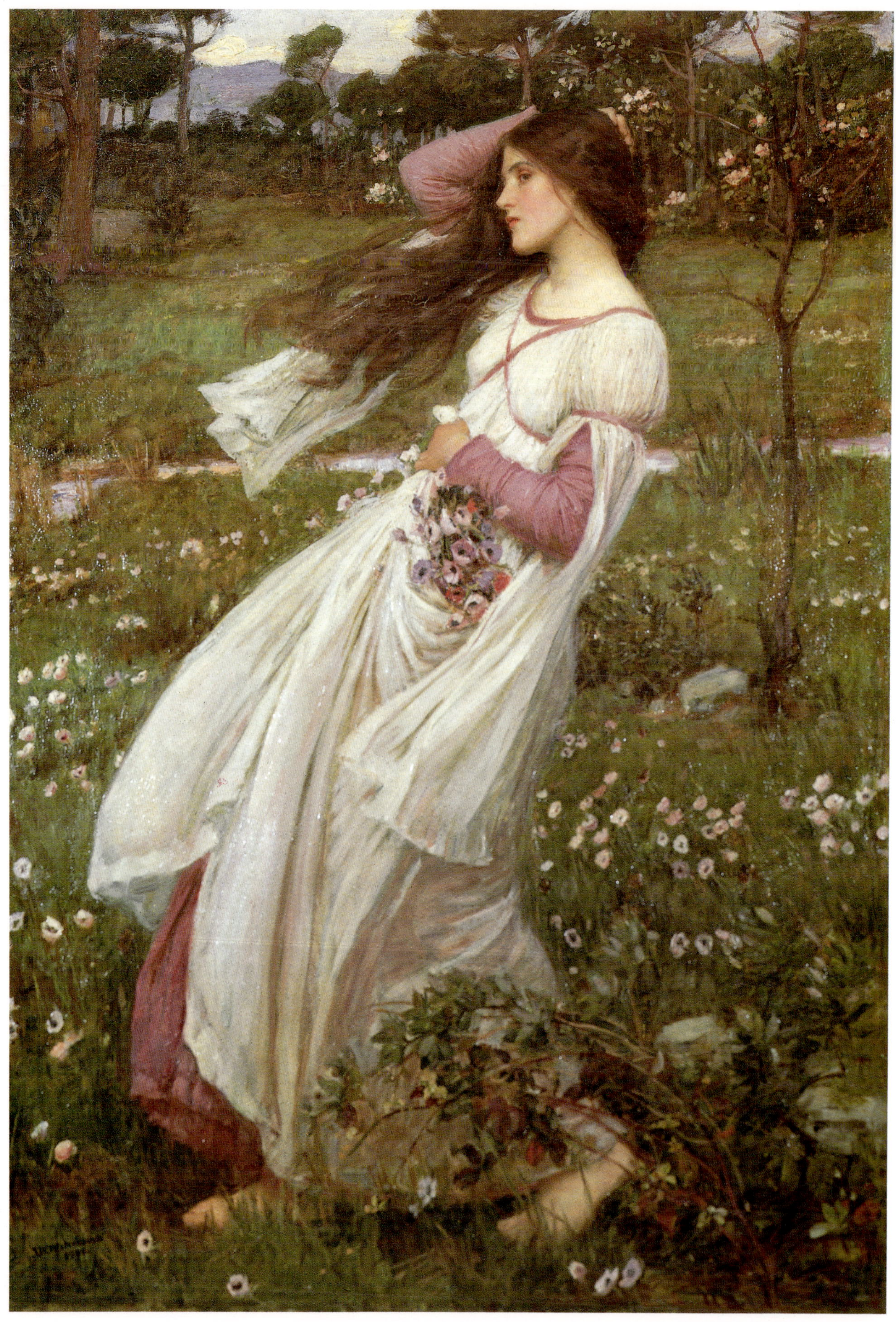

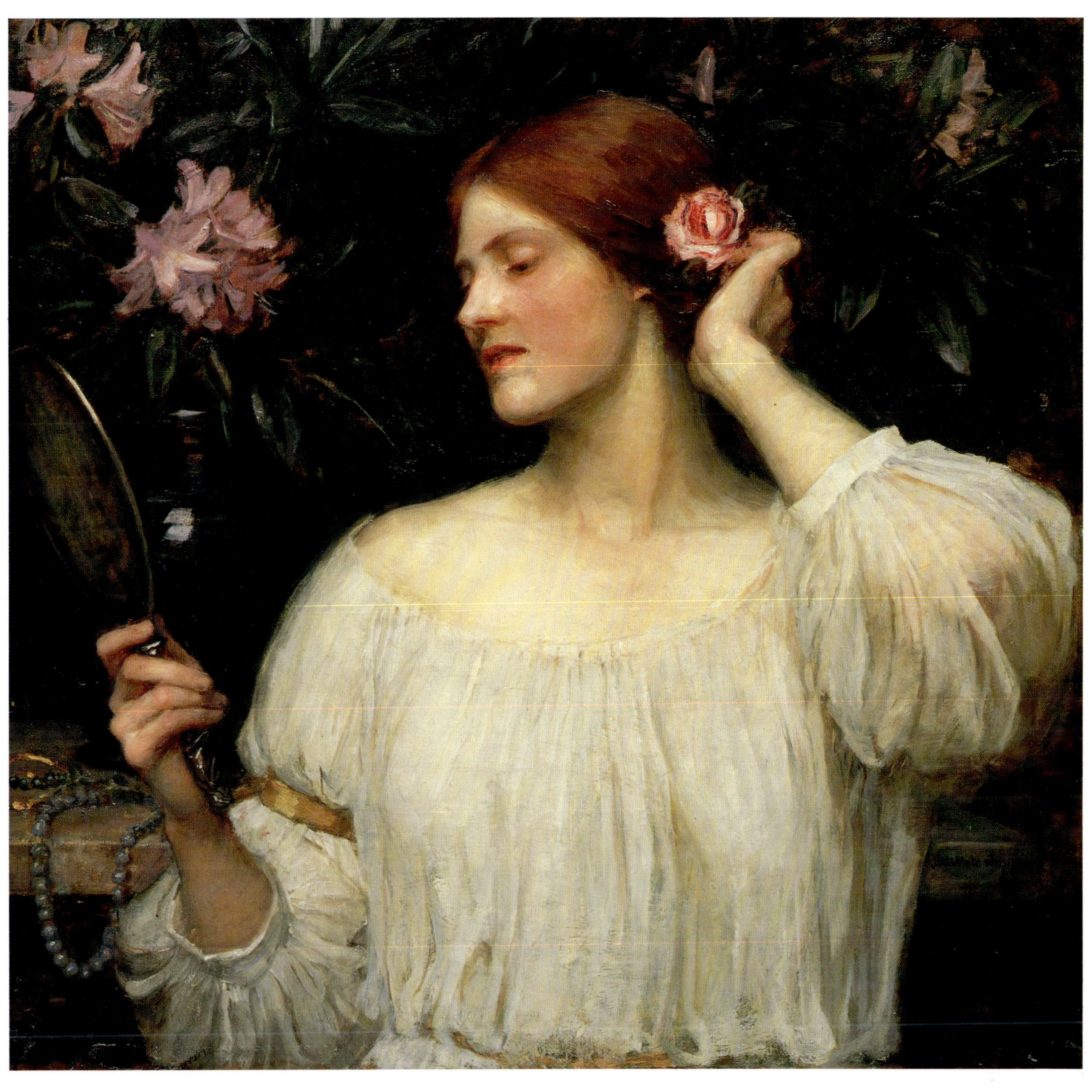

68 *Vanity*, *c.*1910. 26 × 27 in (66 × 68.5 cm). Courtesy Peter Nahum.

67 *Windflowers*, 1903. 45 × 31 in (114 × 79 cm). Private collection

Nino had his duties at the Academy: on the Council and as Visitor in the Painting School, where his comment of 1907 emphasizes the skills which had to underline an artist's creativity: 'The Students . . . ', he wrote, 'seem to have no idea of setting a palette and are too much addicted to the use of small brushes.' The Waterhouses still travelled, but now mainly in Britain. Esther's sister and her husband Peregrine Feeney were visited in Devon and later at Clippesby Hall in Norfolk, and paintings of 1912 record scenes in Scotland. The following extracts from a letter written in January of that year by the curator of the Art Gallery to the Lord Provost of Aberdeen rebutting criticisms of the purchase of one of Waterhouse's major paintings, *Penelope and the Suitors* (Pl. 75), clearly indicate his standing at the time and the continuous demand for his pictures.

69 Study for *Gather Ye Rosebuds*, *c.* 1908.
31 × 22½ in (79 × 57 cm).
Private collection

> There was no commission given to Mr Waterhouse, but as he is a distinguished and individual artist, who has not attained without justification to the position he occupies in the world of art, and as his output is small and his pictures much in demand, my committee, some two years ago, asked him if he would give Aberdeen the option of the next important work which he produced, which he himself deemed suitable for the public gallery, and at the time this particular picture of *Penelope* was, I believe, seen (it was then in its earlier stages), and its general composition was admired and approved . . . The Gallery committee certainly hold no brief for the Royal Academy, but in acquiring a picture by Mr Waterhouse, they have . . . justifiably sought to introduce into the collection a new note . . . of colour and of romance.

The letter then rises to a spirited vindication of the painting which might equally be applied to the rest of his work:

> It was never suggested that Mr Waterhouse had produced a mere reconstruction of an actual scene of Homeric times . . . a diagrammatic illustration suitable for a classical dictionary . . . What Mr Waterhouse has done is to take a classic myth . . . a theme as far removed from reality as from ugliness . . . he has infused into his presentation of it that note of romance and that individual point of view which we look for in the work of a great artist.

Scottish caution about the price is equally rebuffed:

> Diamonds cost more than paste. Mr Waterhouse asks the price he is accustomed to get, and it is not Aberdeen which is doing a favour to the artist; the favour is rather the other way round, for while his price for this particular work is £1,500 to a private buyer, it was £1,400 to us. It is perfectly easy to get thousands of inferior works for a twenty-pound note each, but there is only one Waterhouse.

The letter cites public and private collections containing Waterhouse's paintings, and it is good to note that among these Sir James Murray's collection eventually yielded to Aberdeen another major work, the imposing group of *The Danaïdes*, painted in 1906. The fifty daughters of Danaüs, King of Argos, were

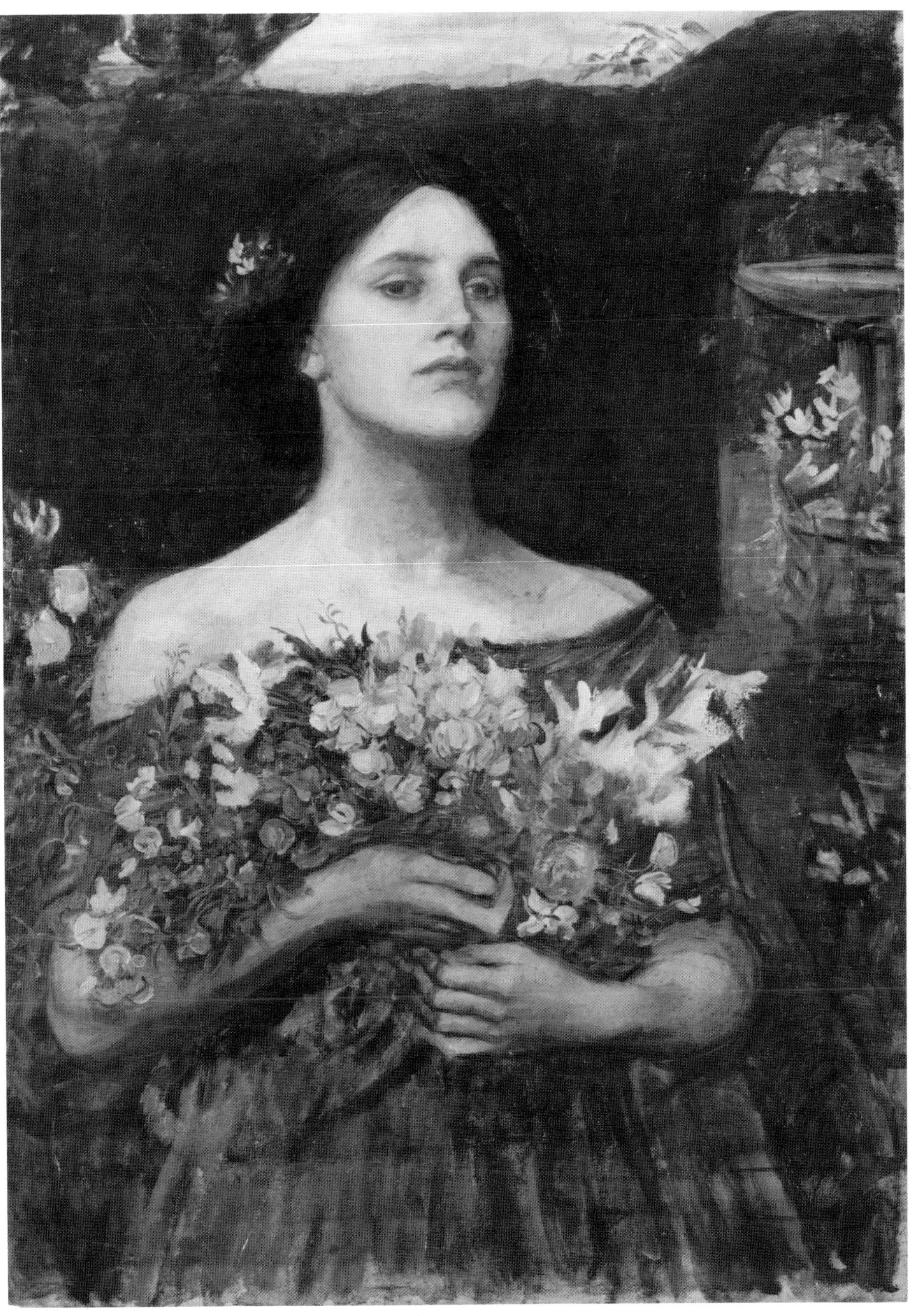

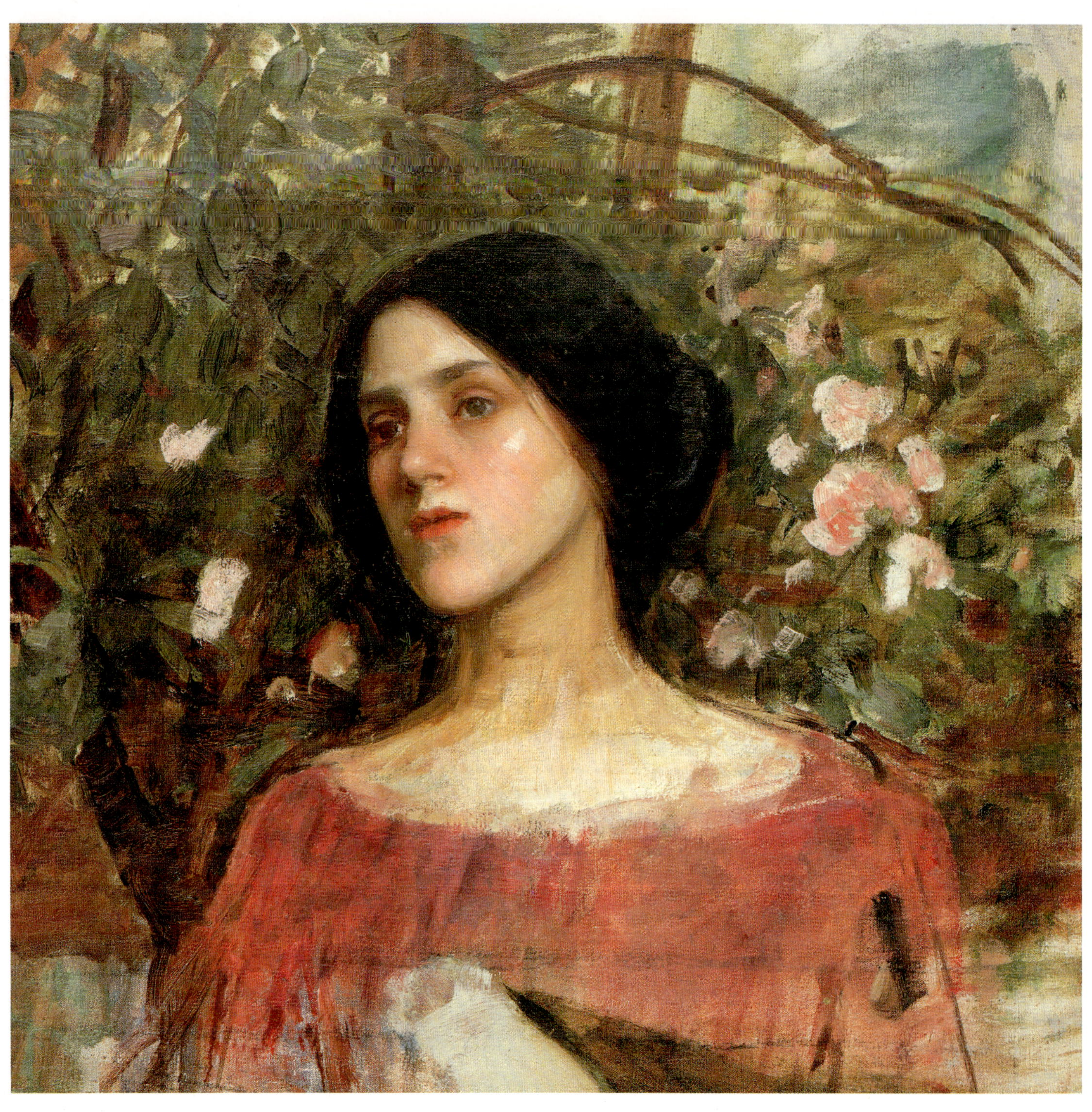

70 *The Rose Bower*, *c.* 1910.
21¼ × 24¼ in
(54 × 61.5 cm). Courtesy
Peter Nahum.

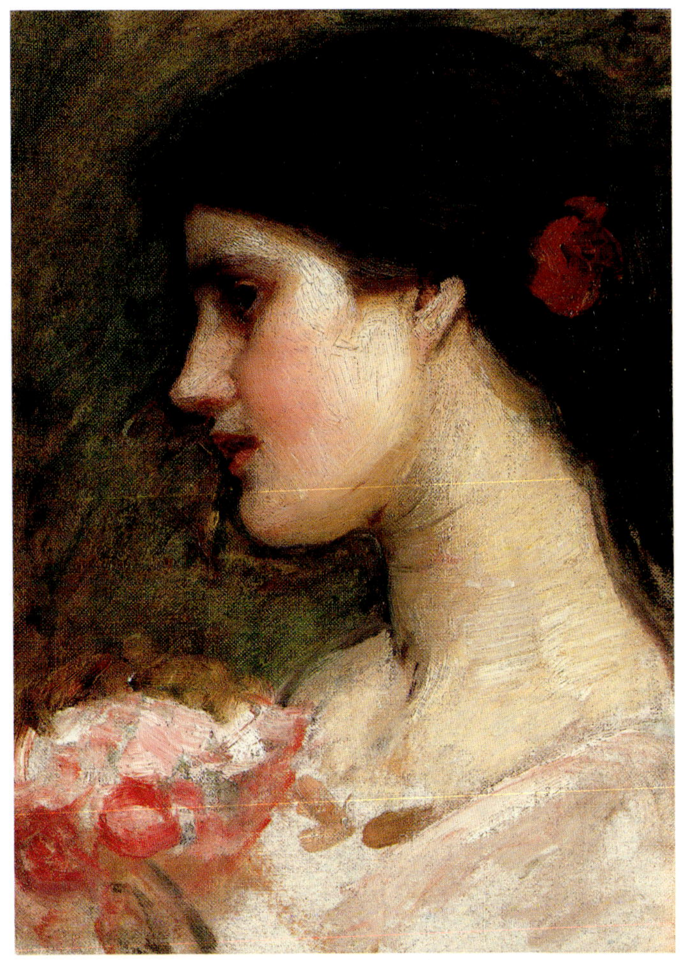

71 *Camellias*, *c.*1910.
13½ × 10 in (34 × 25.5 cm).
Courtesy Peter Nahum

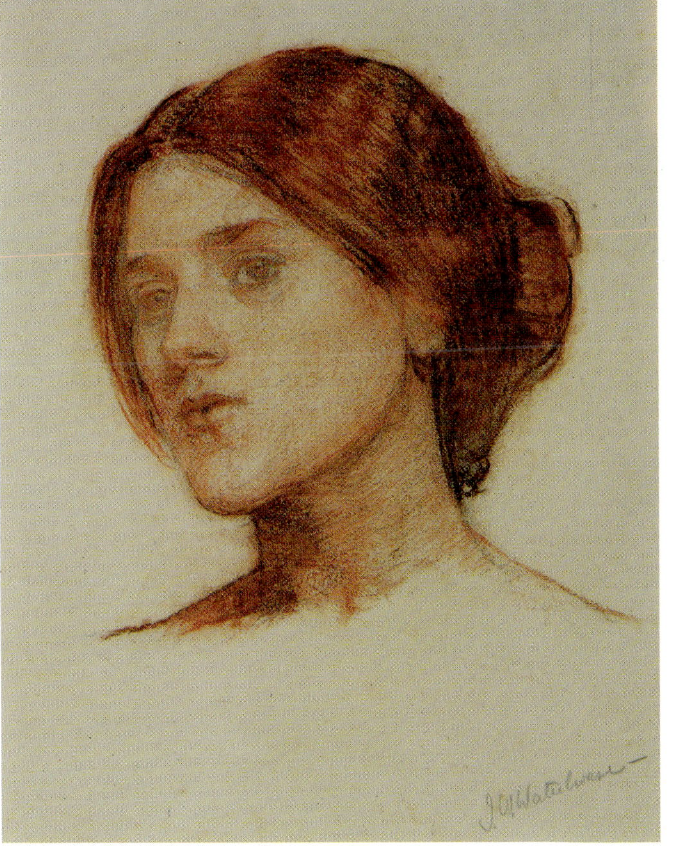

72 Study for *The Rose Bower*, *c.*1910. Sanguine.
Private collection

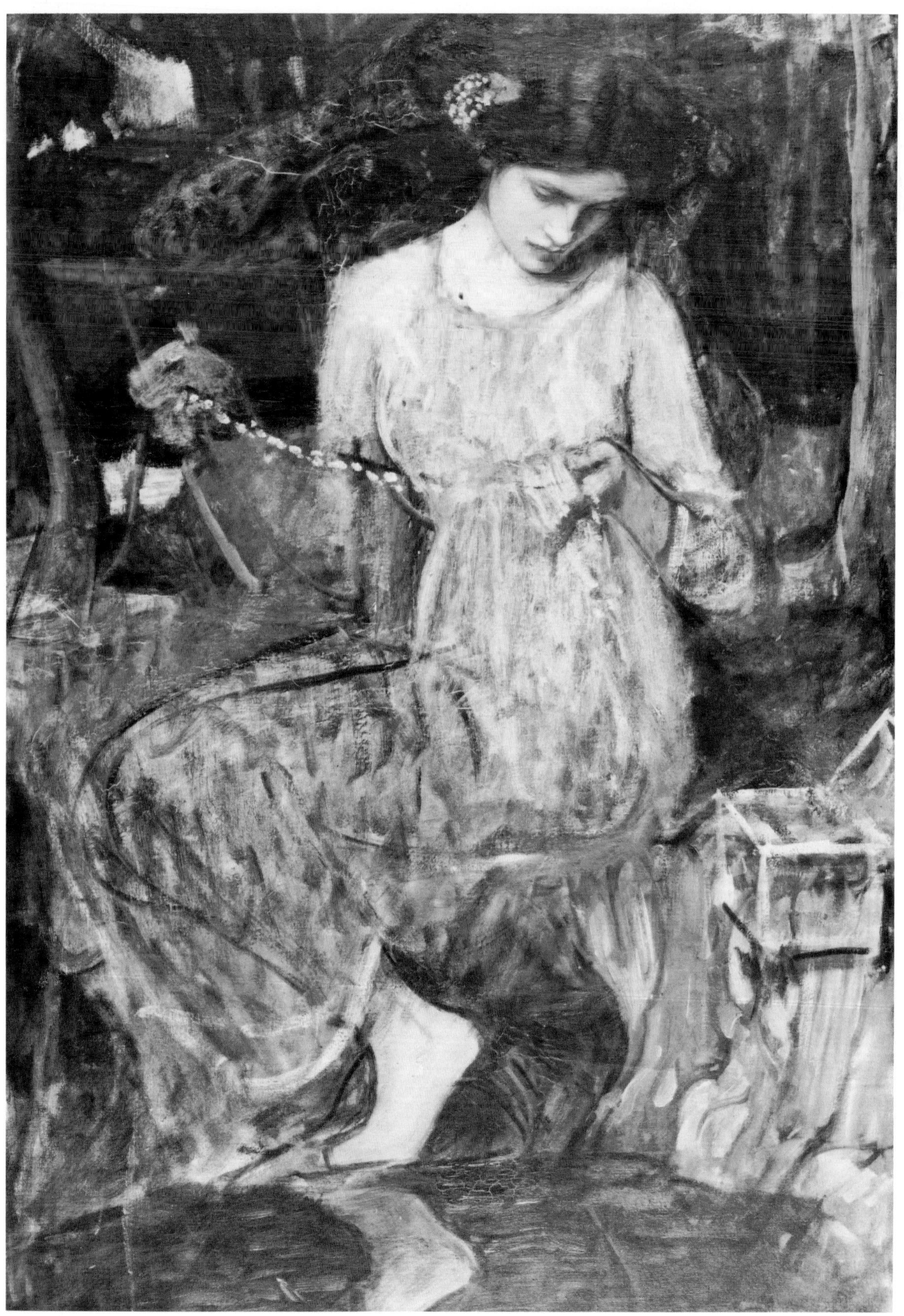

commanded in obedience to a prophecy to murder their husbands on their wedding night; all but one obeyed, and were punished by having to draw water in sieves from a deep well or, as interpreted here, by pouring it endlessly into a vessel from which it continually escaped. The depth of Waterhouse's involvement in this legend is testified by another recently discovered version of the picture, dated 1904 (Pl.79). This has fewer figures, the central ones being reversed from left to right, and is indeed more harmonious than the Aberdeen painting, in which the composition is strangely indecisive.

When Peregrine Feeney died in 1913, Waterhouse designed his graveyard memorial at Thurn, incorporating a line from one of Feeney's own poems: 'To me thy dawn brings ever sweeter rest'. A letter from the sculptor Morris Harding regarding delays over 'the bronzework' and referring to Mrs Feeney's illness suggests that Harding actually executed the bas-relief to Waterhouse's design.

Nino's own health was not robust. Even in the early days at Hall Road he had been referred to as 'happily still with us' in contrast to his vigorous Scottish neighbour, John MacWhirter; although in the photograph of him working in the studio on the 1909 *Lamia* his general appearance matches the alertness of the vigilant Corgi. But by 1913 he seemed gaunt and worn as he sat before the framed *A Song of Springtime*, and he was not to be restored by these nostalgic dwellings upon youth and nature. It may be coincidental that 1914 saw his first and only specifically Christian subject, when *The Annunciation* (Pl.76) was exhibited at the Academy, together with *The Love Philtre* and the portraits of Mrs Arnold Henderson and the Marchioness of Downshire. A photograph of him sketching out of doors at Clippesby in 1915 shows him bent and frail, smoking the accustomed cigarette, and in that year he failed to exhibit at the Academy for the first time since 1890.

His patron Alexander Henderson, by that time a baronet and on the point of his elevation to the peerage, took him to recuperate in Algeciras, whose fine winter climate had long been attractive to invalids. There, on land received from the Spanish Government in part payment for his building of the railway from Madrid, Henderson had erected the Hotel Reina Cristina which, together with the Reina Victoria some forty miles inland at Ronda, provided a refuge for the shy Lady Henderson and a regular wintering-place for the family. But convalescent or not, the painter was always active. His sketchbooks of the period are full of ideas for pictures, and he may well have travelled on to his beloved Italy: the name of Taggia, just inland on the Italian Riviera, is inscribed beside a fine little study of a many-arched bridge. The end was not yet.

73 Study: *The Necklace*, *c.*1909. 37½ × 25½ in (95.2 × 64.7 cm) Courtesy Christie's

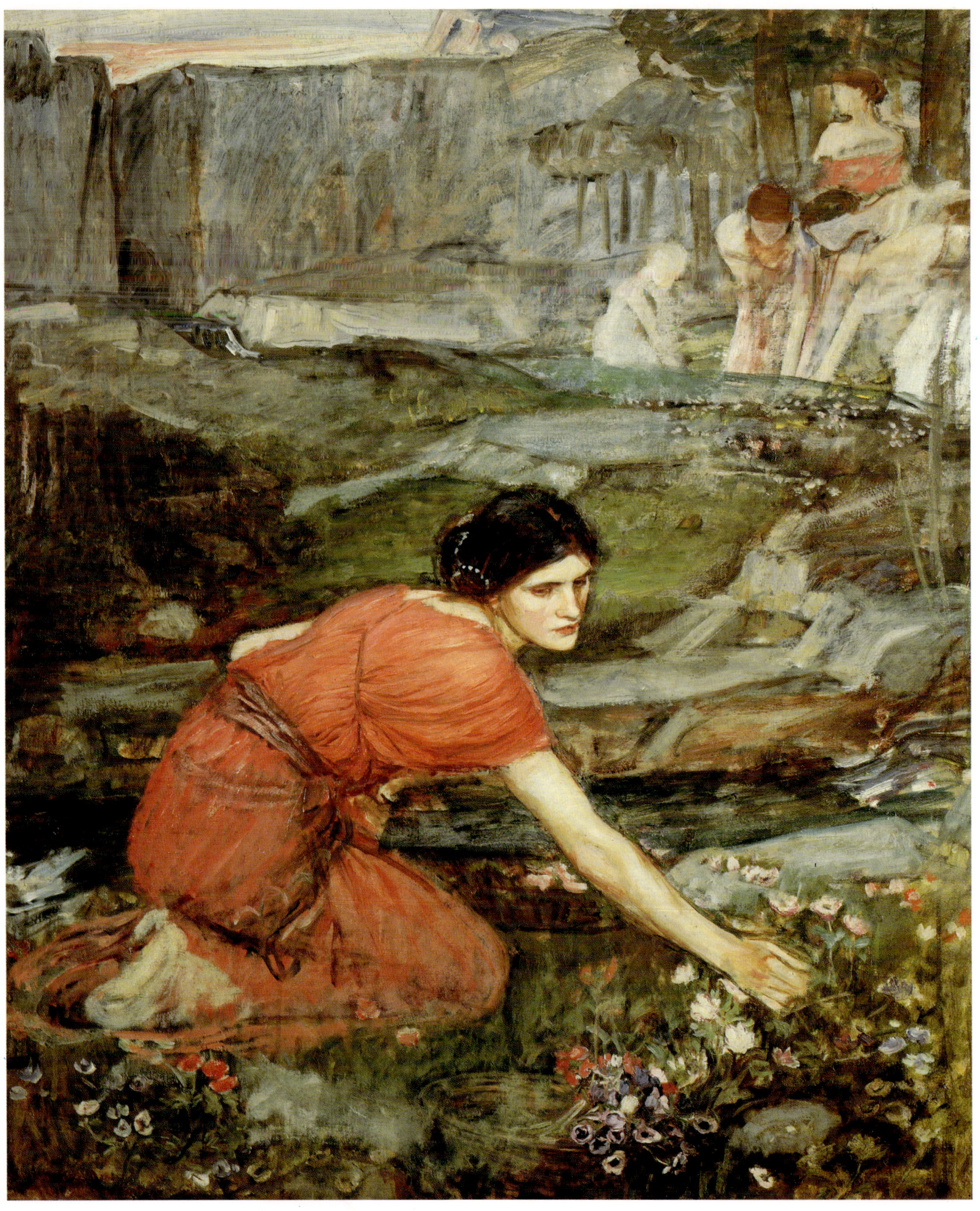

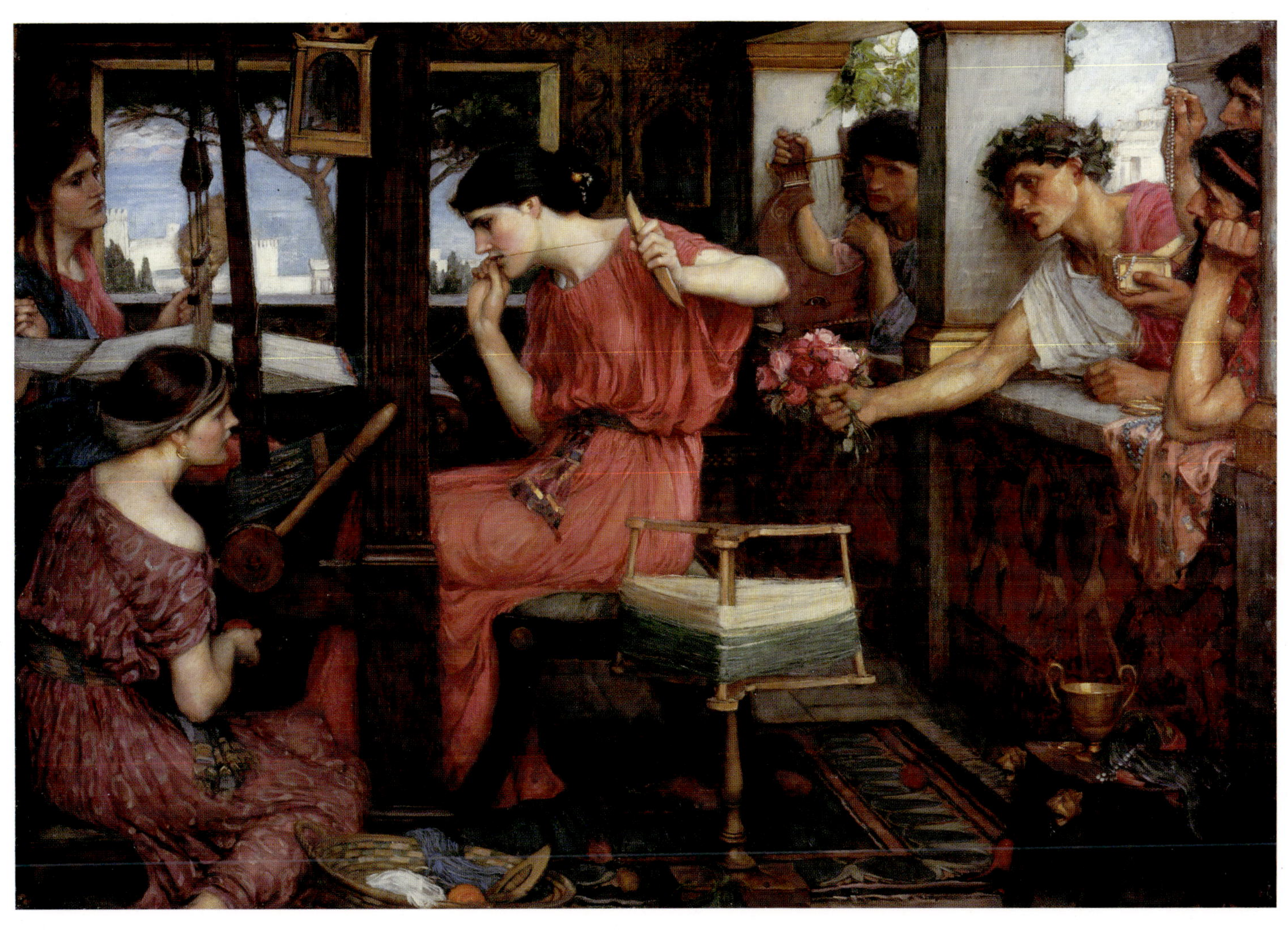

75 *Penelope and the Suitors*, 1912. 51½ × 75 in (131 × 191 cm). Aberdeen Art Gallery and Museum

74 Study: *Maidens picking Flowers by a Stream*, *c.* 1911. 37 × 31½ in (94 × 80 cm). Courtesy Peter Nahum

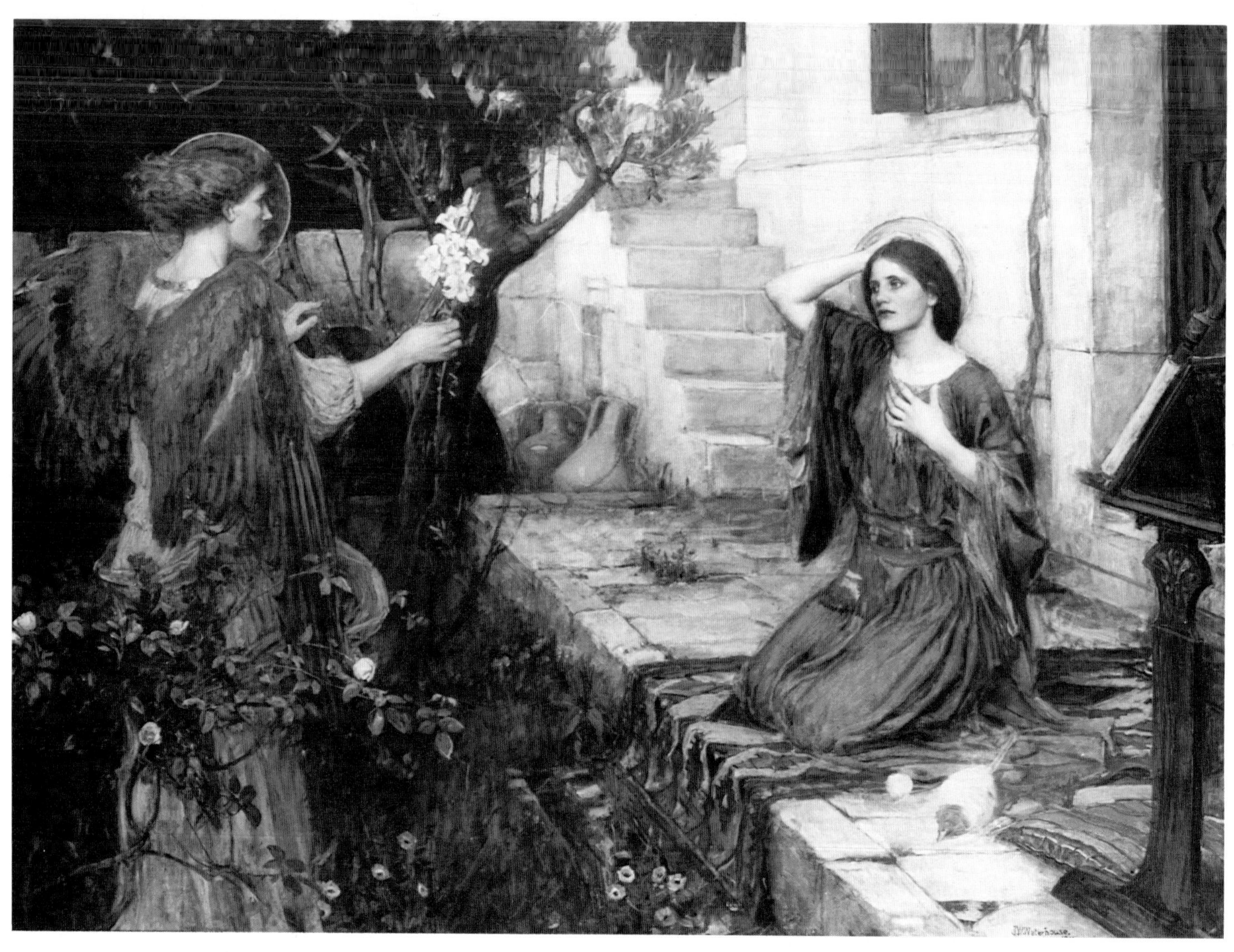

76 *The Annunciation*, 1914.
39 × 53 in (99 × 135 cm).
Courtesy Sotheby's

77 Study for *The Sorceress*,
*c.*1911. 24 × 20 in
(61 × 51 cm). Private
collection

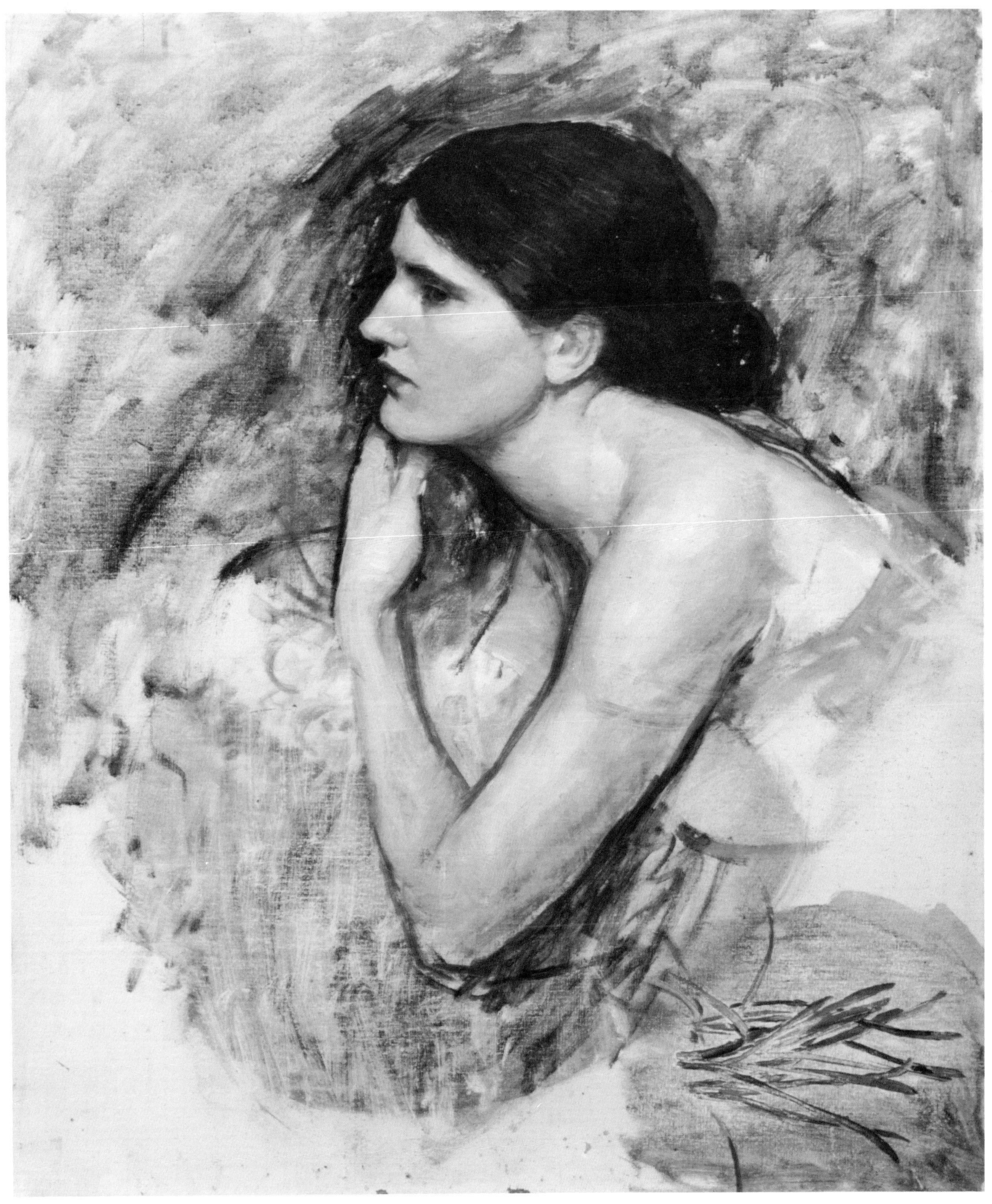

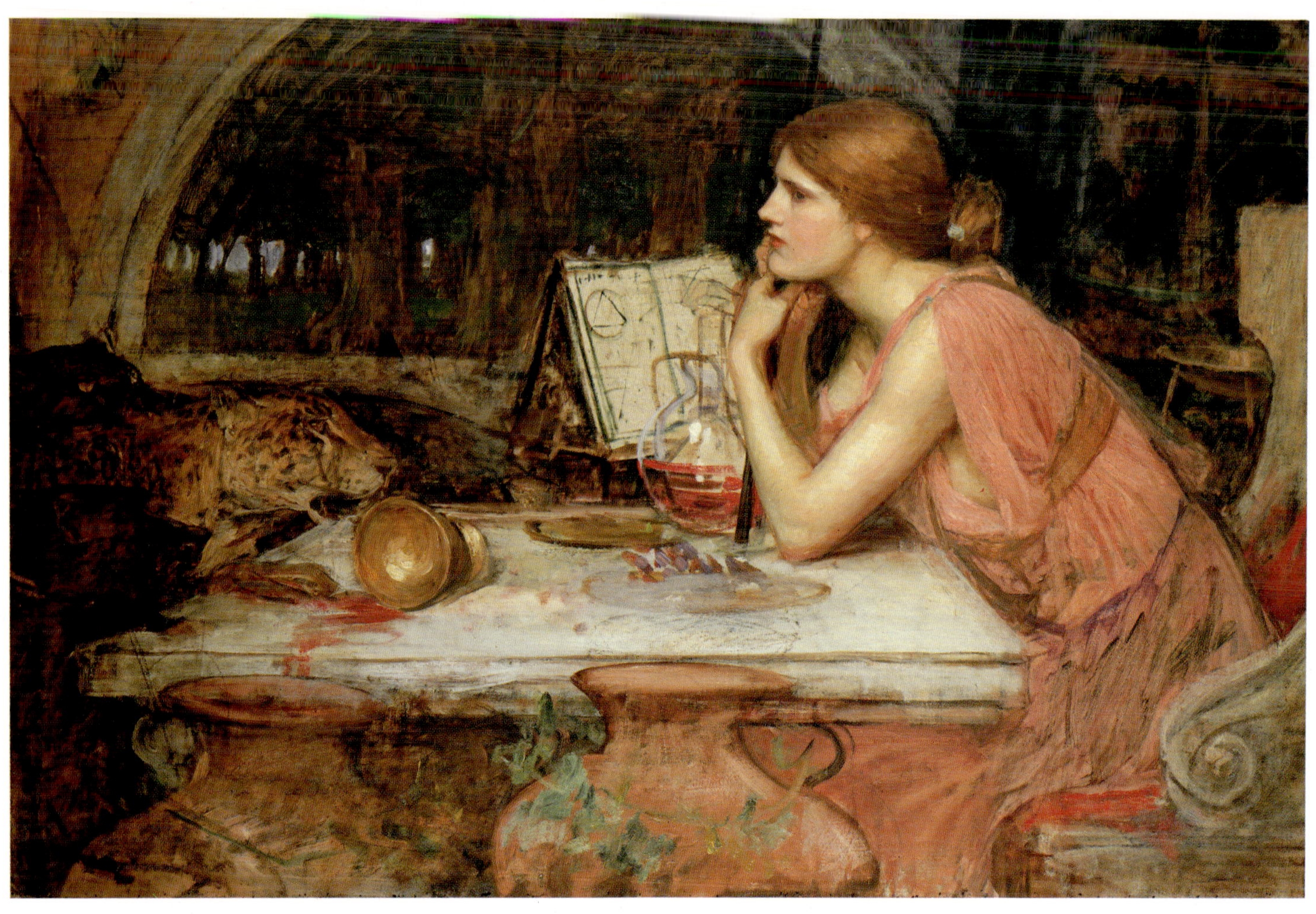

78 *The Sorceress*, *c.*1911.
29¼ × 43 in (74 × 109 cm).
Courtesy Peter Nahum

79 *The Danaïdes*, 1904.
60¾ × 43¾ in
(154.3 × 111.1 cm).
Courtesy Christie's New
York

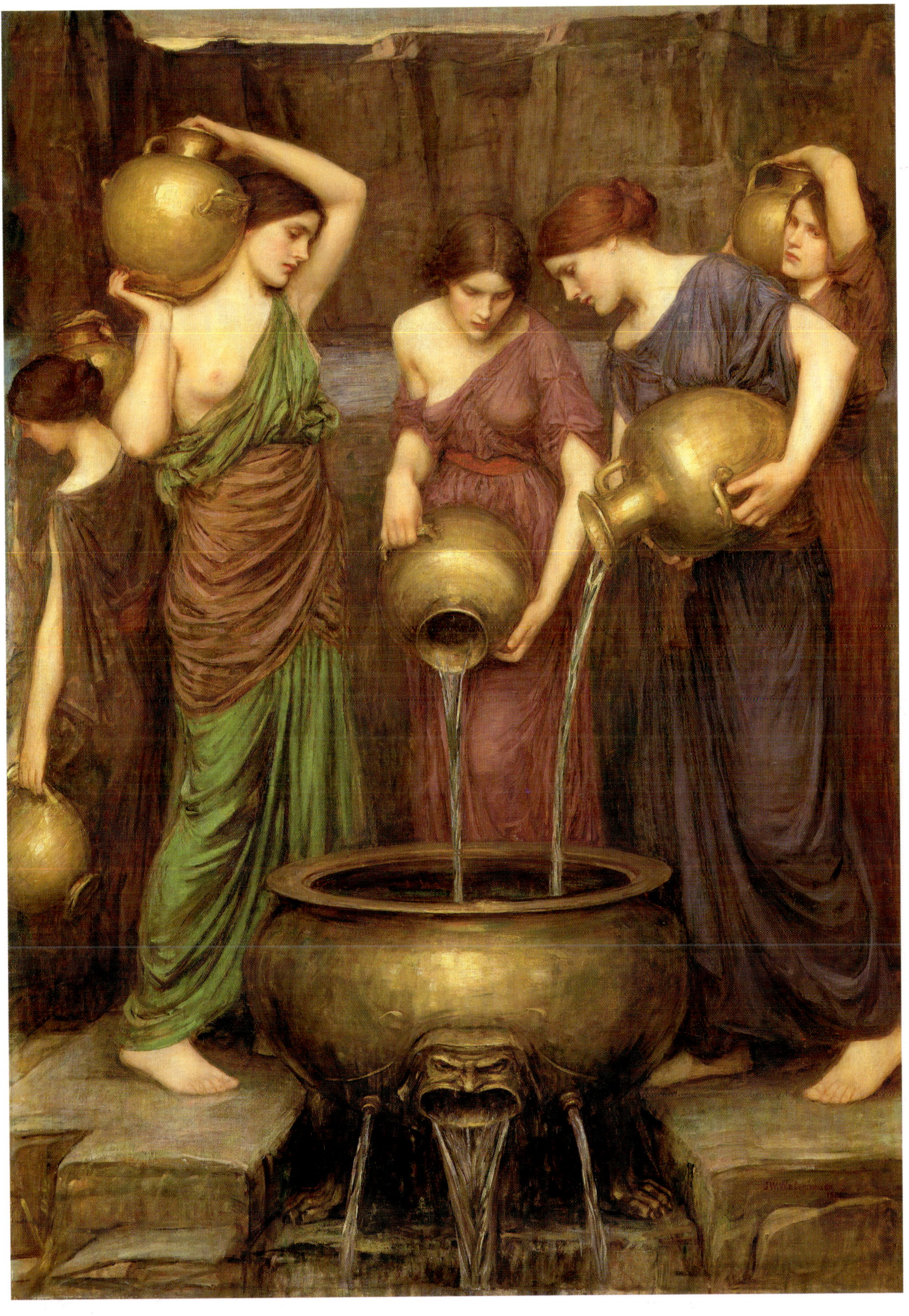

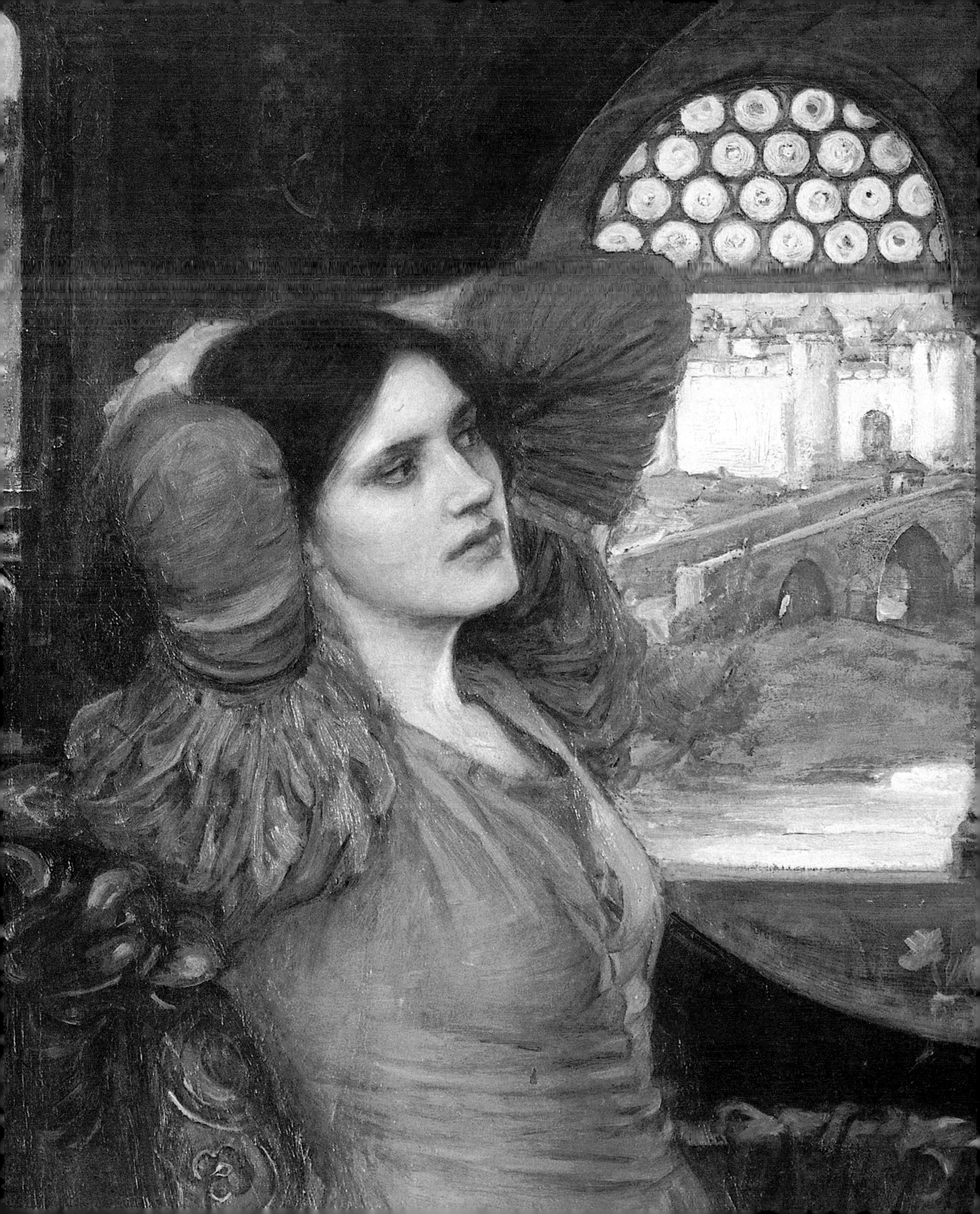

6

Retrospect and Conclusion

80 Detail from *'I am Half-Sick of Shadows,' said The Lady of Shalott* (Pl.85)

WHATEVER THE ideas still in his mind, including those adumbrated in his sketchbooks, Waterhouse's output of work indicates neither a particular sense of urgency in these last years nor, in spite of his ill-health, a perceptible slackening of effort. In 1916, for example, his Academy pictures were in the usual proportion of one group composition to two single figures. The significant change was in subject matter. At this point in his life, he at last abandoned the Greek myths; they were, after all, in spite of their terrors, replete with the hopes and desires of youth. Instead, he reverted to other, earlier images. The romance of Italy was still strong within him, as evidenced by the sketch for *Dante and Beatrice* (Pl.81), but his reading was from Boccaccio, not the classical legends. England also claimed his thoughts, and the English poets: Shakespeare, with another *Ophelia* (Pl.83), Tennyson, and perhaps Malory, as he looked back at the Arthurian tales. And the portraits, whether of patron or model (Pls.82 and 84), were still unsurpassed in their skill and sensitivity.

First in the Academy list of 1916 was the Lady of Shalott. Waterhouse was back in the studio, with the volume of Tennyson and the familiar model, and a wholly realistic painting – his third on the theme of the poem. The model has taken on a few years without losing her beauty, and is more relaxed. Costume and properties are familiar, but never disturb the mood or the story-telling; in the window opening the details of bridge and castle are elaborated while the young lovers wander past arm in arm. The picture takes us back through the poem, past the agitation of the painting of 1894, where the Lady cries out 'The curse is come upon me!', and the sad departure on the river in the great work of 1888 which is one of the Tate Gallery's proudest possessions, to the subdued desires of that early stanza: *'I am Half-Sick of Shadows', said The Lady of Shalott* (Pl.85).

In these pictures Nino gathered his memories around him. What is more comforting to an old man than the presence of former girl friends – if only they are as they were when he was young? For the painter this is always possible, and with one of the finest works of this time he recalled the Miranda whom he had first painted thirty-five years before. In *Miranda – The Tempest* (Pl.86), he refined that earlier composition with all the benefits of his accumulated experience and skill. She stands swaying against the storm, the breakers crash upon the beach, and

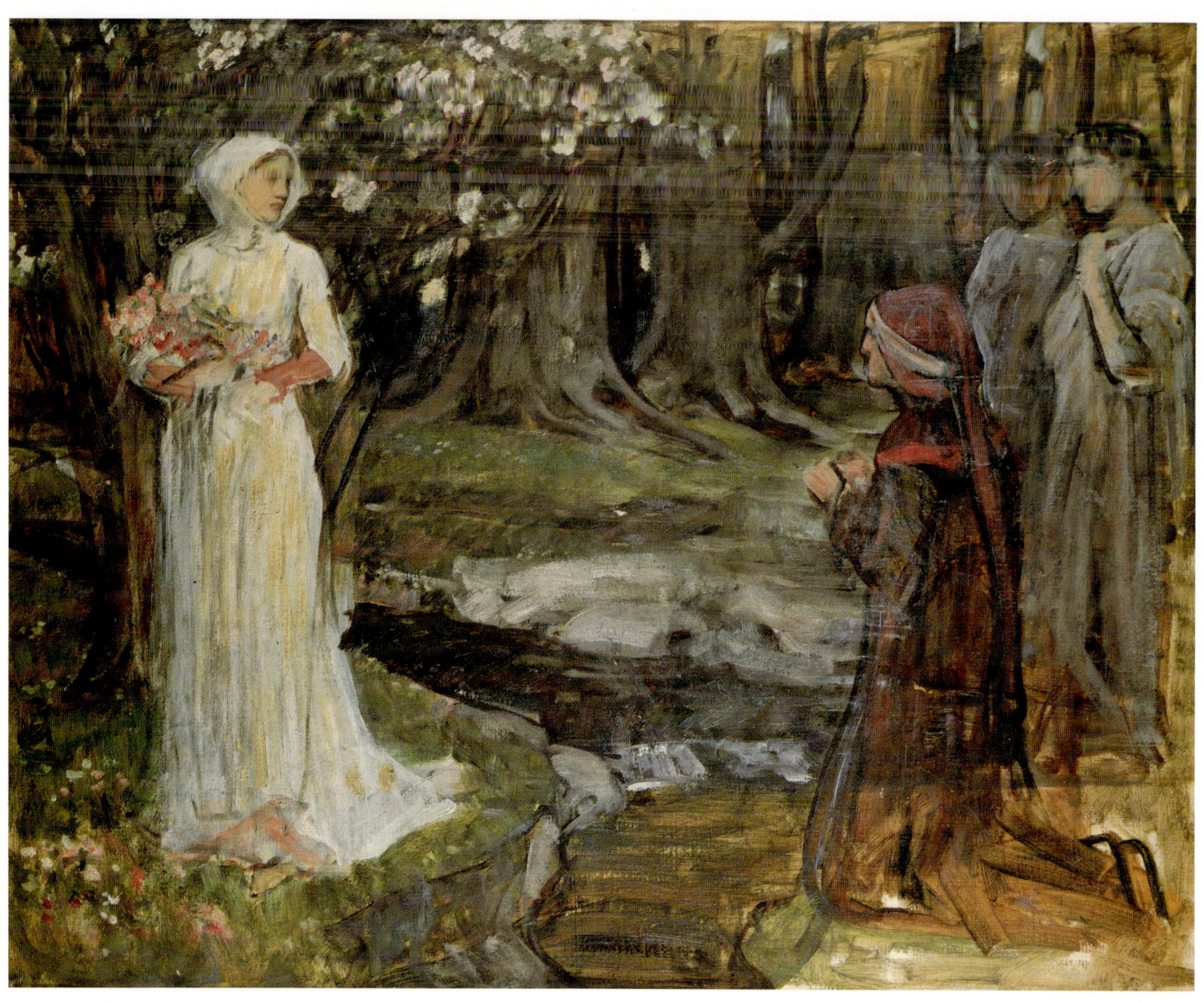

81 Study for *Dante and Beatrice*, *c.*1915. 18½ × 23 in (47 × 58.5 cm) Courtesy Christie's

82 *Mrs Charles Schreiber*, 1912. 30 × 25 in (76 × 64 cm). The Lord Faringdon

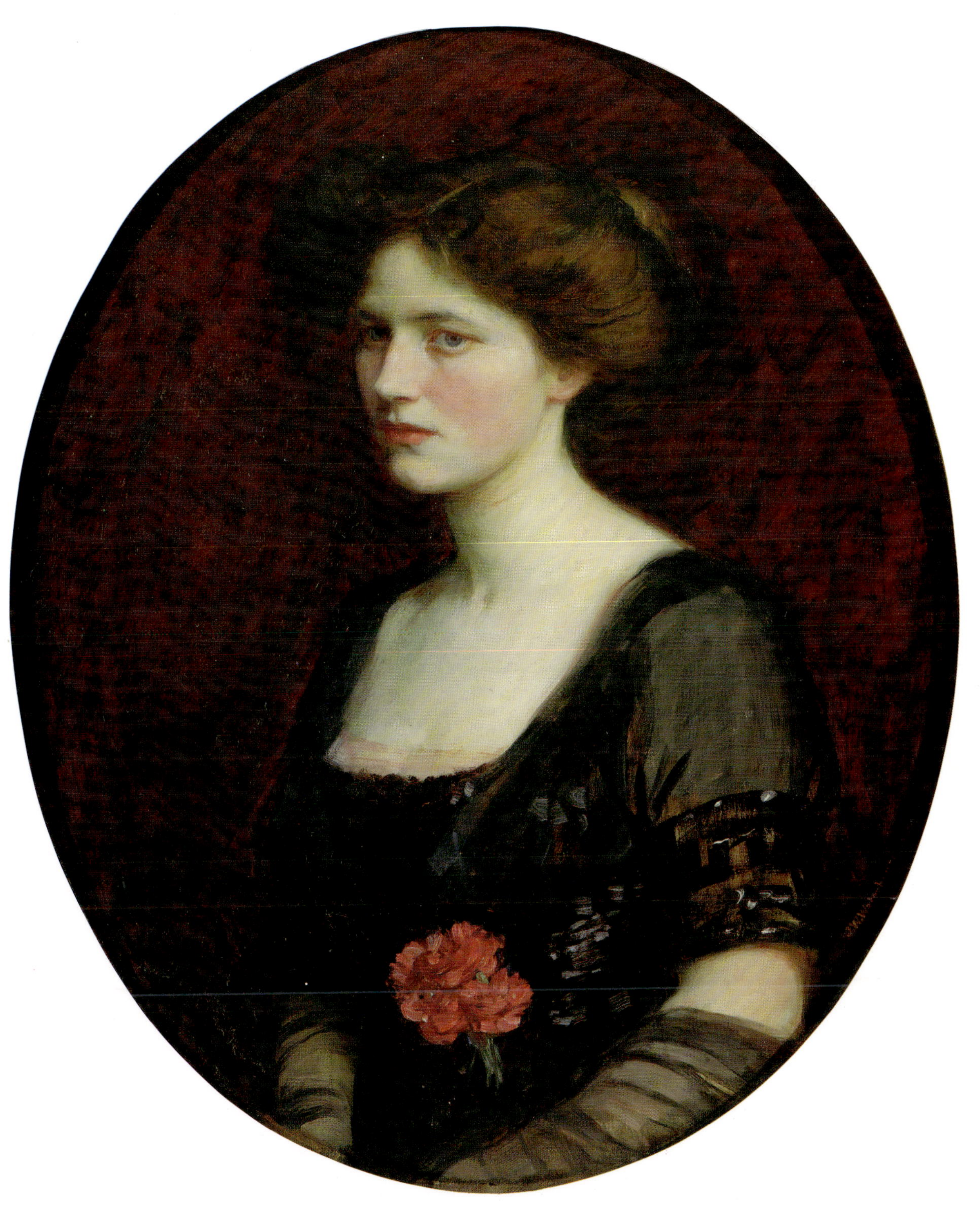

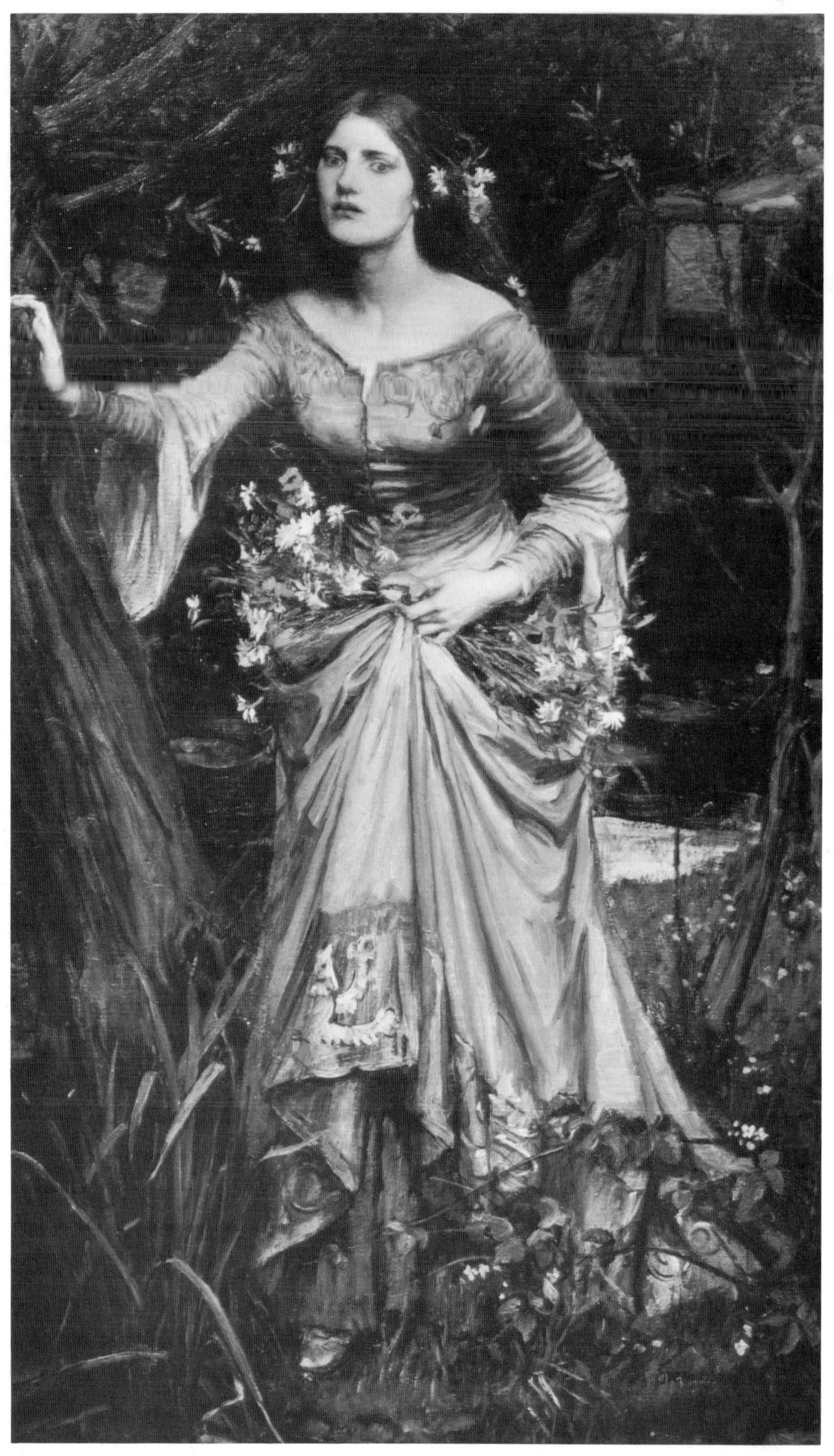

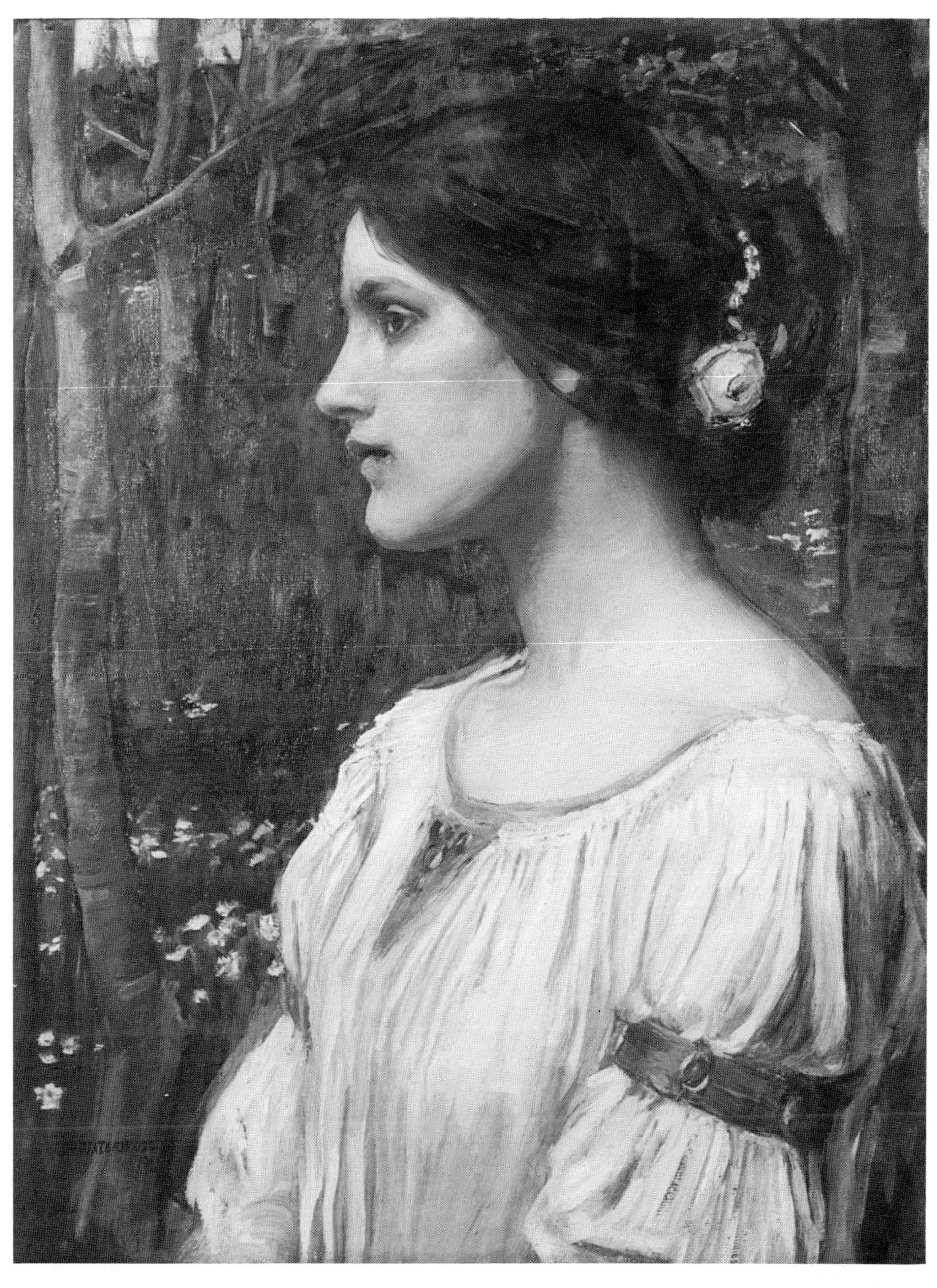

83 *Ophelia*, 1910. 40 × 24 in (102 × 61 cm). Pre-Raphaelite Inc. by courtesy of Julian Hartnoll

84 *Veronica*, 1909. 22 × 18 in (55 × 45 cm). Private collection

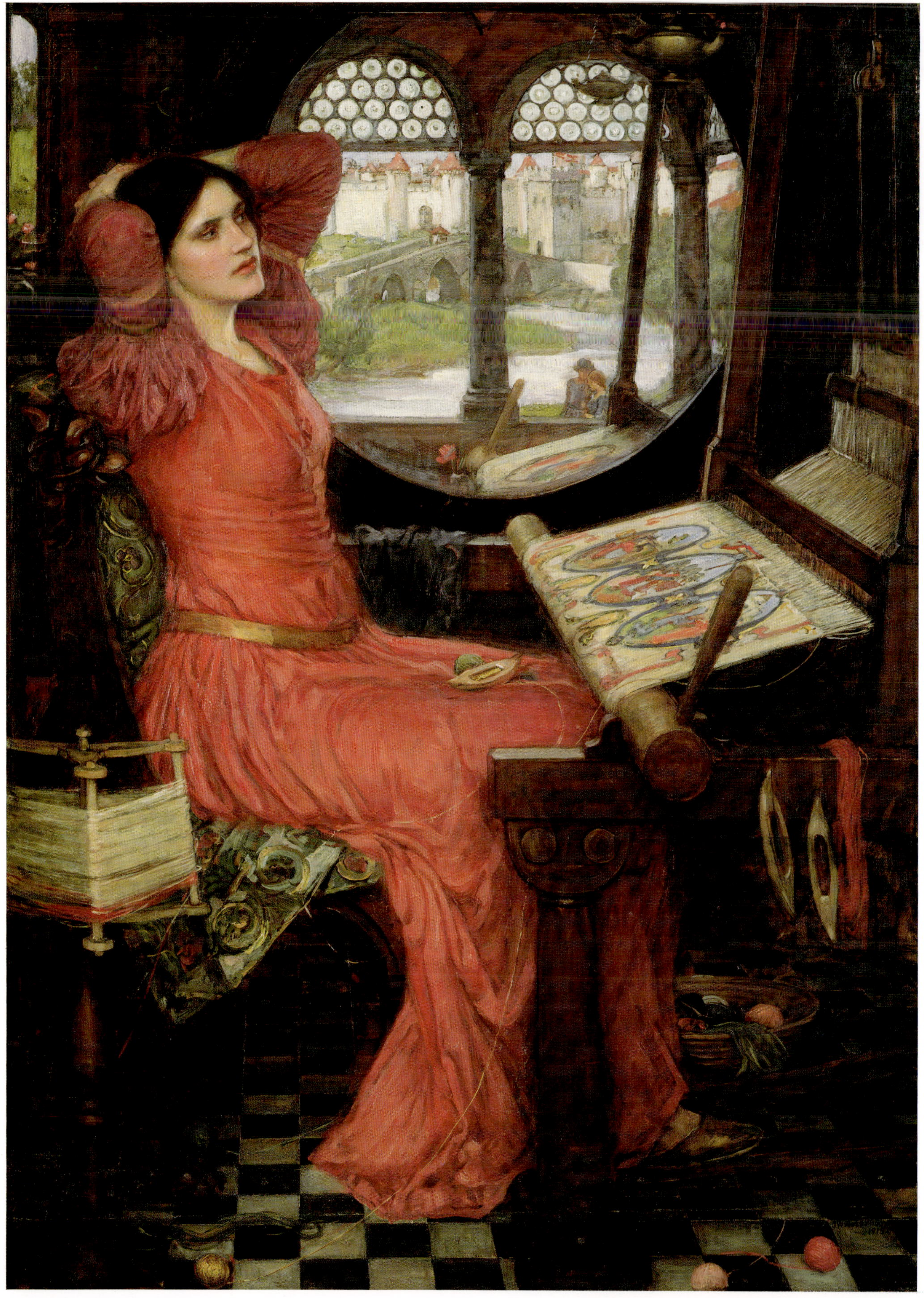

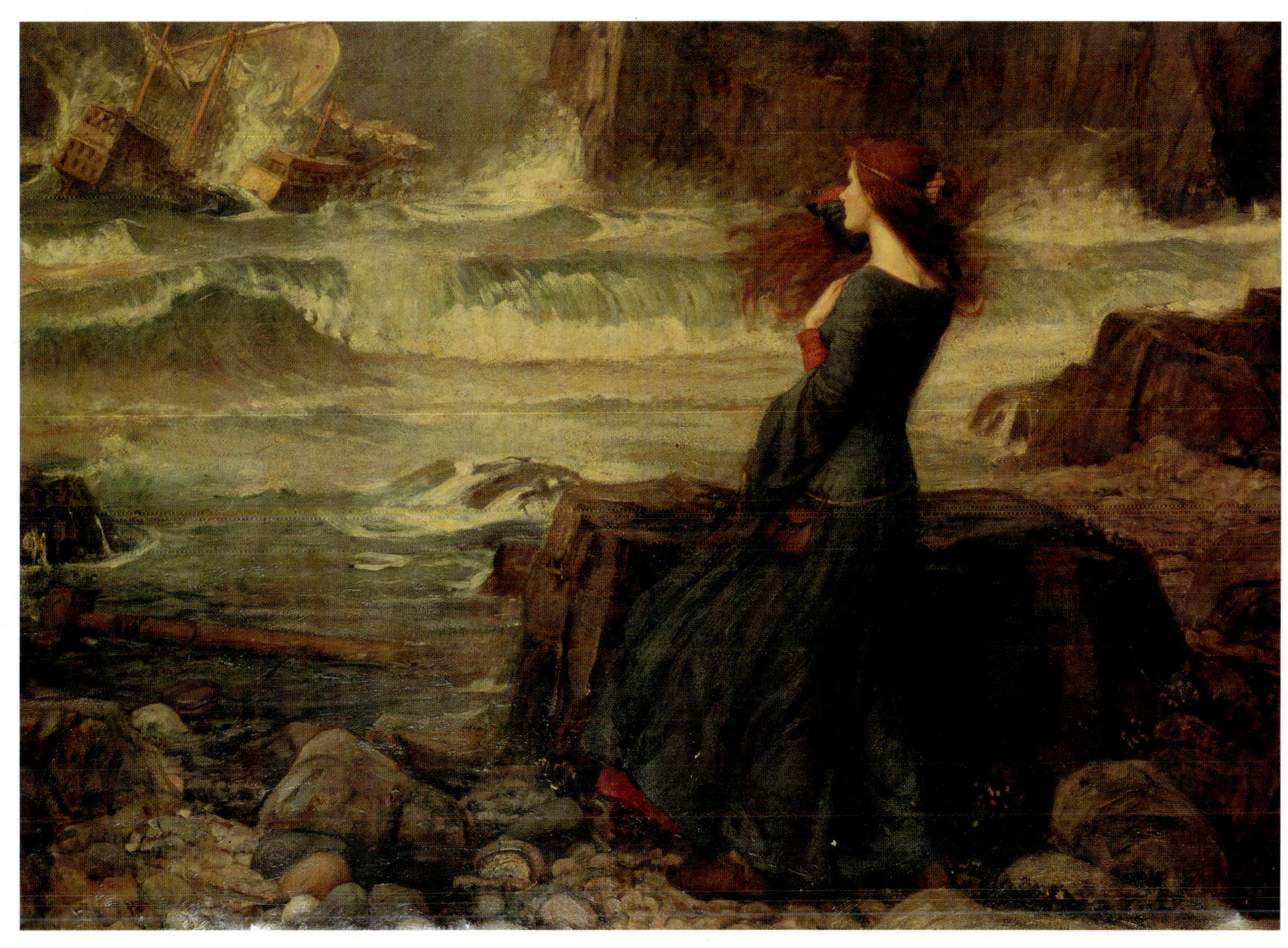

86 *Miranda – The Tempest*, 1916. 38½ × 53½ in (98 × 136 cm). Courtesy Sotheby's

85 *'I am Half-Sick of Shadows,' said The Lady of Shalott*, 1916. 39½ × 29 in (100 × 74 cm). Toronto, Art Gallery of Ontario

under the looming cliffs in a welter of waves the doomed ship plunges like a terrified stallion. The painting of rocks, wild water and the figure of the girl have been brought to perfection by way of the gentle mermaid of his Diploma picture.

There is a study in oils for *A Tale from The Decameron* in a private collection, and another *Scene from Boccaccio* which may relate to it was lost after the artist's sale in 1926. The title of Boccaccio's *Decameron* refers to the ten days during which a group of seven ladies and three gentlemen escape from the great plague of 1348 (when the book was written) to a villa in the countryside where they while away the time by story-telling. Each of them daily recounts a tale, to the total of a hundred, in which the grace and elegance of the prose frequently carry erotic subject-matter more acceptable to Boccaccio's readers than to the Victorians. Waterhouse's painting, however (Pl.88), is not concerned with the tales, only with the telling of them, and he achieves another model of perfection. The quiet harmony of the grouping – the 'keyhole' composition once again – accords with the rapt attention of the girls (one of them crowned 'queen for the day') as they listen in their secluded garden to the tale of romance which takes their minds away from the horrors of the plague. The picture was bought for £700 in April 1916 by Sir William Lever, Bt. (later Viscount Leverhulme), for the Art Gallery commemorating his wife, who had died three years earlier.

In 1916 began the last twelve months of the art and life of John William Waterhouse. The principal fruits of that year's work were exhibited in the Royal Academy of 1917. Another *Miranda* was shown there: lost to us for the moment, it was approximately half the size of *Miranda – The Tempest* but a substantial picture, worth 140 guineas at the later sale of the artist's remaining works. In *Tristram and Isolde* (Pl.89) he returned to the Arthurian legends, characteristically choosing not a tournament or passage of arms but the meeting of lovers for whom there could be no happy ending. Once more, he selected a moment both of stillness and of powerful emotions. On the ship in which Tristram is bringing the daughter of the king of Ireland to be married to his uncle, King Mark of Cornwall, the couple unknowingly partake of a magic potion and, gazing into each other's eyes, become lovers in an instant which also foreshadows their deaths. Nino was still painting as well as ever: the armour of the knight, the ship's timbers and the moving sea, the castle, the Cornish coast which he had visited so often, the veil floating in the wind from the head of his favourite model – all are scrupulously rendered, bringing the romantic illusion to reality.

Fair Rosamund (Pl.94) foresees the sad culmination of another medieval tale, the true story of Lord Clifford's daughter, the beloved of King Henry II. From the window of her secret house, she looks for his coming, but the queen, appearing at the curtained entrance, has followed 'a clue of thredde' through the surrounding maze and, as the chronicler Higden wrote about 1350, 'so dealt with her that she lived not long after.' The costume, the embroidery and the tapestry depicting knightly pageantry fit perfectly, as always, into the precise geometry of the architecture.

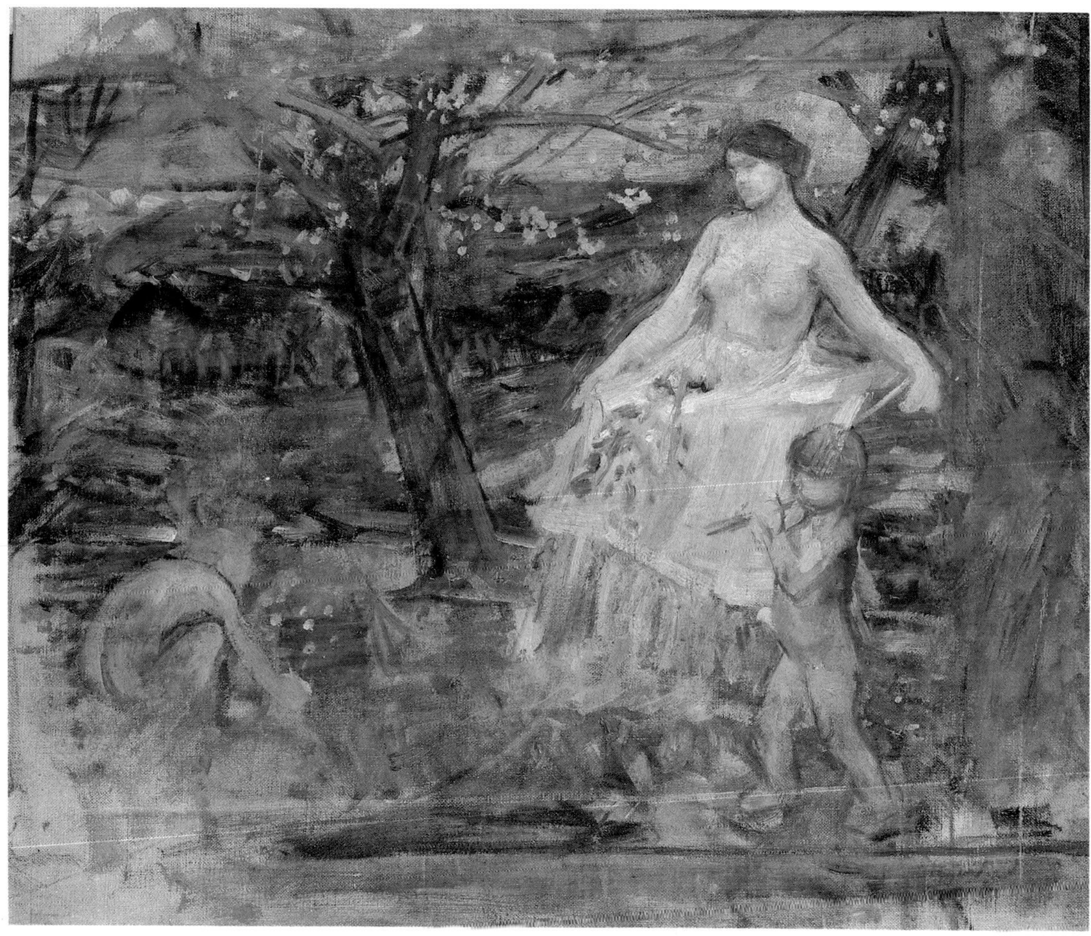

87 Study for *A Song of Springtime*, *c.* 1913. 17¾ × 22 in (45 × 56 cm). Courtesy Sotheby's

It was a tribute to the artist by his peers that the last picture of all was shown in the Academy of 1917 even though it remained unfinished. Nearing the end of his protracted illness, in *The Enchanted Garden* (Pl.91) he summoned up for his comfort the romantic figures in whom his creativity had been personified. From the earliest days he had loved to paint flowers, piled up for sale in *A Flower Stall* of 1880, bound in posies in *A Flower Market, Old Rome* of 1886, gathered in meadows and gardens by the maidens of more recent years (Pls.92 and 93). Now their setting was his last refuge.

He created this haven of warmth in the winter of his life, but almost unwittingly imbued it with a deeper meaning. Past the Dantesque guardian at the entrance, the snow is falling on the steps: it gathers on the entablature above the rounded Renaissance arches which evoke the Italy of his birth, and a few flakes are seen against the shadows of the arcade. But in the garden the roses bloom; one of the girls bends to inhale their scent, and the poppies presage a quiet oblivion. Roses and snow together sum up the duality of desire and restraint in all his work, and because poetry was ever-present in his life, he must also have had Tennyson's Arthur in mind, and 'the island-valley of Avilion, where falls not hail, or rain, or any snow, Nor ever wind blows loudly'.

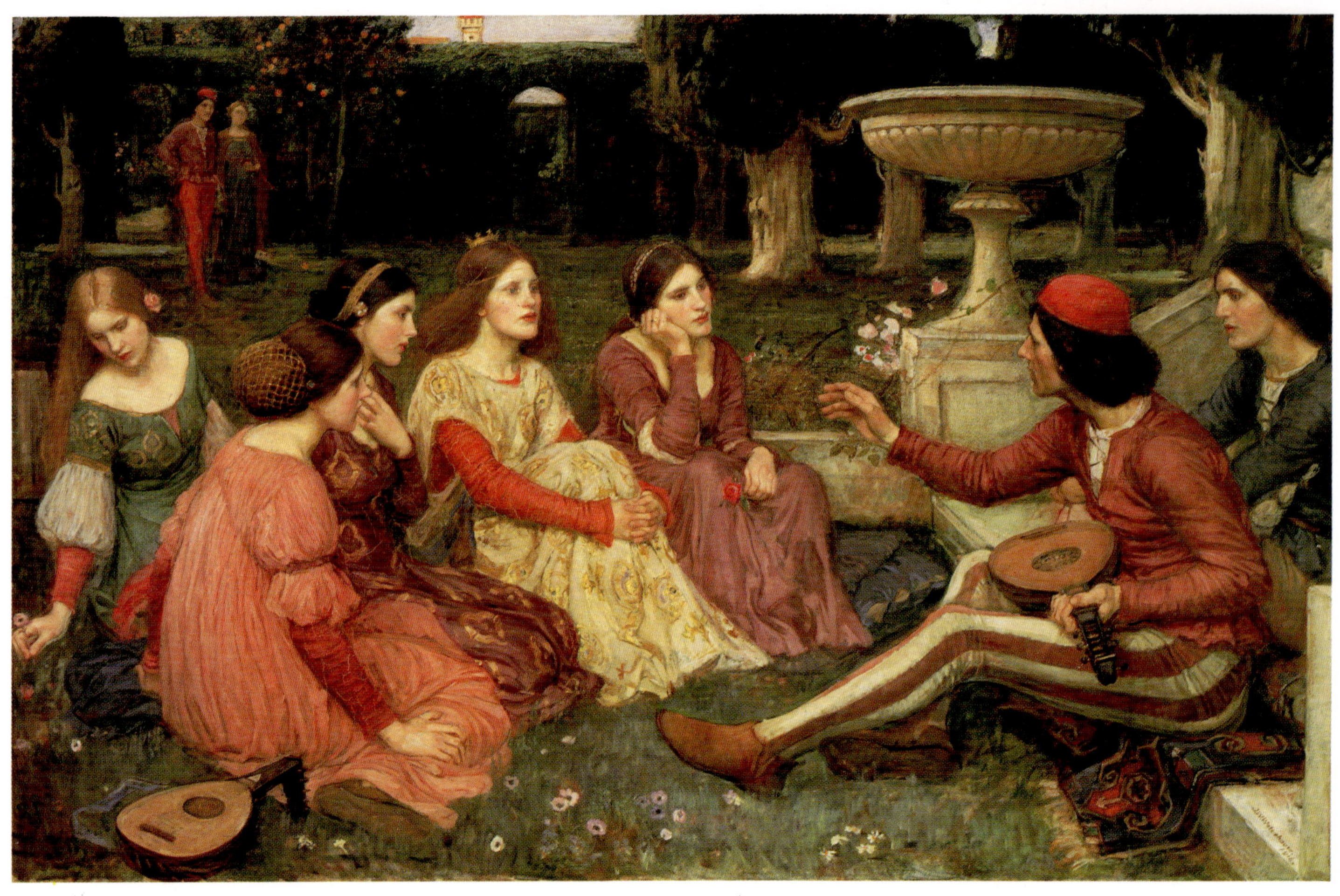

88 *A Tale from The Decameron*, 1916. 40 × 62½ in (102 × 159 cm). Birkenhead, Lady Lever Art Gallery

89 *Tristram and Isolde*, *c.* 1916. 41¾ × 30½ in (106 × 77.5 cm). Courtesy Whitford & Hughes

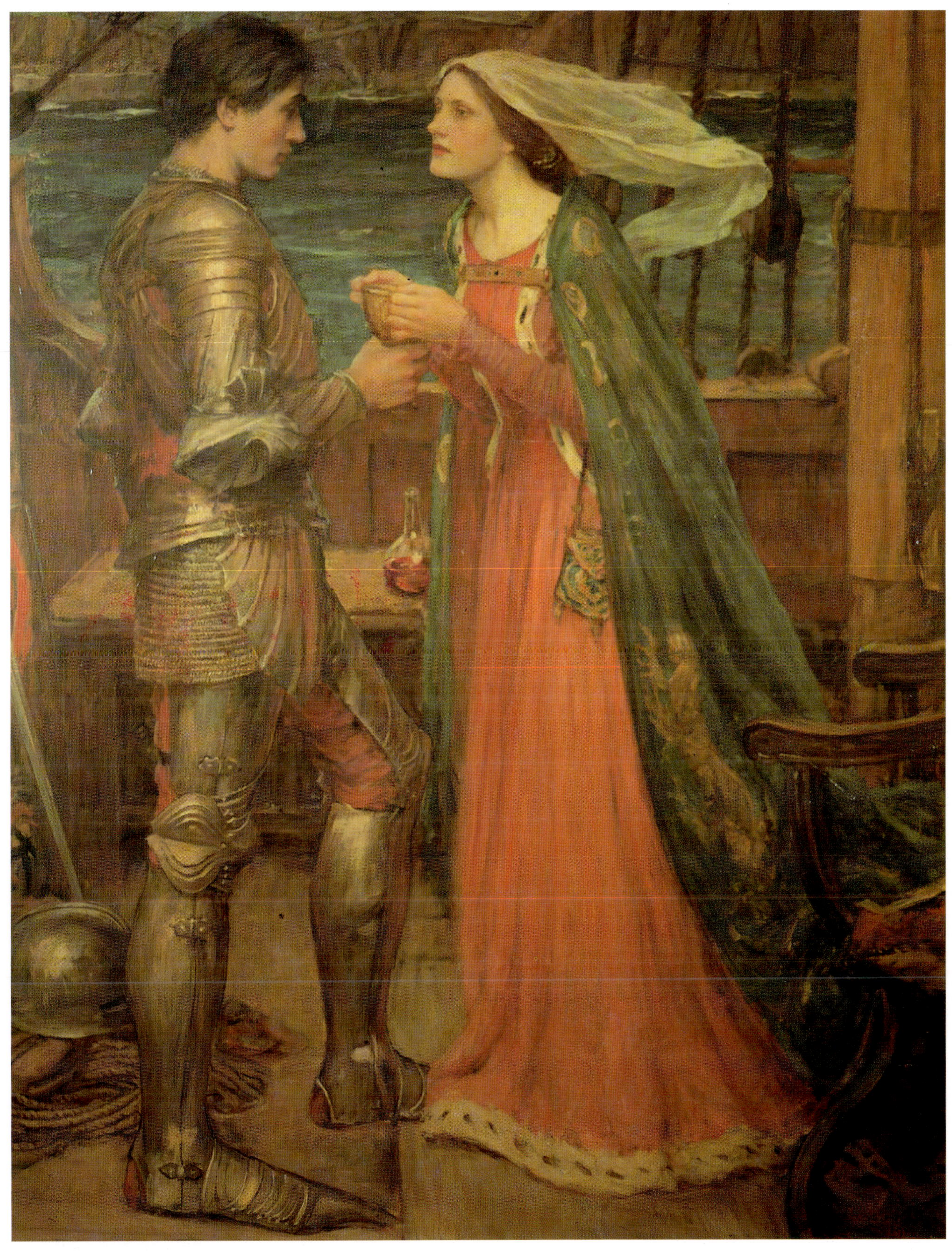

The Times gave notice of the death of 'John William (Nino) Waterhouse ... on the 10th Feb at 10 Hall Rd, St John's Wood, after a long illness borne with great patience', and the Secretary of the Royal Academy performed his 'painful duty' in advising the Members. The venerable President, Sir Edward Poynter, penned the letter of condolence to Esther on their behalf, and led the procession of Academicians at the funeral service held at St Mark's Church, Hamilton Terrace, and the burial at Kensal Green Cemetery. They included contemporaries by then well-known: Andrew Gow, a near neighbour at the corner of Grove End Road, was now Keeper of the Royal Academy; R.A.s Seymour Lucas and W.W. Ouless were Nino's own age, Briton Riviere nearly ten years older; A.S. (later Sir Arthur) Cope had been a fellow-student of the 1870s; Lance Calkin had lived opposite the Waterhouses in Primrose Hill Studios. Younger members of the Academy were present – the sculptors Pegram and Pomeroy and Albert Toft; painters William Strang, the popular self-taught Edgar Bundy, the brilliant Charles Sims, and the neoclassicist Herbert Draper. Whether in art or friendship, they were all indebted to Waterhouse and his example. Those particular patrons the Hendersons were well represented, and among other collectors of his works were Sir James Murray and Mr (later Sir) Frederick Fry.

In its review of the 1917 Academy, *The Studio* said: 'The four pictures by Mr Waterhouse make a pathetic appeal as the last we shall have from a man who for many years past has added much to the interest of the Academy shows – they remind us sadly of the loss we have sustained by his death.' *The Times*'s obituary was complimentary, speaking of his 'taste and learning as well as considerable accomplishments', but a little guarded (perhaps with an eye to the modern movements already gaining ground); although to say that he painted 'always like a scholar and a gentleman' would no doubt have been pleasing to Reynolds.

In Birmingham they were still more enthusiastic, and a 'Special Memoir' in the *Daily Post* would be echoed by many in galleries and salerooms today. With his 'freedom of execution, or rather contempt of tight finish, Waterhouse contrived to give an appearance of reality, truth to nature, and the freshness of first intention which no amount of merely conscientious labour can achieve. ... He was not content with elaborate colour schemes divorced from nature such as may be found in the work of Rossetti and Burne-Jones. ... The colour of his flesh painting has ranked for years with the very best. ... His style is his own, and he has had many young imitators. ... Thanks to the early insight of the late Sir Henry Tate, Waterhouse is well represented in the National Gallery of British Art, while many other public collections contain examples of one of the best painters and colourists our British school can show.' All this is attested by the increasing number of distinguished twentieth-century collectors of his work, and by his place in public galleries both in England and abroad.

It may be wondered why there was no immediate move towards a posthumous exhibition of Waterhouse's paintings; but the times were not propitious. The First World War was still in progress and the fortunes of the Allies were at a low ebb,

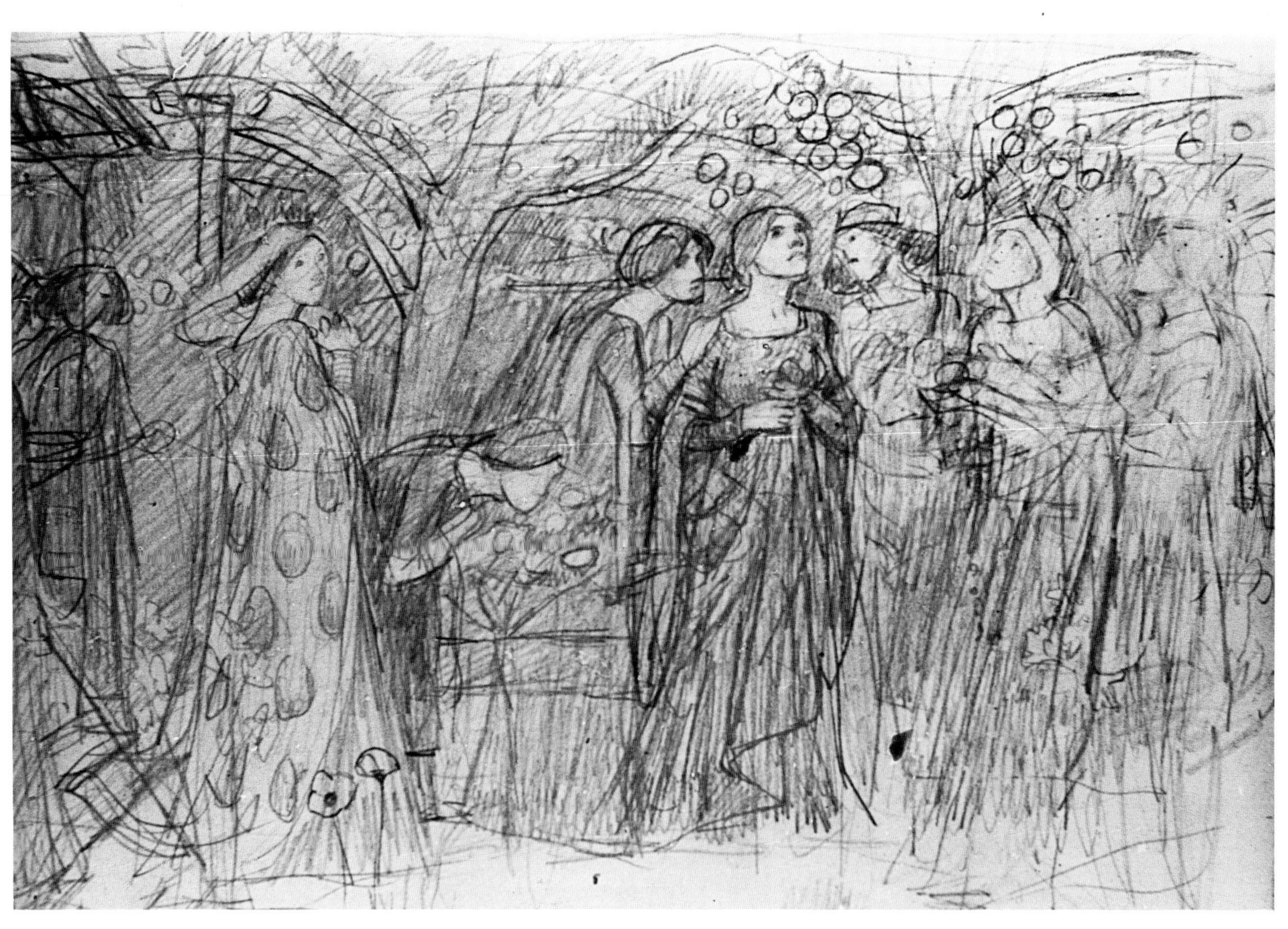

90 Study for *The Enchanted Garden*, *c.* 1916. Pencil. Private collection

with air attacks on London intensifying. Moreover, the reputation of the Victorian painters was even then in decline with the critics, and not until 1978 was a one-man exhibition of Waterhouse's work mounted at the Mappin Art Gallery in Sheffield. In the aftermath of the war the Academy honoured its own with an exhibition in 1922 of 'Works by Recently Deceased Members of the Royal Academy'. This contained thirteen paintings by Waterhouse including *Hylas and the Nymphs*, *Isabella and the Pot of Basil*, *St Cecilia* and *Nymphs Finding the Head of Orpheus*. Esther Waterhouse lent the 1889 *Ophelia*, *Vanity*, *A Hamadryad* and *Apollo and Daphne*, all of which were later sold at Christie's in 1926 among 'The Remaining Works of the Late J.W. Waterhouse, R.A.' The long delay in mounting this sale is difficult to explain. Esther lived on for some time at 10 Hall Road, and in keeping the paintings remaining in his studio she may have cherished the notion of establishing a museum of his works, as had been done for Ingres at Montauban.

To sum up the work of J. W. Waterhouse is more challenging and indeed more interesting than might appear. At the very first glance, his paintings have a virtually universal appeal: skilled in execution and harmonious in colour, they are inhabited by beautiful people and recall well-known stories or instantly acceptable personal situations. His young girls have even proved to be fashionable in terms of twentieth-century dress and hair style, and have been used by advertisers who styled them Pre-Raphaelite. Modern critics have too easily accepted that label, but their invocation of Burne-Jones is wide of the mark: the whole tenor of Waterhouse's work is classical and Italianate, rather than medieval and Gothic as with the Pre-Raphaelite Brotherhood and their followers.

Yet in spite of his Italian birth and sympathies, Nino's paintings are strongly English in spirit, incorporating what the perceptive German historian Gustav Friedrich Waagen had called in 1838 (referring to the work of John Martin) 'the three qualities which the English require, above all, in a work of art – effect, a fanciful invention, inclining to melancholy, and topographic historical truth.'

Over and above the question of style, however, is J. W. Waterhouse's narrative ability. He was an illustrator in the finest sense of the word. Not himself the originator of the tales he chose, he was nevertheless so in tune with them as to extend their literary imagery by his own invention, filling the spaces of our imagination in a manner so natural that we feel it could hardly be otherwise. He achieved this by his expert rendering of natural and man-made surroundings, by compositions which skilfully control our viewing, by his rapport with models who have the appeal of the girl next door rather than the hauteur of goddesses, and finally (since he was not narrating in moving pictures but summing up a story in a still one) by the intuitive selection of the moment at which all movement could be suddenly suspended in a wholly natural pause. The latter is the master's touch. He developed it early and employed it faultlessly, from *Consulting the Oracle* to *Nymphs Finding the Head of Orpheus*, and by displaying, in these situations, beings of such humanity, sympathy and beauty he completes that intimate communication with the viewer which places him among the greatest painters of his time.

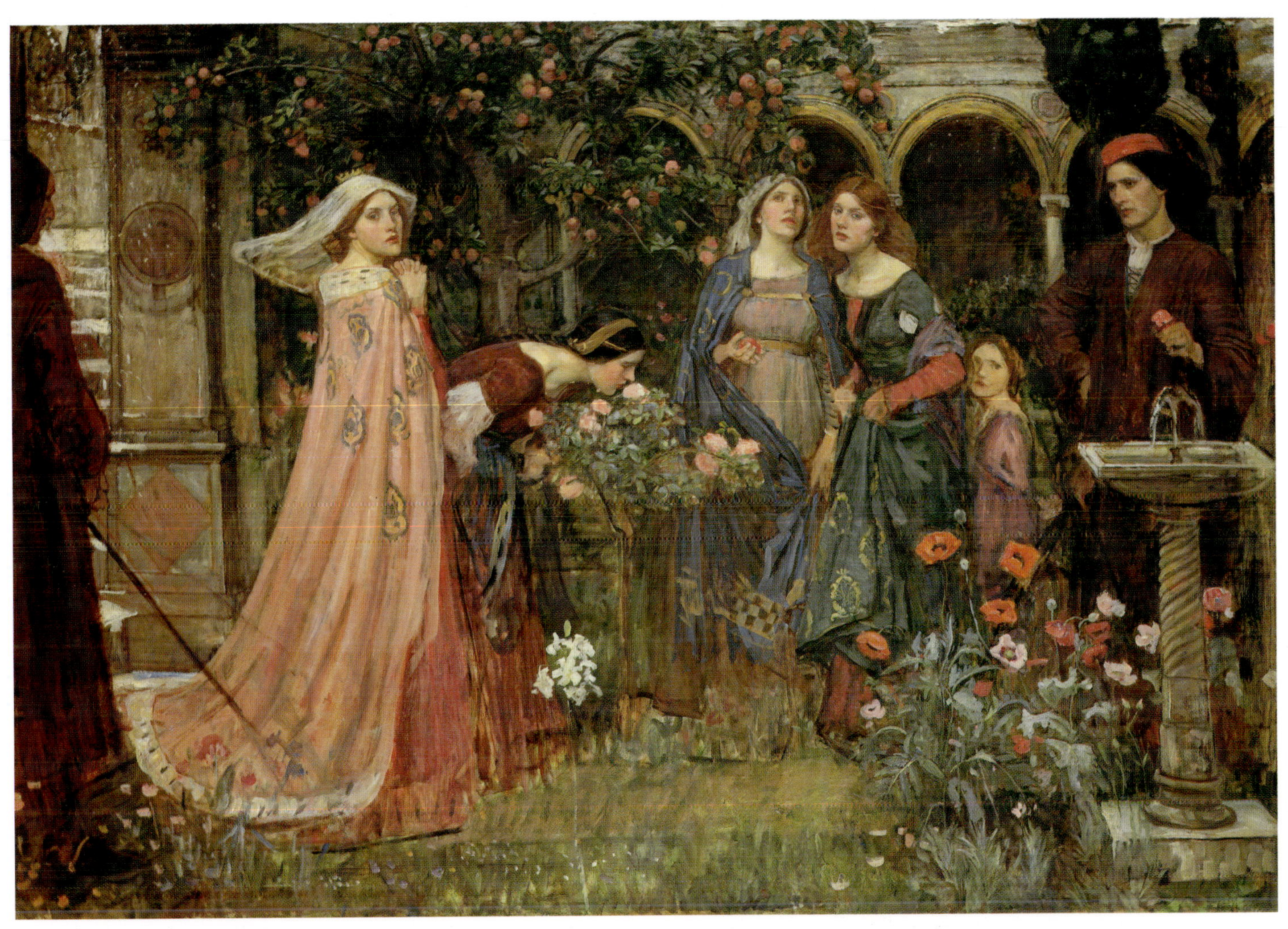

91 *The Enchanted Garden*, 1916. 44 × 63½in (112 × 161 cm). Birkenhead, Lady Lever Art Gallery

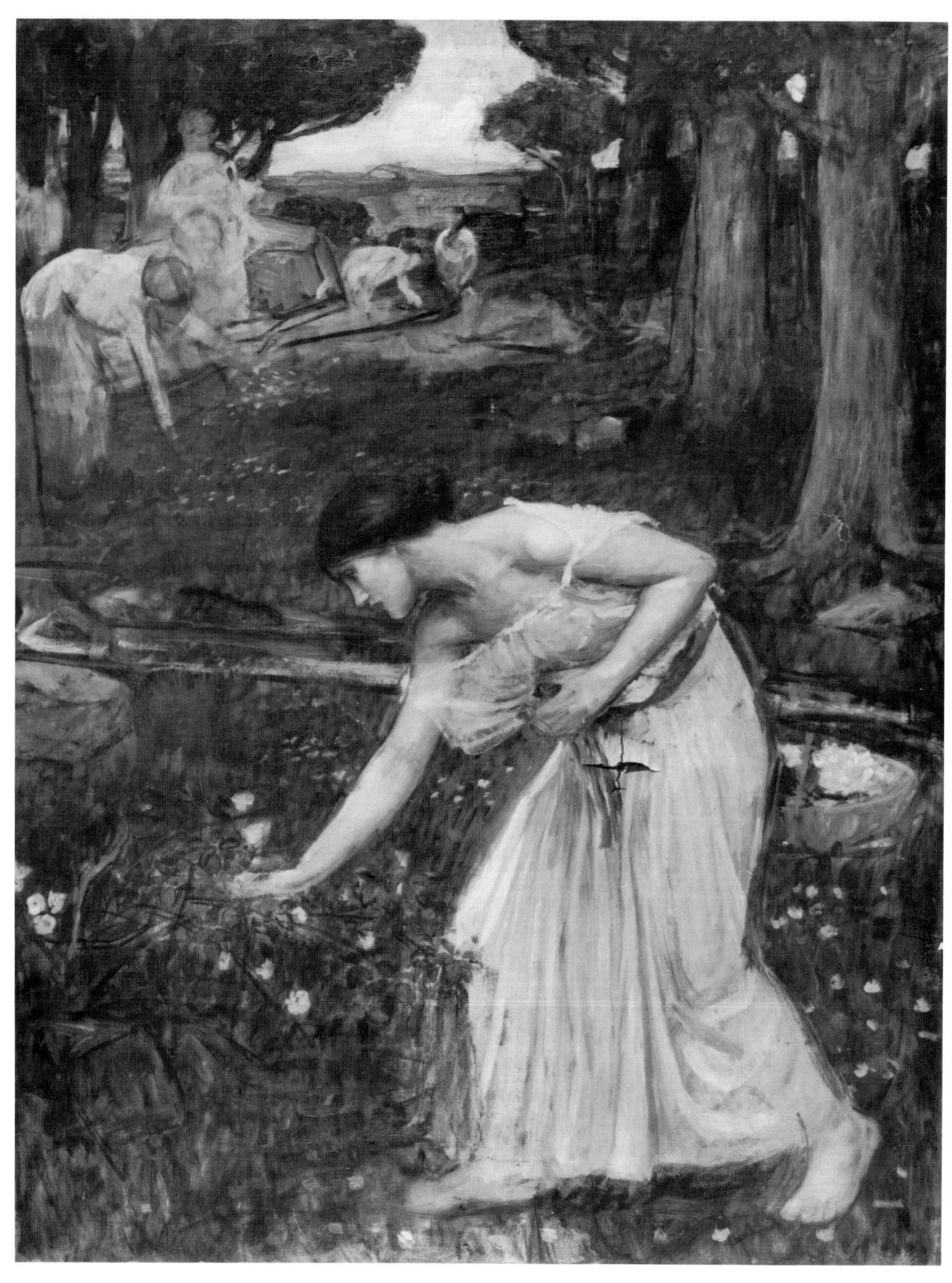

92 Study for *Narcissus*,
1913. 52 × 39¼ in (131.5 × 99 cm).
Courtesy Peter Nahum

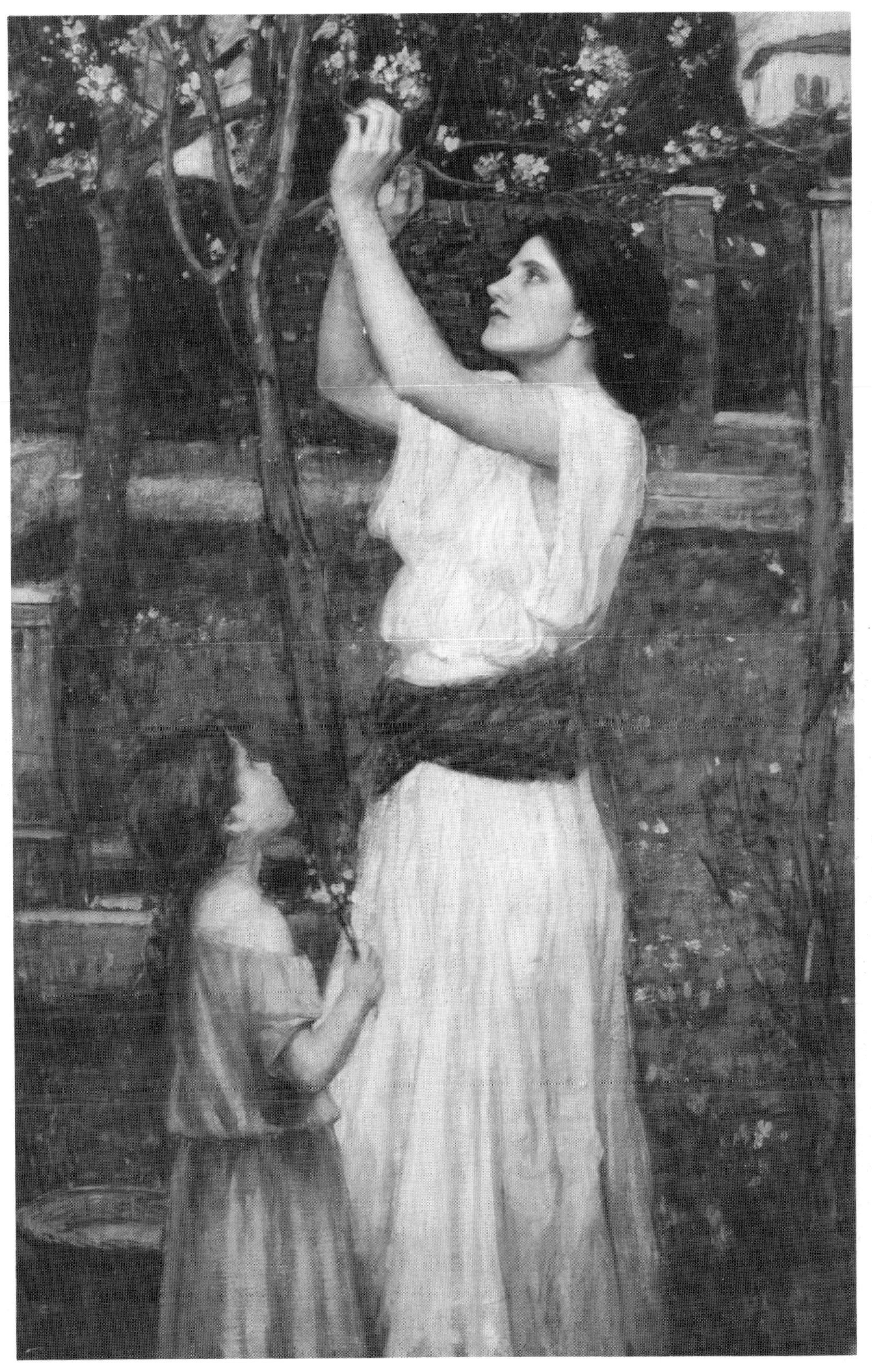

93 *Gathering Almond Blossoms*, *c.*1916. 37 × 24 in (94 × 61 cm). Private collection

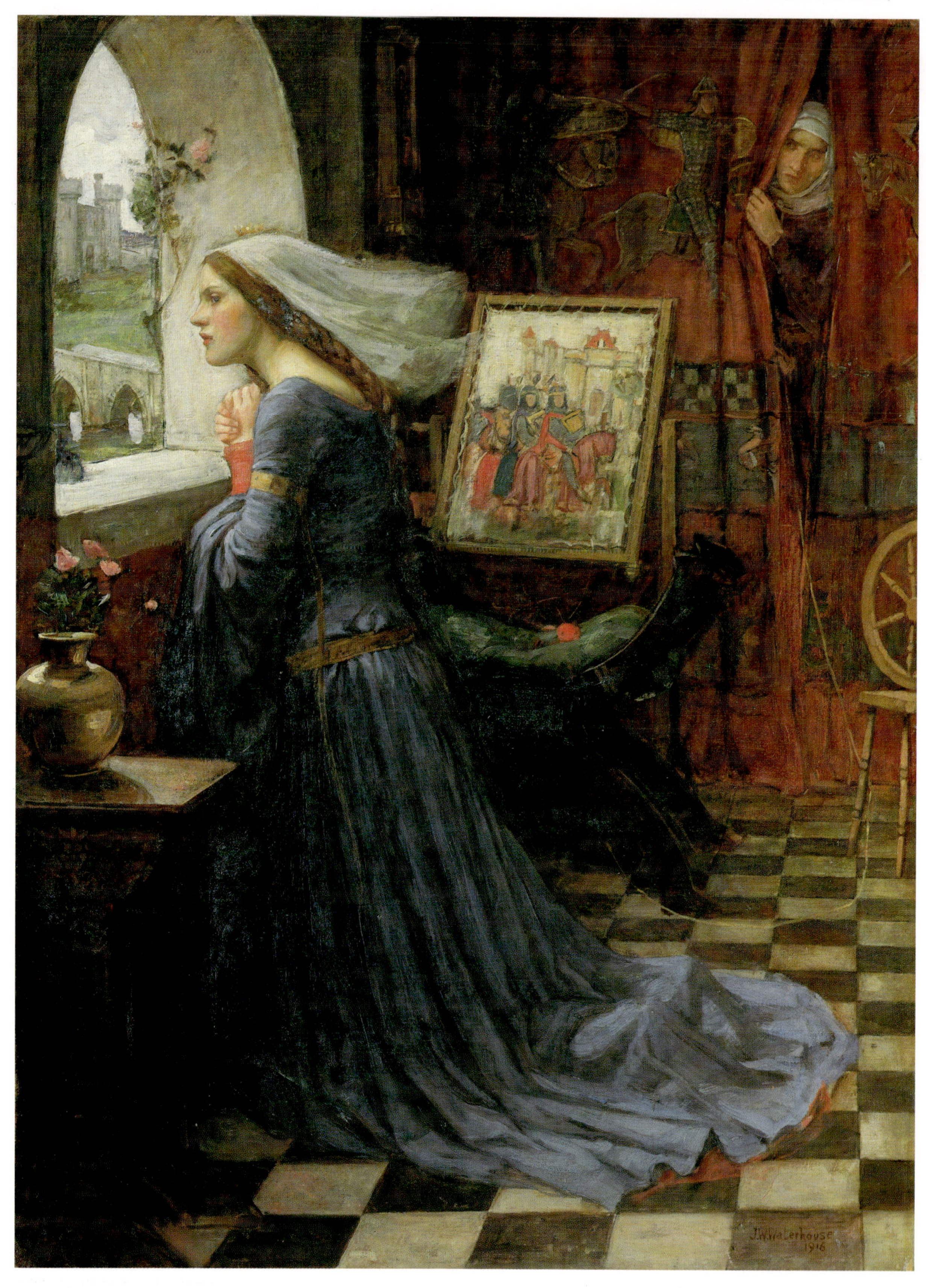

94 *Fair Rosamund*, 1917.
38 × 28½ in (96.5 × 72 cm).
Courtesy Christie's

INDEX